● 中西文化交流系列
East-West Cultural Exchange

丝绸之路
THE SILK ROAD

（澳）许沧洲 著
Writer by Xu Cangzhou

吴松林等 译
Translated by Wu Songlin

多元文化的相融共生
是人类文明社会建构的曙光

An integration of multicultural coexistence is the dawn of the human civilization and the social construction

Contents

Introduction

Part 1 : The Philosophy of Lao Zi

1. What is Dao ? Is it a pseudonym of God? （17）
2. The mystery of creation. （43）
3. In achieving understanding of The Word, one relinquishes perverse desires daily （49）
4. Do not live for oneself – live without selfish desires. （55）
5. Reduce the surplus and supplement the scarcity. （65）
6. Wealth and Authority. （73）
7. The paradox of Softness and Hardness. （84）
8. The paradox of "Nothing" and "Something" （94）
9. Retire after accomplishment or success （100）
10. Superior goodness like that of water （106）
11. The Heart is Buddha. （110）
12. The Way of Man （118）
13. Return to the Origin （138）

目 录

前　序

上篇　老子的哲学

第一章　什么是道？道是否是上帝的别号？	（18）
第二章　创造的神秘	（44）
第三章　为学者日益，闻道者日损	（50）
第四章　不自生，无私欲	（56）
第五章　损有余而补不足	（66）
第六章　金玉满堂，莫之能守，正复为奇，善复为妖	（74）
第七章　柔胜刚	（85）
第八章　逆义的无和有	（95）
第九章　功遂身退	（101）
第十章　上善若水	（107）
第十一章　心即是佛	（111）
第十二章　人之道	（119）
第十三章　复归	（139）

Contents

Part 2: The Ethics of Confucius

14. What is his name?
The Lord-on-high or Heaven and Yahweh, The Lord. (150)

15. What is the son of God? (166)

16. Christians Before Christ (178)

17. Dao exists among the heavens and the earth and people (182)

18. Search for Truth, Goodness and Perfection. (192)

19. The difference between God and Man (200)

20. The Ambiguity of Sin in the Chinese Language. (206)

21. Love others as yourself (216)

22. In the beginning the nature of man was originally good. (222)

23. Ancestral worship or veneration? (228)

24. Self-discipline, Family Management, National Government, and World Peace. (236)

25. In a company of three, definitely there is my teacher. (242)

26. Bringing up children without discipline is the fault of the father, Uncut jade not finely honed does not represent something precious. (250)

27. "The Righteous shall live by Faith", Peter's Vision (256)

Postcript

下篇　孔子的伦理

第十四章　上帝、天、耶和华或主 …………………（151）
第十五章　什么是神的儿子？ ………………………（167）
第十六章　基督出生以前的基督徒 …………………（179）
第十七章　道于天地人 ………………………………（183）
第十八章　寻求真善美 ………………………………（193）
第十九章　神与人的区别 ……………………………（201）
第二十章　汉语"罪"的模糊性 ……………………（207）
第二十一章　爱人如己 ………………………………（217）
第二十二章　人之初，性本善 ………………………（223）
第二十三章　崇敬父母 ………………………………（229）
第二十四章　修身，齐家，治国，平天下 …………（237）
第二十五章　三人行必有我师 ………………………（243）
第二十六章　养不教，父之过；玉不琢，不成器 …（251）
第二十七章　公义者因信得生；彼得的异像 ………（257）

后　记

Introduction

The Silk Road was a major highway between Cathay (China) in the East and the rest of the world – the Middle East, Turkey, India, Europe and South-east Asia. It was a popular trade route, through which silk, precious stones and other commodities were bartered. The exchanges were not restricted to merchandise. The Silk Road was also a place where cultures met, and customs, religions, perceptions, and philosophies engaged one another in fruitful dialogue.

Since it was introduced during the reign of Tai Zong in the 7th Century, the Christian gospel has been preached to the Chinese people. At that time, due to the influence of the Syrian trader, Alopen, who was a Christian a royal decree issued by Emperor Tai Zong (635 C.E.), ordered churches to be built in every town in China. Alopen was made a minister of the royal court. In spite of this early acceptance of Christianity, and the fact that three further bursts of missionary endeavoured to ripple through China in the last 13th centuries, the Christian faith remained a foreign religion.

Buddhism arrived in China in the same period that was seen in the introduction of Christianity. However, unlike Christianity, it was more readily welcome. Its scriptures were re-written, with additions and alterations influenced by Chinese philosophies, especially the Taoism. It intermingled with Daoist and Confucian thought, dovetailed with many aspects of Chinese culture. Buddhism adopted Chinese architecture and clothing styles, even incorporating Chinese gods, legendary heroes and heroines. Buddhism, being indigenized, was much more easily absorbed than Christianity, with its Western, monotheistic exclusiveness.

The authors agree with Father Matthew Ricci, a Portuguese missionary, who arrived in Macao, China in 1582, that ancient Chinese philosophies would benefit from a superintending deity to compliment their ethical transcendentalism. The Christian God fulfilled this role. However, [1]this Christian God, together with the theology he inspired, and the society dedicated to his worship, needed to accommodate Chinese culture. This God would not be accepted totally as he was seen to be a foreign God.

前 序

从中国人的观点看基督教

　　丝绸之路是东方的大秦（中国）和世界其它国家和地区如中东、土尔其、欧洲和东南亚之间的通衢。这条路为通商之路，沟通着丝绸，珠宝和其它物资贸易。贸易往来不单单是物物交换，不同文化在丝绸之路互相碰撞，风俗习惯、宗教、思想和哲学的对话富有成效。

　　从七世纪唐太宗统治时代，基督徒向中国传教，当时，受叙利亚商人、基督徒阿罗邦的影响，朝廷一道圣旨，太宗赦令全国各市镇兴建教堂。阿罗邦任职侍臣，这就是中国最初接受基督教的情况。后来，全国突飞猛进地搞了三次传教运动，十三世纪后期，信仰基督仍没有跨出洋教的藩篱。

　　佛教与基督教同时传进中国，然而，人们接受佛教是比较顺利的。禅宗曾受中国哲学，尤其是道哲学的影响，增添并修订了很多内容。其实，它综合了儒家的伦理和道家哲学思想，参进了许多中国文化的内涵。佛教采用中国传统建筑设计、服装设计等，甚至也吸纳了中国神话中的鬼神。佛教汉化以后，比基督崇拜西方一神论更容易被吸收。

　　作者认为，1582年，来自澳门的葡萄牙传教士雷马太的观点是有根据的：中国古代哲学需要一位专神来支配他们的伦理超验主义。基督之神正符合这个需求。但是，基督之神与他所倡导的神学及其受膜拜的社会是需要融汇中华文化的。如果上帝是夷神，那么，完全被接受的可能性是不存在的。

Introduction

Christianity began as a sect in Judaism. Its message, however, was considered more radical and less legalistic. At first, Christianity resisted, but later embraced Hellenistic philosophy, logic and science. It enshrined Graeco-Roman, and later Germanic, Gallic, Anglo-Saxon, Scandinavian and Slavic customs. Because Christianity came to China later, it was only tentatively accepted, but never effectively integrated into Chinese culture. Associating with European colonialism, Christianity remained a foreign religion. While Christianity, influenced more by its roots in Western culture than by the open and universal message of its founder, rejected the few tentative moves that were made to bring together the essence of Christianity and the distinctive elements of Chinese culture. Such a conflation would have been the natural, inevitable and fruitful outcome of the merging of the two great cultures.

The "Three Self-Movement," which recognizes a need to dissociate the essence of Christianity from the horror of imperialism and colonialism, is set to play an important role in the propagation of the Gospel in China because of its commitment to indigenizing Christianity.

The West needs to demonstrate greater understanding of the horrendous suffering and political dislocation to which the Chinese were subjected over the last two centuries. The Church, in particular, needs to demonstrate love, compassion, repentance and humility, qualities which they argue most to characterize their God. China should be allowed to develop a unique, indigenous expression of Christianity

No one should blame China for being suspicious of the intentions of "Christians," because of considering their evangelism a covert expression of political espionage. The experience of Chinese, in spite of the admirable qualities of many missionaries, made them suspicious that many Westerners were really wolves in sheep's clothing. They were the servants of the imperialistic governments to which they owed allegiance, and who protected them with their gunboats.

It is important, facing the future, for Christians, both Western and Chinese, to be transparent in their motives, and to ensure that the freedom they promise does not become a means in re-enslavement. Christians need to ensure that they abide by the dual commandments – to love God and neighbours. One expression of this, the encouragement given to Chinese to explore close parallels between Confucian and Taoism, [2]accords with the Christian call to be transformed by the renewing of one's mind. [3]When such comparisons are made, it will become evident that Chinese Philosophy, no less than Greek Philosophy, anticipated the Gospel.

The following chapters hint at the possible interchanges that might have taken place along the Silk Road many years ago. The authors are interested in exploring similarities discernible in the ethical and contemplative traditions of China and the Christian West. They consider the sources of both to be the same God.

前 序

基督教本来属于犹太教教派，其教义极端，不怎么受制于律。起初，基督教不承认希腊哲学、伦理和科学，然而，后来还是接受了。基督教也容纳了希腊-罗马以及日耳曼、高卢、盎格鲁-撒克逊、斯堪的纳维亚和斯拉夫的风俗习惯。基督教传到中国比较晚，虽然暂时占下了，却没有汉化。作为夷教，基督教与欧洲殖民主义有着挥之不去的联系，它根植于西方文化，和宗教始祖豁达包容的精神相背离，甚至把体现基督精神并以之为鉴的寥寥教规和中华文化色彩的成分拒之门外。两大文化最终是要融合的，但冲突也是在所难免的。

"三自运动"主张把基督精神与殖民主义、帝国主义分离开来，这样，才能使基督教本土化，才能在中国传播福音过程中有所作为。

西方必须深入理解上两个世纪中国所历经的苦难和政治误国局面。基督教会尤其要弘扬最大体现上帝意志的仁爱悲悯。中国应该培育出土生土长的基督教来。

不要责怪中国疑心"基督徒们"居心何在，认为他们怀着政治阴谋到处传道。以往，不少传教士的精神是可嘉的，然而，经验也告诉中国人，也有很多西方人羊皮是假，狼性是真---他们是帝国主义国家靠着炮舰保护起来的忠实奴才。

面向未来，中国人也好，西方人也罢，信基督的干什么都要讲究透明，都要保证他们所允诺的自由不会为奴化人们的精神服务。基督徒要谨守"两大诫命"，爱上帝，也爱邻人。对此，儒道哲学讲究"尊道而贵德"，倒与基督教洗心革面的号召不谋而合（罗马书八章）。通过比较，人们会看到，中国哲学和希腊哲学差不到哪儿去，是会期待福音到来的。

下一章讲到，多少年以前，丝绸之路可能应该会发生贸易互动。但是，作者的兴趣在于审视中国和西方基督宗教和思维传统的共性。作者认为，它们的神都是同一个。

Introduction

Hans Kung identified the three great religious watercourses Hinduism/Buddhism of the Indus Valley, Judaism/Christianity/Islam in the Middle East, and Chinese religion/philosophy in the lowlands of the Yellow River. (4)

The major premise on which this volume is based is that these three "rivers" originated from the same source. The water flowing through each river represents the universal grace and revelation of the one god----the creator of the heaven and the earth.

However, it is the same water that flows through each of the rivers.Colour and quality of the water will reflect the geological character of the regions through which the water flows. There is a sense in which the different cultures and revealed truth are embodied, emphasize different dimensions of this truth. Each has been given a different gift to share.

The Chinese received in the "Philosophies Before Qin", earlier than 500 years before the birth of Jesus Christ, anticipatory understanding of the Christian gospel. These philosophies were mainly concerned with behavioural standards, which imposed certain social obligations, partly moral and partly physical, on those for whom they were designed. However, Chinese did not consider that these moral standards were imposed by divine fiat. Heaven was too far to have any bearing on behaviour. In one sense, the Chinese were like sheep without a shepherd. Fortunately, God, embracing them in his love, had not been forsaken the Chinese. With the high culture they inherited, it would have been a simple step for them to accept and worship the Creator God, whose "Word" had been the backbone of Chinese culture for thousands of years.

Father Matteo Ricci might have argued that Taoism and Confucian Thought were ethical teachings that fulfilled what Jesus described as the second greatest commandment "Love your neighbour as much as yourself." It was because of this high estimation of Chinese philosophy that he argued that what the Chinese needed was a deity to compliment this philosophy. This was no mere ruse on his part, and attempt to gain the confidence of the Chinese, was based on a genuine appraisal of Confucian morality. In his view, the Chinese with their culture were worthy of the son of the Creator God. Morality and spirituality is an indivisible unity. Those who are truly moral, not necessary perfectly moral, are close to God. When God gave Moses the Ten Commandments, six of them are dealt with ethics.

前 序

孔汉斯认为，世界有三大宗教：印度教/佛教、中东犹太教/基督教/回教、黄河下游平原的中国宗教哲学。

这部书主要是根据"三大源流"为同源的理论。每条源流的淙淙流水都是宇宙世界的创始者神的启示及其普世的恩慈。

然而，流过每条河的水并没有变。水的颜色和质量反映着它必经的地质特征。其意义在于它所蕴涵的不同的文化及其反映的真理，这种真理的维度不同。而每种文化各分天成。

前秦时代，也就是耶稣诞生500多年以前，中国哲学就已经悟到了基督福音。这些哲学主要观照行为规则，推行某些既定的道德或物质的社会责任。然而，中国人认为，这些道德规范并非神谕，"天"过于遥远，绝对不会约束人们的行为。简直之，中国人好似"散羊"。有幸的是，上帝仁慈的怀抱中，他们并没有被抛弃。有了高尚的文化，接受创造神的道不是不容易的，而这种"道"便是中国几千年文化的脊髓。

雷马太也许认为，儒道伦理满眼时间是耶稣所说的第二诫命："爱你的邻居如同自己"。雷氏高姿态评估中国哲学，认为中国人达到哲学上的圆满只需要一个神就够了。他并不是想讨好中国人，也不是强求他们信仰什么，而是在见到儒家道德观以后才说出了心里话。他认为，有中华文化的中国人无愧于创造神的子嗣。道德与灵性是个整体，是不可或缺的。那些真正有道德的，虽然称不上是全道，也是离上帝不远的了。上帝由摩西赐下十诫的时候，其中六条是关于伦理。

Introduction

Taoism and Confucian Thought reflect aspects of the principle of the Creator God, of his "Word," which Christians argue was incarnate in Christ. It can be argued that such a God can be seen to transcend all political, cultural and religious boundaries. These incarnations, in the context of different traditions, are the result of the revelation of the Spirit of God from differernt angle. This Spirit is the Go–Between God, who facilitates communication between God and people, between individuals and between cultures. Not all beneficiaries of this communication are aware that how it was facilitated, or what its Source is. It is the task of Christians, and others who are accessed by one Spirit, to help identify this transcendent Presence. For those who have benefited from the richness of Chinese culture, its ethical philosophy and psychology, will involve an openness towards the possibility of there being a transcendent Source of all that is best within the Chinese experience. For Christians, it will involve a recognition that the God they worship is far greater than their theology, and can only be truly known by the one who is invisible. Discussing traditions calls for humility all round, for repentance on the part of all dialogue partners.

True Spirituality, the awareness of and sensitivity to the Spirit presents in all of life, transcends all cultures. No matter how important each culture is, as the matrix of individual and social development, and as the springboard from which we can discover the deeply ecumenical connectedness of all peoples, it is the underlying spirituality that represents what is best in all cultures. This spirituality is foundational and of paramount importance. This truth is recognized by the contemplatives of all traditions. It is on the basis of such recognition that can only be appreciated by its being lived, and by a shared awareness that manifests. As the grace which gifts and shapes our lives, we can appreciate the underlying unity, the basic spiritual unity of all cultures. Without this awareness, we will be conscious of little more than our differences, and contend with each other to assert the correctness of our traditions.

It is only one on the basis of this deep spiritual awareness that we can sympathetically appreciate the distinctiveness of religious, philosophical and ethical traditions other than our own. It is also on this basis that we can incorporate aspects of those traditions into our own to enhance our understanding of inherited insights, and complement them where they are weak and deficient. It is this awareness that makes possible dialogue between traditions that reaches beyond the thinly veiled defensiveness that sometimes passes for dialogue.

It is as a consequence of this perspective – the result of meditative awareness, a meditative awareness fostered by all religious traditions – that we are emboldened to suggest that the marriage of the high culture of the Chinese, and the essence of Christian gospel, would represent a flourishing union.

前 序

儒道思想反映了普世创造之神，也反映了他的道，从基督徒的角度看，就是基督再生。由此，此神是超越所有政治、文化和宗教范畴的。在不同传统中，这些再生系统是神之灵从各个角度启示而来的。这灵便是保惠师，是他使神际、人际、个体和文化之间得以沟通。这种沟通所受惠的人并非全都能够完全知晓何沟通的方式和它的源头的。基督徒和其它受灵性点染的人可以证明这种超验的灵的存在。对于饱学中国文化的人而言，哲学和理学能够从中国人的经验中坦然地证实这位超世的灵的存在。基督徒也会公认，他们所崇拜的神超出他们的神学，不同的是，看不见的才为致知。知言成俗，言谈要谦恭、足戒。

至真的灵性也就是神灵的感知和敏锐体验，它存在于所有的生命当中，超越了一种文化。每种文化无论如何重要，作为个人和社会进步的母质，衔接着我们能够发现的各民族普遍深切勾连的内涵。这种潜伏的灵性代表着最优秀的文化，最基本的，也是最重要的。一切传统都源自思想，思想的结果便是真理。在这种认识论基础上，才会欣享生活经验，分享到昭示人间的共同意识。我们被赋予了形体，赋予了生命，我们便可以欣赏到所有文化的内在同一性及其根本的神合。如果没有这样的体认，那么，我们的认识要小于我们之间的差异，我们彼此之间就会为匡正各自的传统而发生争执。

只有深深地意识到这种灵性，我们才能以同情的态度来看待外面的宗教、哲学和道德上的差异。也只能基于这点，我们才能把我们的那些传统融汇到自身当中，以此来强化我们的内在认识，克服弱点，弥补缺陷。只有这种体会，传统和传统才可能进行对话，捅破横亘在对话之间的薄薄的心理防线。

从这点来看，一切教派要一改俗成，要韬光养晦；我们在此也斗胆地认为，中华文化和基督教福音的精髓一旦结合，必定天作之合，硕果累累。

Introduction |

Human inadequacy and cultural preoccupation, which have not been subject to adequate analysis, will frustrate any attempt at effecting a marriage between Chinese culture and Christianity. Therefore developing an indigenous Chinese Christianity draws upon Chinese ethical, cultural, religious and philosophical traditions in a way that goes beyond merely recognizing their historical importance. Part of the problem, both in China itself, and among overseas Chinese, is that many are either poorly educated in Chinese, particularly the sort of Chinese traditions we have been talking about, or are too Westernized to make a significant contribution to the dialogue

These problems are pivotal but not the only ones. There are others:

1.Some Western missionaries were ill-equipped to cross the cultural barrier between East and West. Some were not sufficiently educated in the high culture of the Chinese. The Theology of others was too orthodox or autocratic. They insisted on the superiority in their cultures, or their interpretation of Christian Scripture. Many of their interpretations would not have a foothold today, particularly among serious Biblical scholars. Some of these "orthodox" teachings are entrenched in the faith of some Western-educated Chinese.

2.The Westernized, ethnic Chinese are not sufficiently educated in their own culture to recommend Christianity to Chinese schooled in Confucian traditions. Some, because of their ignorance, misunderstand Chinese "values". Others are so well grounded in the culture of the country of their adoption that they do not have the inclination or posses the means to marry Christianity with Confucian culture.

3. Many overseas-born, educated Chinese Christians are either burdened with a sense of inferiority in their theological study, and lack the courage to venture into the unfamiliar and risky wilderness they must cross it if they are to teach Chinese compatriots schooled in the Chinese classic and brought up in traditional Chinese culture. Some may even prefer for it not being known that they are Christian in their approach or commitments. They would rather not ripple the waters. Their lack of knowledge, or timidity, have placed them in this dilemma.

4.Others are "peace lovers, " who have attained a considerable degree of theological depth, prefer to be held stationary, like the three monkeys, who see no evil, hear no evil, and speak no evil. The task of bringing together the best in Chinese culture and the essence of Christianity is a gargantuan undertaking, which will need to be re-worked in each generation, as new insights come to hand, as new attitudes develop, and as new opportunities arise for in-depth dialogue.

前 序

如果不搞清楚了人性的缺点和文化的偏见，那么中华文化和基督教的结合必然受到挫伤。如果要建立本土化的中国式基督教，需要从中国的道德、文化、宗教和哲学的传统着手，从历史的角度得到超越。问题是，中国也好，海外华人也好，不少人汉语水平贫瘠，尤其是我们从来提到的哪类传统型的华人；也有不少人西化了，想对话也是无从谈起的。

上述是问题的关键所在，然而也不止如此。

1. 有些西方传教士们不具备跨越中西方文化的素质，有些人连象样的汉文化教养都欠缺。有些人的神学观过于正统，过于武断。他们只认同自己的文化多么多么优越，什么都手不离圣经。现在，圣经阐述论中的许多观点已经站不住脚了，一头扎进神经的学者们尤其如此。这些"正统的"说教有些深深地陷入西化教育的华人信仰之中。

2. 西化的华裔自身的文化底蕴不足，却要给儒学的华人传授基督教。有些人因为自己无知，才误解了中国人的价值观。有些人深深地根植于他们所适应的国家的文化，不敢奢望、也无法把基督教和儒家文化结合起来。

3. 许多受过教育的华裔基督徒在神学领域是自卑的，没有勇气迈进这种未知而迷茫的险境，他们有的无非是教教受过华夏经典教育并在中华文化传统背景下成长起来的华裔同胞。有些人在人情往来过程中，不愿意让别人知道自己是信奉基督的。他们不想无事生非。他们知识的匮乏和性情的懦弱使他们自己进退两难。

4. 其它人"熬好和平"，神学底蕴相当深厚，但却不闻，不问，不看，事不关己。因此，要把中华文化和基督教的精髓实质拢在一起，工程莫大如是，需要每一代人都要反复劳作，产生新的见解，产生新的观点，产生新的机遇，以此来进行深入的对话。

Introduction

The Silk Road does not pretend to be a substantial academic undertaking, let alone a definitive study. It offers little vignettes, teasing suggestions. These are premised, as we have indicated, upon what we claim to be a shared awareness of the creative, sustaining, and illuminating Spirit that is the essence of reality, a Presence that Christians claim was incarnate in Christ. This Spirit is the source, not only of all life, but of all best in all religious traditions and philosophies. It is on the basis of this conviction that the brief studies that make up this book were put together. They are intimations of the thesis we have been arguing.

The Apostle Paul argued that, in spite of superficial differences between people, all share a common humanity. Beneath the colour of their skin, and the cultural differences that distinguish them, all human beings are the same clay pots bearing the signature of the creator. These clay pots are the receptacles of the Spirit of God.

It is our conviction that the grace expressed so imperfectly in us all, and in nature, was uniquely present in Jesus of Nazareth. It was for this reason that he was described as the Word of God, that is, the incarnation of the creative Word of God, the full-blown manifestation of the Spirit that indwells us all, that constitutes our eternal essence. Being able to relate to the incarnation of the eternal Word in Christ, we can find release from our selfishness and parochialism. We can find healing. We can be "saved." We can discover a new dimension to living, and find ourselves having been possessed by the values of the Kingdom of what Jesus spread of.

The Silk Road was the old well-trodden highway between Chang An and Baghdad-Damascus-Tyre-Byzantium and beyond. It was a strategic position for travel and trade. The Silk Road seeks to effect a different sort of religio-cultural exchange, between China and Western Christianity. We invite you to sample the exchanges that are attempted. We do not anticipate that the merchandise will appeal to all readers. But we do invite you to hold a tolerant attitude as your contribution.

前 序

丝绸之路不可能成为饱学之路,也不可能规定人们去研究什么。它所做的无非是调个味、逗个乐而已。我们曾经说过,这些都是假设,假设的基础是大家都能意识到的创新精神、可持续精神和维明精神---这,便是事实的精髓,而这种精髓也就是基督徒所称的基督化身的存在。这种精神是生命源头,是一切宗教传统和哲学流派中的精粹。基于这个信念,写作本书所需要的寥寥素材也便拢在一起了。而这些素材一直围绕着我们所谈的主题进行。

使徒保罗有言,人们表面上相异,而博爱却是共同的。在我们不同的肤色和文化差异之下,人类无非都是同炉陶罐,盖着创造者的戳记。这些陶罐就是用来收藏上帝之灵的。

我们相信,上帝的慈爱在我们所有人身上或在自然界中是不可能体现得十全十美的,而在拿撒勒人耶稣身上,却倍加青睐。正因为这样,耶稣被称为上帝的道,就是全能上帝的道化身的,也是永恒的圣灵与我们同在,真理就是这样形成的。我们在基督这里领会永恒的道的化身,就可以从自私和偏见当中走出来。我们找到了医治的方子,我们得救了。我们还会找到新的生存领域,拥有耶稣所传的天国的价值。

古代丝绸之路把长安和巴格达-大马士革-泰来-拜占庭以及其它地区沟通起来,是商旅必经之路。这本《丝绸之路》旨在寻求中国与西方基督教在宗教和文化上的交流。我们敦请读者重点看看交流,并不敢奢望读者都对贸易感兴趣。尚希包涵赐教。

The Philosophy of Lao Zi

The Word,

that can be discussed,

is not the eternal word.

老子的哲学

道可道，非恒道也。

CHAPTER ONE
What is Dao? Is it a pseudonym for God?

The word that can be discussed is not the Eternal Word.

The origin of Taoism in China can be traced back to the matriarchal society that existed c. 6, 000 B. C. E. Between 1953–1957 many sites of ruins and relics of that period have been excavated in the south of the Yellow River. A good example is Banpo Village, in the eastern suburbs of Xian city in Shanxi Province.

The question of survival, the society where the infant mortality rate was extremely high, was of vital importance at that time. It is little wonder that reproduction was considered to be great significance. As a consequence, women at that time played a more central role than men in that primitive society. They assumed the dominant role in the family as well as in the community. This led to a focus on "women, " "mother earth, " and feminine "reproductive organs." These emphases found expressions in Taosim. This focus was reflected in such phrases as: "mother of all creation"; "value the mother of life-nourishment"; "the gate of reproduction is called the root of heaven and earth". It is also of interest to note that femininity was associated with gentleness, tenderness and weakness and with peace and harmony in society. (5)

At the time this matrifocal society was superseded by a patriarchal society men who needed to protect and defend the community when it came under attack. According to legend, the Yellow Emperor (2697 B. C. E.), a peace-loving leader, following the principle of Taoism, fought and defeated his half-brother, Yan Di, a war-monger who were disrespectful for the teachings of Dao. Four classics, which were attributed to the work of Yellow Emperor, contributed to the philosophy of the Dao. (6)Peace reigned through the time of two other legendary emperors who followed the Yellow Emperor. They were Tang Yao and Yu Shun. Both voluntarily abdicated in favour of younger and wiser men. This represented the teachings of Dao, which advised "retreat after accomplishment" (功遂身退 gong sui shen tui), "do not contend", "do not live for yourself", and "sacrifice yourself for your love of the world".

第一章

什么是道？道是否是上帝的别号？

道可道，非恒道。

中国，道哲学的起源可以追溯到公元前约6000年时母系社会。1953-1975年间，黄河南面发掘许多这一时期的遗址、遗物。陕西省西安市东郊的半坡村即是一例。

当时的社会，婴幼儿死亡率极高，生存问题至关重要。因此，人口繁衍问题极其重要。在当时的原始社会里，女人至上，位处核心，里里外外一把手。这就导致了"女性崇拜"、"母地崇拜"以及女性"生殖器崇拜"。道家特别推崇这些说法，如从"万物之母"、"贵食母"、"玄牝之门是谓天地之根"等语辞中均有所反映。值得注意的是，从女性的身上联想到的是温柔和柔弱，还有社会的平安和谐。

母系社会被父系社会取替，男人要担负起防护群落免受袭击的责任。据说，部落之首黄帝（轩辕氏，公元前约2697年生）爱好和平，尊道而行，打败了好战背道的嫡弟炎帝。黄帝所著的四书对道学亦有所贡献。道学往往被人称作"黄老哲学"。黄帝之后，传说中的唐尧和虞舜这两帝治国平安，都自动禅让给年轻贤达之士，这便引出了道学所倡导的"功遂身退"、"不争"、"不自生"和"爱以身为天下"。

What is Dao? Is it a pseudonym for God?

Lao Zi brought together the teachings of Dao Philosophy into the Dao De Jing, the Classics of Dao De. He considered that God was Lord-on-high or "Heaven", and that Dao was associated with the "Lord-on-high" or "Heaven." From the study of the Dao De Jing, which was written during the period of Spring and Autumn Warring States, some 2,500 years ago, it is obvious that Dao was not regarded as God. Dao was, however, as mysterious as God and man by himself can understand it. As Lao Zi, put it, if "Dao can be discussed, it is not the eternal Dao". Nevertheless, this Dao according to Lao Zi, "'pour'down" from Heaven. Lao Zi "wonders whose offspring it is" and "whether it existed before God". Such comments suggest that the Dao belongs to the spiritual realm, beyond this physical world. [7]

A meeting between Lao Zi and Confucius, as reported by Zhuang Zi in Tian Yun described the mysterious nature of Dao. The narrative reads:

When Confucius went to the south to meet Lao Zi at his age of fifty-one, Lao Zi asked him, " I have heard that you are a wise man in the north. Here, you come. Do you possess the knowledge of Dao?" Confucius replied, "I have not attained it." "How did you quest for it?" Lao Zi asked again. Confucius said, "I have tried from a number of systems for five years, while, I have not attained what I quest for!" Lao Zi added "What else did you do to quest after it?" "For another twelve years I searched from the doctrine of paradox yin yang to attain the knowledge of Dao and still I have achieved nothing!" Confucius replied. Lao Zi then said, "That is right! If Dao can be presented as an offering, people will respectfully present it to the emperor. If Dao can be presented as a gift, people will piously present it to their parents. If Dao can be told, people will tell it to their brethren. If Dao can be given as an inheritance, people will bequeath it to their descendants. However, such a thing is not possible. There is no other reason. If the heart inside (a person) does not accept it, Dao will not stay there. If outward deeds do not bear witness about it, Dao will not be popularized. Speaking from his heart (that is, with sincerity), the sage will not teach people, if it is not accepted by them. If the hearts of people do not accept anything coming from outside them, the sage will not dwell on the subject.' "

老子把道学一股脑地写入《道德经》。他认为，神即上帝或"天"，道属于"天"而不是"天"。我们可以从大约2500年前春秋战国时所著的道德经中找到答案：道并不是上帝，却和上帝同样神秘，单靠人的天质是没有办法明了的。所以老子说："道可道，非恒道也"。老子认为，道即"道冲"。老子发问道："吾不知其谁之子也？象帝之先"。这种说法意即道超出了物质世界，属于灵界。

庄子在《天运》中描写老子和孔子相会，谈论道的神秘。文章是这样说的：孔子行年五十有一而不闻道，乃南之沛见老聃。老聃曰："子来乎？吾闻，子北方之贤者也，子亦得道乎？"孔子曰："未得也。"老子曰："子恶乎求之哉？"曰："吾求之于度数，五年而未得也。"老子曰："子又恶乎求之哉？"曰："吾求之于阴阳，十有二年而未得。"老子曰："然。使道而可献，则人莫不献之于其君；使道而可进，则人莫不进之于其亲；使道而可以告人，则人莫不告其兄弟；使道而可以与人，则人莫不与其子孙。然而不可者，无它也，中无主而不止，外无正而不行。由中出者，不受于外，圣人不出；由外入者，无主于中，圣人不隐"。

After that conversation, Confucius went back and told his students that he had visited the one who was like a dragon, meaning someone who was as omnipotent as a dragon. (Note: Confucius had 3000 students and 72 scholars). He was considered a great teacher and a wise man, but he just could not understand what the Dao was. It was not something that he could firmly grasp or that he could teach. (8)

The Christian theologian and author, Hans Kung, asked whether "Dao" is a synonym for God?

Lao Zi argued that the Dao came from above, meaning, Heaven, and was "the source of everything" created. He further contended that "In being used, the Dao is never exhausted". He described this Dao as "invisible, inaudible and intangible. "Following it, we cannot see its back, confronting it, we cannot see its face". This was why Lao Zi considered that "Heaven (or God) seems to have no shape, and that the dao (his word) is hidden without a name". He went on to argue, however, that "upon careful study and observation of the Dao, it can be seen to be a substance replete with essence, truth, and faith". He said that Dao existed before everything, even "before heaven and earth". It is, in fact, "the mother of heaven and earth". Lao Zi explained, "I do not yet know its name, and so I nickname it 'Dao'". "What proceeds from Dao, " he argued, "is bland and tasteless" Lao Zi contended that the Dao was eternal but nameless, but full of humility. (9) From this it can be argued that the Dao is not God, but is rather "The Word of God".

If Dao is "The Word of God, " how does Lao Zi explain it? Lao Zi argued that one of the characteristics of Dao was that it was intangible, that we "need to spend effort to understand the teaching of the Dao." This exploration should be what we get out of".

言毕，孔子归，谓弟子曰，此今于是乎见龙！（注：孔子有三千学生和七十二贤士）孔子被尊为至人、圣师，但什么是道，他不明白，把握不好，也教不了。

基督教神学家兼作者汉氏康发问：道是不是上帝的别号？

老子认为，道是上面来的，意思是从天上来的，是"万物之宗"，"而用之有弗有盈也"。他把道形容为"微，希，夷"，"随而不见其后，迎而不见其首"。老子由此认为，"天像无形，道隐无名"。他又说，道之物，"唯望唯汤…中有象…中有物…中有精。"他说，道乃"先天地生"，又言，道"可以为天下母"。"吾未知其名也，字之曰道"。"道之出言也，曰：'淡而无味'"。老子主张，道恒而名朴，满有廉讓。由此可见，道不是上帝，却是"上帝之言"。

如果说这是"上帝之言"的话，老子是怎样解释的呢？老子认为，道者难明，须用心入道，"明道如费；进道如退"。

As the Dao is an eternal entity, it is difficult to comprehend or describe. Hence, we have to put in great effort to engage it, and the achievement will be proportionate to the effort. Confucius, at the age of fifty, still did not understand the Dao, an understanding that he so much desired it. Dao is not worldly knowledge, but is spiritually discerned.

Though Judeo-Christianity and the philosophy of Lao Zi come from two different traditions, there are certain similarities in the teaching of "The Word of God" and the "Dao." The Israelites were forgetful following the Way of God that God was so disappointed and frustrated that he wanted to inscribe his Law in their hearts. One conclusion that being drawn from this similarity is that the inspiration behind the Judaeo-Christian tradition and the philosophy of Lao Zi are from the same source.

"Whatever a man plants that shall he reap." This is true that all the conditions for cultivation met. The state of the ground plays a very important part. This is illustrated in the story told by Jesus of Nazareth about a Sower. The condition of the ground, which represents the heart, that is, an individual's receptivity, is important. If the seed of the gospels falls on a well-trodden path, the seed will not germinate, and will be eaten up by the birds. If the seed falls on rocky ground with little soil, the seed may germinate, but will not cope with extreme weather changes and will die, owing to lack of support. Seed that falls on ground covered with thorny bushes, where the warmth of the sun cannot reach it, will be stunted and finally choked by the bushes. Only the seed that falls on rich soil will germinate and grow. With preparation, including a little fertilizer, the harvest will be 30 percent. With a little more, it will be 60 percent. With sufficient fertilizer it will yield 100 percent. (Matthew 13). This parable teaches the importance of both the state of readiness of one's heart and the effort we need to put in to pursue the teaching of the Word. The more we empty our hearts in humility, the more we can accommodate the Word of God, which Christians believe was incarnate in Christ.

Spiritual advancement and worldly riches are like weights on alternate sides of a balance. Those who pursue spirituality seem to be troubled less by the burden of riches, and the reverse is also true. Jesus of Nazareth said that it was easier for a camel to go through the eye of a needle than for a rich man to enter the kingdom of God. It appears that worldly burdens hinder the pursuit of spirituality. Siddhatha Gautama gave up his future kingship, and all the luxuries of palace life, in his search for Enlightenment.

There are many demands of the Dao of Heaven, or the Way of Heaven. These demands are not preconditions for attaining a knowledge of Dao, but rather the result of attainment, much as Jesus sermon on the Mount is not so much a list of do's, but rather a description of a life lived in the energies and under the direction of the Spirit.

道有常，不易明了，不易描述，非下苦功夫，否则难以有成。孔子欲得道，可是活到五十岁还不明白什么是道。道不是世上的知识，而是灵性的参悟。

虽然犹太教/基督教与老子哲学传统不同，然而，"上帝之言"和"道"也有许多共同之处。以色列人没把上帝之道当回事，上帝便失望了，便想把自己的意志刻到他们的心里。从这个相同点可以得出一个结论，就是藏在犹太和基督教传统以及老子哲学背后的灵感是同一个渊源。

"种瓜得瓜，种豆得豆"，假设耕种条件具备，那么，这句话便说得真切。土质非常重要，关于这一点，拿撒勒人耶稣撒种的比喻说得好。土壤好比心脏，其重要程度体现在它的接收能力。假如福音的种子掉下踏平的路上，种子发不了芽，就会被飞鸟吃掉。假如种子掉在石头上，土壤很少，种子即使发了芽，因为得不到外力，天气一变，也就枯死了。假如种子掉进荆棘，温暖的阳光够不到，发育受到了阻碍，最后还是被荆棘扼死了。只有掉在肥沃的土壤里，种子才能发芽生长。备耕点肥，收成会达到三成。再加点粪肥，收成可达到六成。粪肥充足，收成圆满（马太福音第十三章）。这个模拟说的是，心理上做好准备，行动上付出努力，按照道之道去指引自己的行动方向。我们越谦虚，越融进上帝之道，基督徒化身基督就是这个道理。

灵性的文明和世间的财富好似天秤各执一端。追求灵性的人不被物累，反之亦然。耶稣说，富人进天国好比过针眼儿。显然，物累阻碍了对灵性的追求。释迦摩尼放弃王位继承，放弃了宫殿里奢华人生，反而去寻求开化了。

"天之道"有许多条件，但求道并存在先决条件，得道之后，也就有了条件。耶稣"登山宝训"不是一个串门徒该做的事，这里描写的是在圣灵教导下力所能及的生活。

Among the demands of the Dao are the following:

(1) Know the Dao and put it into practice:

Lao Zi argues that "knowing the teaching of the Dao, one should "use" it, that is, putting into practice the insights acquired. The effect of the Dao on a person is not to free him from passion into "emptiness", or "passivity", where one "does nothing ". On the contrary, it brings a demand to "perform work without acting against the teaching of the Word, and to put the Word into practice without babbling on about it" The Dao demands action. It is far from retreating to inactivity and passivity, or "non-action, " and "doing nothing". One is supposed to empty oneself of worldly materialism and covetous desires, and to do things that are "not against" the teaching of The Word.

When persons empty themselves in this way, they become selfless, humble and caring, with a "love that compels them to serve the world like a common servant or a hired hand", and to "sacrifice themselves for their love of the world". When one is selfless, he gives up worldly wealth, status, authority, power and glory. Like the Desert Fathers, in the Christian tradition, he makes do with minimum physical reserves. In such a state of humility, he is not afraid of losing himself.

Jesus argued that those who knew the Word of God and put it into practice were his brothers, sisters and mothers. He asked those who wanted to be his disciples to deny themselves and to take up their crosses and follow him. To deny yourself is to empty yourself of your excessive wants, but this does not necessarily make you an ascetic. On the contrary, denial of yourself is a call to selflessness, and to free yourself into humility, as Jesus did. The next step is to take up the cross by doing the Will of God, that is, to prepare to serve the world. Jesus said that he had come to serve the world and not to be served. Jesus of Nazareth did not claim equality with God. In humility, Christ took up the human form, assuming the nature of a servant to serve the world: obeying the Will of God to the point of death.

St. Augustine realized the importance of service. For this reason, monasteries became centers of education and health. Therefore, they lived up to the demand of the Second Great Commandment "Love your neighour as yourself."

(2) Do not contend:

If you have attained the teaching of Dao, "your good behaviour will be like the character of water". The qualities of water have been appreciated by Chinese sages. Water nourishing, never asks any reward in return; it gives and gives ceaselessly. In service, it flows to the lowest level, a level often despised by others.

"道"的要求如下：

1. 识道遵行

在老子看来，"知"道为了"用"道，也就是把既得的认识付诸实践。得道的结果并不是让人脱离激情，进入"虚空"甚至"无为"。相反，得道要"居无为之事，行不言之教"。道，要求行动，而绝不是要人退到静虚状态，达到无所作为的结果。人应该摒除尘世的物欲和贪念，要无违"道"而行。

如果人能舍己，那么，自私的因素也就没了，有的是谦逊，和"爱以身为天下牧"，甚至能爱以身为天下。如果脱离了自私，那么他就会放弃世间财富、名位。也就像基督教里的"沙漠神父"一样，物欲要求少之又少。人都到了这个不能再退的境界，还有什么舍不得的呢。

耶稣认为，谁听上帝的话，照上帝的旨意去做，那么，谁就是他的兄弟姐妹，就是他的母亲。他告诉想做他弟子的，要舍得出，要扛起十字架跟着他。舍己就是要摆脱过多的欲望，但不等于禁欲。实际上，舍己呼唤的是无私，就像耶稣那样，把自己解脱出来，进入悲悯状态。然后，扛起十字架，遵行上帝的旨意，时刻准备着为苍生服务。耶稣说，他来到人世，就是要服务世人，而不是要世人服务的。耶稣从来没有说过和上帝平起平坐，他以谦卑的姿态幻化人形，以仆人的身份来为人民服务：秉承帝旨，死而后已。

圣奥古斯丁意识到了服务于人的重要性。为此，寺院成了治病育人的地方。这也兑现了第二大诫命上所倡导的：爱人如爱己。

2. 不争

如果你已经得道，那么，你就会"上善若水"。中国古代圣贤赞美水的质量。水滋养万物，不争报答，不停地给予。在给予的过程中，水流向最低的地方，流到了别人时常瞧不上眼的地方。

It "does not contend", but accommodates itself to everything it encounters, whatever its size, shape, condition or colour is. Its tolerance is beyond description. Water is soft, gentle and yielding. The softness of water can overcome the hardest thing in the world. Drops of water can wear the rock onto which it falls; rivers alter their courses as they go, and waves change coastal lines. "Gentleness overcomes agitation" and "Agitation forfeits mastery", when one loses self-control. It is wise to maintain calmness and coolness, when one gets agitated quickly, he often loses his head. When this happens, instead of problems solving we make hasty decisions that often turn out to be wrong.

(3) Social Equality or No Distinction of Status:

If "the scholar are not much honoured", people will not shoot for class status. This advice is designed to promote equality in society. When there is no class distinction, people are more inclined to be selfless. They will not yearn for distinction and will not be arrogant. This arrogance creates ill-feeling, even among best of friends. Treat a person as a person, without putting her on a pedestal for her achievement, so that she will have less inclination to become arrogant, and to regard others as inferior. This advice, however, is not intended to discourage excellence. It is invidious distinctions, not excellence that does the damage.

Jesus of Nazareth similarly fostered an ethos in which distinctions fell away. The Apostle Paul, wishing to further this spirit in the church, argued that "There is neither Jew nor Greek, slave nor free, male nor female, for you are all in Christ." This is true freedom and equality.

The Dao De Jing goes on to suggest that when there is "no demand or no desire for things that are rare and expensive", thieves and robbers will not be encouraged to ply their trade. Luxury arouses covetousness, which in turn creates disharmony. We should seek to maintain a basic level of comfort rather than an exaggerated level. Food "is for the stomach and not for the eyes". Eat food for its nourishment, and do not be too concerned about fanciful colours or exotic flavour. That is, we should eat to live rather than living to eat. When we do this we will not crave for things that are difficult to obtain.

(4) Be contented

The Dao urges us to live with "simplicity with no covetous desires", which makes it easy for one to "be contented". This is why "the sages can forgo extremities, luxuries and extravagance". Lao Zi argues that "when one is contented, one is rich".

水不争，不管碰到了什么，不管所碰到的东西是大是小，是什么形状，是好是歹，是什么颜色，它都能一概包容。它的包容雅量大得难以形容。水是柔软的、温顺的、谦让的。"天下者至柔，驰天下之至坚"。滴滴的水能穿透盘石；河流改变航道；波浪变更海岸。"静为躁君，躁则失君"。明智的是冷静、沉着，如果冲动，难免失去理智。如果失去理智，也就解决不了问题，还会急功臆断，事与愿违。

3. 平等社交或不分阶级

"不尚贤"，人们也就上不了层次。这就是说，社会本来应该是平等的。如果社会没有阶级，人们往往也就无私了。他们不求什么身份，不摆什么高姿态。看不起人是要坏事的，挚友之间也是如此。要把人当人看，不要谁有才就把谁捧了上去，只有这样，人才会戒骄戒躁，也不会瞧不起别人。这么说并不是打消积极性。人们反感的是被划定了身份，坏事的绝不是因为谁做得优秀。

耶稣所推崇的性格就是消除人和人的不同。使徒保罗在教会里推行这种平等精神，他说："你们受洗归入基督的…不分犹太人还是希腊人，不分奴隶还是自由人，不分男人还是女人，在基督耶稣这里，你们就是一切"。这才是真正的自由、平等。

《道德经》上说："不贵难得之物，使民不为盗"。奢华引起贪欲，贪欲产生不和。我们应该寻求一种维持祥和局面的基本水平，这个水平是不能夸大的。食物"为腹而不为目"，吃是为了营养，而不是为了追求色泽和香气。我们吃是为了活着，活着而不是为了吃。这样，我们才不会汲汲以求难求的东西了。

4. 知足

"道"要求我们生活"见素抱朴，少私寡欲"，这样，才能易于知足。为此，"圣人去甚，去太，去奢"。老子说："知足者，富也"。

The advice is not altogether unequivocal, as we each draw the line at a different place. But it is important for us to consider drawing a line. "No calamity is greater than for one who does not know what is enough".

There are three economic levels——subsistence, comfort and luxury. The first level may describe those who have just enough to survive on basic staple foods, slightly better than from hand to mouth. The second category represents those who have no worry about where the next meal will come from, but whose wants are not excessive. This middle income group may have to sacrifice other things to occasionally enjoy something luxurious. Those were given to luxury demand the finest quality, or the rarest type of food. Their appetites are far in excess of what is required. More often than not, such excess is waste. The high-income group can afford all the niceties without worrying about impoverishing themselves. However, the level of wealth one aims at depends on where he draws the line. The attitude of being contented is a form of wealth.

Jesus of Nazareth taught his followers, saying, "Look at the birds of the air, they do not sow or reap or store away in barns, and yet your Heavenly Father feeds them …," but "Seek first the Kingdom of God and his righteousness, and all these necessary (material) things will be given to you." He also made reference to a poor rich fool, who wanted to build large storehouses to house his bumper crop. He was not able to enjoy what he was putting away because he died shortly after he decided to build more capacious barns. He told this parable to illustrate that we should be contented, and give generously of what we have.

(5) Be generous:

"Do not live for yourself only". Lao Zi suggests that the reason "heaven and earth last forever" is "because they do not exist for themselves". Its existence is for the sake of the life they sustain, the life of men, birds and animals. They have "no self-desire".

Jesus argued that we should live generously. We should "give to the needy, without letting our left hand know what our right has done."

The Apostle Paul, taking up the same theme, told the Philippines not only look to their own interest, but also to the interest of others.

(6) Be moderate and humble:

Lao Zi argued that people are "created by the word and nurtured by integrity", and should "adopt moderation" in attitude and behaviour. "Knowing your ability, you do not trumpet your own virtues; respect yourself, do not over-value yourself".

这则戒言并非毫不含糊，关键是这条"知足"的线划在哪里，因此，划线是个问题。"祸莫大以不知足"。

从经济角度来讲，可分为生存、温饱和奢靡三类。第一类是活着全靠基本的主食来勉勉强强地糊口。第二类是上顿不愁下顿，所求也不太多。这类人的收入平平，想偶尔享受一下，别考虑其它的了。至于穷奢极欲的人来说，他们要最好的，吃最奇的。他们的胃口常常超过所需，然而，多了往往属于浪费。高新一族不必犯愁穷困，最好的也能买得起。不过，认定财富的标准取决于线划在哪里。知足也是一种财富。

耶稣教诲弟子们说："你们看天上的飞鸟，也不种，也不收，也不仓储，但是，你们的天父养活他们"。又说："先去找上帝的王国，再去找上帝的义，一切都会赐给你的"。耶稣拿那个无知的财主作了个比喻，他想盖个大房子来收藏丰收的庄稼，他所收藏的他无法享受了，因为他刚想盖个大仓子，他就死了。他用这则寓言来说明，我们应该"知足"，我们应该对自己所有的处理得要大度些。

5. 要慷慨

"不自生"。老子说："天地能长久，以其不自生"。存在就是为了维持生命---人的命、鸟和兽的命。它们"无私欲"。

耶稣说："我们应当慷慨地活着"，我们应当"施舍穷人，但是，不要右手做了什么，不要让左手知道"。

使徒保罗告诉腓立比人说："不要只考虑自己，也要考虑一下别人"。

6. 中庸和谦卑

老子认为，人是"道生之，德畜之"。人的态度与行为要"守于中"，要"自知而不见，自爱而不自贵"，要记住："自伐者无功"。

"Those who flaunt their virtues have no more merits". Whatever you do to serve others, you "should not seek to justify your own action, boast, or be conceited". One should be humble and accommodating, as valleys are low lying and receptive. If one "wishes to lead the people, one must put oneself last".

Jesus told a parable of the Pharisee and the Publican who went to the temple to pray, where the Pharisee overstated his righteousness and the Publican beat his chest in repentance, highlighted a similar ethic. Jesus advised his disciples, "When you pray, you do not stand in the temple or at the street intersection to make youself be seen by others just like the hypocrites' doing."

(7) Do not overhoard:

Do not "hoard treasures in your house", because they will catch thieves and robbers' eye and be difficult to protect. The Taoist suggests that we should not seek necessity for life of excess. What is more, gold and jade are subjectively appraised. If no one craved gold or jade, their value would diminish.

The owner of Yuyuan in Shanghai, which is a tourist spot today, collected rare jewels and precious stones. These treasured objects cost all his money. In his will, he advised his descendants not to repeat this foolish activity. In human history, many kingdoms decomposed after the expensive tastes, pleasures and extravagances of their rulers.

Jesus suggested that his disciples should not worry about tomorrow, but rather deal with tomorrow's worries. They should "… store up treasure in heaven, where moth and rust can not destroy it, and thieves can not break in and steal it."

(8) Service before self:

When you "govern a state and care for the people", you should not do so solely for your own aggrandizement. You should "treat the wishes of the people as your own desire". Lao Zi argued that leaders should be like fish, which should not leave deep water, that is, they should stay close to the wishes of the people. One of the three qualities of good leaders is that they follow the aspiration of the people". They are also instructed to be "compassionate" and "thrifty".

无论给别人做了什么，都应该"不自视，不自见，不自伐"和"不自矜"。人要谦卑、随和，好比峡谷一样，位置是低了，但可以过得去。"欲先民，必身后"。

　　耶稣有则比喻，说的是法利塞人和税吏去教会祈祷。法利塞人自夸有多么仗义，税吏则一顿捶胸，表示悔悟，也唱起了同样的高调。耶稣劝告门徒们说："你们祷告的时候，不要站在教堂，也不要站在街中央，不要让人看到，那样纯粹是伪君子干的"。

7. 不要多囤积：

　　不要"金玉满堂"，因为贵重之物很难保护，而且也会招贼。道家认为，身外之物不要求。金玉是人定的，人不爱金玉，金玉必然贬值。

　　上海豫园是旅游圣地，它的主人收藏了稀世珍宝，让他倾囊而出。主人在遗嘱中劝告子孙不要重复他的愚笨行为。人类历史上，许多王国的衰落都是因为统治者骄奢淫逸。

　　耶稣认为，门徒不需要为明天忧虑，但是要应对明天的忧虑。他们要"积财宝于天堂，也就是贼不能近、虫也不能蛀的地方"。

8. 服务为身先：

　　当你"爱民治国"的时候，不要单单考虑自己往上爬，应该"以百姓之心为心"。老子认为，领导者要像"鱼不脱于渊"，要贴近人们的意愿。成功的领导者应具备的三种品性，其一就是"退其身而身先"。其它两个品行是慈爱和勤俭。

While you may excel, because of your abilities and industry, you should not "dominate others". After you have "completed a task, you should retreat", that is, not dwell on your accomplishments.

In all forms of government, those who aspire to leadership are tempted to use their power to serve their own desire, aggrandize themselves and preserve their positions. As Lord Acton argued "Power corrupts and absolute power corrupts absolutely." [10] This is strongly against the principle of Dao.

Jesus of Nazareth said to his disciples that those who wanted to be leaders of other people must first be their servants. [11]

Unfortunately, the hearts of men have not been changed greatly by Dao Philosophy or the Christian Gospel. We have the same selfish, self-centred hearts, hearts that are reductant to yield to the Way of God.

(9) Identify with the Dao:

Lao Zi argued that when we "identify with the teaching of 'The Word', " we will possess it. On the other hand, when we are out of touch with Dao that subsidiary virtues such as benevolence, righteousness, piety, and faithfulness etc., we arise unselfconsciously and take on an independence that can gut them of true virtue". That is, they become virtues to be striven for, accomplishments that evoke the praise of others. In this context, the 'forced' acquisition of such virtues can lead to hypocrisy and treachery. The assistance we give to others needs to be sincere, "without conceit, boastfulness, and self-congratulation".

Abraham obeyed the Way of God and was credited with righteousness. It is said that Enoch walked with God so closely that God took him away and he did not experience death.[12]

The Apostle Paul argued that, "If anyone is in Christ, he is a new creation, the old has gone, the new has come." This is another way of saying that true virtue arises as a consequence of discerning and following the intuitions of the Spirit, or the way of Dao, "The Word." Putting it in slightly different terms, Paul contended that "Those who live according to natural inclinations have their minds set on what nature desires; but those who live in accordance with the Spirit have their minds set on what the Spirit desires."

你的能力和才干可以胜过他人，但千万不可用来宰制他人，也就是"长而不宰"，而要"功遂身退"，不可居功久留。

无论是什么样的政府，都是一些谋权者弄权自利，使权膨胀，用权自守。阿克顿大人断言："权利造成腐败，绝对权力造成绝对腐败"。这与道大相径庭。

耶稣告诫门徒："想领导别人，必须首先被别人领导。"

不幸的是，人们的思想并没有因为道学或基督教福音而改变，人们照例自私自利，对上帝之路寡然止步。

9. 同于道

老子说："从事而道者，同于道"。换句话讲，如果人离开了道，那么，仁义悯信等配套的品德也就落空了，就是说，"大道废，安有仁义-孝慈-贞节"。守德也就成为令人赞扬并奋力争取的美德。而这些美德一旦是被迫争取来的，也就会导致伪善和欺诈。我们帮人，应该出于诚实，应该做到"毋骄、毋矜、毋伐"。

亚伯拉罕听从上帝的道，他就因信称义。据说以诸与上帝同行，上帝把他接去，他没有过死亡的经历。

使徒保罗说过："如果人信了基督，他也就有了新生，原来的人没了，换了个新人。"换句话说，人受了领悟，随从圣灵直觉或者是道的启示，真正的德行也就出现了。用保罗的话稍微换个说法，也就是："随从肉体的人，体贴肉体的事。随从圣灵的人，体贴圣灵的事。"

(10) Do not kill:

"Resort to arms is an inauspicious act and one should do it only when compelled to do so". The teaching of "The Word" discourages the use of unnecessary force. It favours gentleness and peace. Lao Zi argued that when "a man is alive and well, he is soft and tender, however, when he begins to be tough and hard, he is obviously walking towards death". The teaching of The Word forbids threatening others with death, or making a spectacle of execution. "The people do not fear death, what is the purpose of threatening to kill them? If people always make spectacle out of such death by killing, I will kill those who organize and carry out such executions".

In Ancient China massive slaughter was carried out by warlords. They were merciless in their treatment of each other, and each other's forces and peoples. Rivals and their families were unceremoniously eliminated. Relations were wiped out to prevent possible retaliation. They "not only cut the grass, but also removed the roots". Public execution of young and old upon the gallows was wholly without sanction in the Way of Heaven.

This type of savagery was also practiced between Israel and its enemies. [13] "An eye for an eye, and a tooth for a tooth," was illustrative of legislation designed to restrain killing to that which represented fairness. "Thou shall not kill," in the Decalogue, was a further attempt at curbing unrestrained violence.

In the Sermon on the Mount, in Matthew's Gospel, Jesus of Nazareth was depicted as probing beyond actions to motives. He argued that we should not only refrain from murdering others, we should not even nurse hatred towards them in our hearts, or get angry with them, much less act that anger out. Jesus urged his followers to go beyond the principle of "an eye for an eye and a tooth for a tooth," and love their enemies and pray for those who persecuted them.

What did Zhuang Zi say about the Dao?

Zhuang Zi (c. 369–286 B. C. E.) was recognized as a great sage in the period of the Spring and Autumn Warring States. His writings were based on Dao Philosophy, in contradiction to Confucian teaching, which enjoyed great popularity at that time. Dao Philosophy has sometimes been referred to as Lao Zhuang Philosophy. Therefore, it is equally important to know what Zhuang Zi said about the Dao.

10. 不要杀生

"夫兵者,不祥之器也---不得已而用之"。道的教化不鼓励任意逞强。它主张安顺平和。老子说:"人之生也柔弱,坚强者,死之徒也"。道教禁用死亡来恐吓他人或者是以死刑示众。"民不畏死,奈何以杀惧之也?若民恒是死,则而为者,吾将得而杀之"。

古代中国,诸侯大开杀戒。他们彼此绝不留情,对他国军民也绝不手软。对手及其家族毫不客气地根除。为了避免报仇,连他们家族的亲属也被剪除,不但斩草而且要除根。老老少少公开勒死,这是灭天理的行为。

以色列人和敌人们也有这种野蛮的处刑方式。"以眼还眼,以牙还牙,"是律法上的用典,但是不可开杀戒,公正还是存在的。十诫里说"不可杀人",就是试图进一步禁止无度的暴力。

马太福音"登山宝训"中,耶稣被说成是越级试探。他认为,我们不要杀害他人,不要心存仇恨或怨气,更不要一股脑地发泄出来。耶稣基督劝告跟随者们,不要理会"以眼还眼,以牙还牙"这个说法,"爱你们的敌人吧,为迫害你们的人们祈祷吧"。

庄子如何解释"道"?

庄子是春秋战国时代的思想家,他的著作以道学为本,和时尚的儒学相反。道学也称为"老庄哲学"。认识庄子论道也同样重要。

What is Dao? Is it a pseudonym for God?

Zhuang Zi argued that the Dao had "its own origin, its own root, and existed in the beginning before the heavens and earth were created". He placed the Dao on a plane above and beyond the universe: "Above the highest point of the universe, it is not considered high; beneath the six levels of the earth, it is not regarded as deep; existing before the creation of the heavens and the earth, it is not considered to belong to antiquity; existing in the distant past, it is not considered old". The Dao "created the heavens and the earth and was beyond special and temporal extremities". It is not confined by the limits of these extremities, which are termed "Wu Ji". In other words, it is beyond the limits of human thought.

In the Gospel according to John, "The Word," translated as "Dao" (道) in Chinese, was said to be with God in the beginning. This "beginning" represented a dimension of existence prior to the creation, that is, before the coming into being of space-time. The understanding of the origin of Dao from two different traditions seems to be from the same source.

When Zhuang Zi was asked by his students what existed before the Dao, he answered that the Dao was not part of our space-time world, so that there was nothing "before" the Dao. It was not itself created. Rather was it the "non-matter that created matter". As Lao Zi expressed it, this "Nothing is the beginning of everything". Zhuang Zi argued that the Dao, "as it is not part of the creation, can not be destroyed, and is omnipresent". The Dao "is in, but above all creations".

什么是道？道是否是上帝的别号？

庄子说："道是自本自根，未有天地，自古以固存"。他把道放到了上方的位置，超过了宇宙。他说："在太极之先而不为高，在六级之下而不为深，先天地生而不为久，长于上古而不老"。道"生天生地，在太极之先"，是不能被限制在这些极端的范围里的，它是无极的。换句话说，"道"超过了人类的想象。

在约翰福音中，WORD翻译成"道"，是太初与上帝同在的。太初代表创世以前的景象，也就是没有空间和时间之前的存在维度。

庄子的学生问他，道以前是个什么样子，他说，道与时空无关，道以前是无，道不是被造之物。毋宁说，道是"生成物之非物"。老子说："无，名万物之始也"。庄子认为，道是"无成无毁，无所不在"，"道在万物中，但高于万物"。

The Johannine Gospel argued that all things were made through "The Word," and that "The Word" was life – the life that sources all things. The Apostle Paul in his letter to the Colossians, contended that Christ, "the incarnation of the Word," was the first born of all creation, and was the energy in which all that was created inhered.

Zhuang Zi once rebuked his student, Dong Guo Zi, for inquiring where the Dao was instead of what the Dao was. He argued that "people able to discern the Dao find it as comfortable to be immersed in the Dao, as fish do in water." That is, people take the Dao for granted, because it can be discerned as part of the natural environment.(14)

The prologue to the Gospel of John argued that "The Word", "Logos" in Greek and "Dao" in Chinese – is in the world, but that the world does not recognize it. While we need the teaching of The Word, just as fish need water, many don't discern its presence. The Apostle Paul contended that the god of this age – which might be wealth, power, pride, arrogance, greed or jealousy etc. - has blinded many so that they do not discern the light of the Gospel of Christ. They are unable to identify "The Word" in Jesus Christ.

From this cursory comparison, it is evident that the "Dao" of Dao Philosophy bears many similarities to the "Logos," or "Word" in Christian theology. It is little wonder that Chinese translators, in translating the prologue to John's Gospel, used the expression "Dao" to translate "The Word."

As wisdom is universal, in spite of the diverse cultural contexts in which it is found, it should not surprise us to discover that there are many similarities between the Dao and the Logos of Christian theology. From a Christian perspective, it can be contended that God revealed the essence of the communicative Dao, Word, or Spirit to the Chinese through the philosophy of the Dao. Again, from a Christian perspective, it can be argued that there were people in touch with the Word, or, Dao, in China before Christian missionaries brought the message of a unique incarnation of that "Word," "Logos," or Dao in Jesus of Nazareth. In a similar sense, Justin Martyr argued that all Greek philosophers before Christ were Christians, as their wisdom came from the Creator God.

Incarnation of the Word.

Plato argued that it was the Logos, Word or Reason, that was the active agent in creation.

Zeno (c.464 B. C. E.) defined the Logos as the maker of all things, as the mind of Jove and Universal law.

约翰福音认为，万事万物都要经过道，道就是生命，生命是万物的源泉。使徒保罗在给歌哥西书信中说，基督是道化身的，是创造万物的首胎，也是万物承受的能源。

有一次，庄子的弟子东郭子问道在哪里，而没问道是什么，庄子驳斥说："鱼相造乎水，人相造乎道"。也就是说，认道乃自然而然，不用不费事。

约翰福音序言中讲，世上就有LOGOS，有WORD，有"道"，但是，世人却不认识。人之于道，好比鱼之于水，许多人认为，道并不存在。使徒保罗认为，当今大家所认准的是财富、权力、骄傲、贪欲、嫉妒和仇恨等等，人们蒙蔽了视线，看不到基督福音之光，认不出基督耶稣的道。

当然，这种模拟难免草率，然而，道学之道与基督神学里的LOGOS或WORD有许多相同的地方。从基督教角度看，上帝通过道学，向中国人揭示了交流过程中道或神灵的本质。而且，人们也认为，在传教上通过化身耶稣传道（WORD或LOGOS）之前，世上已有许多人接触了"道"。同样，贾斯廷认为，所有希腊哲学家在基督降生之前就是基督徒，因为他们的智慧来自造物之神。

道化身：

柏拉图认为，"道"是创世最活跃的因素。

泽若（公元前464年）把"道"界定为万物的创造者，是左夫神的心智，是具有普遍性的规律。

Cleanthes (c. 330–232 B. C. E.) argued that this Spirit, as God, pervaded the living Universe.

Tertullian regarded Spirit as the substance of the Word, or Reason, or Power. When the Spirit gave utterance, it was called Word; when the Spirit ordered and disposed all things, it was called Reason, and when the Spirit achieved effects, this was called Power. According to Tertullian, this Logos came from God, and was called "Son of God." The Logos had the same nature as God, the God who was also described as Spirit.

Tertullian went on to argue that, just as a ray of the sun is a portion of the whole, the sun is in the ray. The ray is an extension of the sun, and not a division of its substance.

While light is lit from light, the original matter remains whole and undiminished, even if you take many rays from it. Therefore, what comes from God is God's Son, and is God, for both are one. The Spirit that issued from God is God; God is Spirit. This ray of God descended from above into the womb of a virgin, where it became flesh. This flesh mingled with God and was born as a person. This person was nourished by the Spirit, grew to manhood, spoke and taught. This was Jesus of Nazareth, the Christ, or Messiah. (15)

The doctrine of the incarnation of the Word is not the same as the Buddhist belief in reincarnation. Christians believe that after death souls return to the Creator and that every person will find himself accountable for the way he has lived. The purpose of the Incarnation of the Word was to bring salvation to humankind. God is love and God gives people the opportunity to repent and trust themselves to him through faith in Jesus Christ.

克类地斯认为，灵即是上帝，遍及这有生命的宇宙。特尔徒连认为，灵是道，是道理，是权力。当灵发言的时候，叫做"道"；灵发出指令，料理万事，叫做道理；灵取得，叫做权力。根据特尔徒连的说法，"道"来自上帝，叫做"上帝的儿子"。"道"与上帝性格相同，上帝也同样称做灵。

特尔徒连还认为，日光是太阳的一部分，太阳存在于日光中。日光是太阳的膨胀，不是太阳的本身。

光是从光中点燃的，初始物质完整无损，没有减少，即使从这种物质当中取出许多光线，它仍然是完整的。来在上帝那里的是上帝的儿子，是上帝，因为他们是一体的。来自上帝的灵是上帝，上帝就是灵。上帝之光来自上苍，射入处女的子宫，变成了肉体。肉体和上帝相合，出生为人。人受圣灵滋养，长大成人，有了说话和受教育的能力。这就是拿撒勒人耶稣、基督。

道可以化身的教义和佛教还身不同。基督徒们相信，人死后，灵魂回到创造者那里，每个人都会看到，他要为有生之年的所作所为负责。道化成肉身的目的是拯救人类。上帝是爱，上帝给人间悔改的机会，通过信仰耶稣基督来相信上帝。

CHAPTER TWO
The mystery of Creation

Philosophers and prophets of all nations have tried to probe the mystery of creation. Qu Yuan, a national of Chu State during the Period of the Spring and Autumn Warring States, wrote the following poem:

"Face Skywards to Query Heaven,"

"Let me ask, in the beginning, before anything was in existence, who was present to preach and propagate the Dao?

When heaven and earth had not been defined, how was it possible to examine them?

Who can clarify this state of affairs, when there was only darkness and emptiness?

How can one determine what was hovering about and floating around?

Light emerged out of bottomless darkness, making one wonder what caused it?

One wonders about the origins of Yin/Yang, and their composites, and how they alternated?

If heaven has nine levels, who managed them?

Such a majestic work! But, who created it?" (16)

Similar questions were asked by the author of the 《Book of Job》 in the Hebrew Scriptures. (17)

"Can you fathom the mysteries of God?

Can you probe the limits of the Almighty?

They are higher than the heavens – what can you do?

They are deeper than the depth of graves – what can you know?

Their measure is longer than the earth and wider than the sea …"

第二章

创造的神秘

所有国家的哲学家与先知们都试图探索创造的神秘。屈原（公元前229年逝世），春秋战国时代楚国人，在《天问》中写道：

邃古之初，谁传道之？　（sui gu zhi chu, shui chuan dao zhi?）
上下未形，何为考之？　（shang xia wei xing, he you kao zhi?）
冥昭瞢暗，谁能极之？　（ming zhao meng an, shui neng ji zhi?）
冯翼惟像，何以识之？　（ping yi wei xiang, he yi shi zhi?）
明明暗暗，惟时何为？　（ming ming an an, wei shi he wei?）
阴阳三合，何本何化？　（yin yang san he, he ben he hua?）
阛则九重，孰营度之？　（huan ze jiu zhong, shu ying du zhi?）
惟兹何功，孰初作之？　（wei ci he gong, shu chu zuo zhi?）

希伯来经文《乔布书》里记载乔布（公元前二世纪之间）类似的发问：
你能看透上帝的神秘吗？
你能探索到全能的上帝的极限吗？
他们的智慧高于天，你呢？
他们的智慧比阴间还深，你知道吗？
他们的维度比地长、比海阔……。

Lao Zi in the "Dao De Jing" wrote:

"... a whirlwind does not last a whole morning,

Nor does a rainstorm last a whole day.

Who causes these phenomena?"

Greek philosophers also sought to explain the origin of the universe. Thales of Miletus (624–547 B.C.E.) considered water as the origin of the universe, as it was the most essential element sustaining life. Chinese legendary leaders, some 6,000 years B.C.E., under the matriarchal family system, entertained a similar concept regarding the female element, and water, as sources of life. They promoted the concept of "Water integrity", which underlay Daoist Philosophy. The account of creation in Genesis begins with an enormous expanse of water.

Xenophanes of Colophon (c. 570–480 B.C.E.) propounded a refined and enlightened monotheism, whose God was the greatest of all gods, and who resembled neither the shape nor thought of mortals. He was regarded as the founder of natural theology. He ridiculed the doctrine of the transmigration of souls, and criticised luxurious living. Incidentally, many regard Dao Philosophy as a form of natural theology. (Lao Zi b. 568 – B.C.E.)

Heracleitus of Ephesus (c. 540–480 B.C.E.) studied cosmology. He believed that fire was the origin of life, and was concerned about men's understanding of "Logos." He argued that people could never discover the limit of the soul in the spiritual realm, which was in the hidden dimension. Furthermore, only the souls of wise men possessed the inclination to follow the upward path to Fiery Intelligence, which called for self-discipline and appropriate conduct. This was very close to Confucian Philosophy. (Confucius b. 551 – B.C.E.)

Pythagoras of Samos (c. 580 – 500 B.C.E.) argued that the dynamics of world structures was based on pairs of opposites, and that the Earth and other planets rotated around the Sun. He introduced the doctrine of the immortality and the transmigration of the soul.

Buddhism promises Nirvana, which involves the extinction of the suffering and the incarnation of the soul to a better next life.[18]

Zoroaster/Zorathushtra (c. 628 – 551 B.C.E.) of Persia, now Iran, founded Zoroastrianism, believing in monotheism, dualism and eschatology. Zoroastrians worship fire. It is said that Zoroastrianism influenced Judaism, Christianity and Islam. Incidentally, Zoroastrians, Tibetans and the Qiang tribe practised the same type of burial, called by the Chinese "sky burial". Zhuang Zi was opposed to extravagant funeral and burial customs and he did not object if his dead body was exposed to vultures.

老子在《道德经》里说，

飘风不终朝，（piao feng bu zhong zhao）

暴雨不终日，（bao yu bu zhong ri）

孰以此？（shu yi ci）

古希腊哲学家也想解释宇宙的起源。米列多士的达耳氏(624-547)认为宇宙起源于水，水是维持生命的最基本元素。公元6000多年前，传说中国母系社会时期也同样认为水和母性是生命的源头。她们提倡水德概念，也就是道学的根本。创世记开篇便是洪荒。

可罗坊的先诺芬氏（公元前570-480）推出一个完美的启迪性一神教，该教的上帝是众神之神，长相不像凡人，思维也不像凡人。人们说，他创造了自然神学。他看不起灵魂转世说，批评奢华生活。无独有偶，许多人认为，道学就是一种自然神学（老子生于公元前568年）。

以弗所的赫拉克勒特斯（公元前540-480年）学习宇宙哲学。他认为，"火"是生命源头，关注人对"理性"的认识。他认为，人不可能发现隐秘的灵界之中灵的极限。而且，只有智者的灵魂才能把握住通向上智之路，但这需要自律，需要行为正当。这非常贴近儒学（孔子生于公元前551年）。

萨摩斯的毕达哥拉斯（公元前580-500年）认为，构成世界的动力是建立在对立体的基础上的，地球和其它星球环绕太阳旋转。他阐述的学说是人的灵魂不死，人的灵魂可以转世。

佛教讲究涅槃，说的是结束苦难，灵魂转世以后去更好地活下辈子。

波斯（现在的伊朗）琐罗亚斯德教始创崇拜火，信仰独一神、二元论和末世论。琐罗亚斯德教为拜火教，据说还影响过犹太教、基督教和回教。琐罗亚斯德教徒、藏族、羌族们的葬礼相同，中国人叫天葬。庄子（公元前369-286年）反对奢靡的殡礼和丧葬风俗，尸体被兀鹫吃了他也不在乎。

The mystery of Creation

The Prophet Isaiah described the creation, thus:

"He sits enthroned above the circle of the earth, and its people are like the grasshoppers.

He stretches out the heavens like a canopy, and spreads them like a tent to live in.

He brings princes to naught and reduces the rulers of this world to nothing ···

Lift your eyes and look to the heavens; who created all these?

He who brings out the starry host one by one, and calls them each by name.

Because of his great power and mighty strength, not one of them is missing ...".

先知以赛亚是这样描述创世的：

他在环形大地的上空登基而坐，它的人民多如蝗虫。

他铺张帷幔一样的穹苍，像帐篷一样展开入住。

他使君王归于虚无，使地上的审判官成为虚空...

抬眼看看上苍吧，看是谁创造了这万象?

他领出了多如星斗的主人，一一称其名，

他能力大，力量强，数出来的一个也不缺 …

CHAPTER THREE
In achieving understanding of The Word,
one relinquishes perverse desires daily,

The Confucian Chinese say that as we live until we are old, so we keep learning into old age. There is no end to acquiring general knowledge through experience. We divide academic learning into primary, secondary, and then higher learning, or tertiary education. It is a process of continuing accummulation – the reservoir of knowledge continues to fill. This type of academic learning not only increases in quantity day by day, but speed and retention also increase. To comprehend what we are taught, or what we read, requires a degree of effort on our part. Otherwise, it would be a waste of effort teaching someone who does not understand you or who refuses to accept your teaching. A common Chinese saying describes this situation as "playing music to the bulls". However, it is indisputable that we increase in knowledge as we persue academic learning day after day.

On the other hand, when we develop a deeper understanding of "The Word", we become less the victims of perverse desires. It is suggested that the process of shedding perverse, coveteous, selfish desires is slow and gradual. There is much to unlearn, much of it hitherto regarded as normal. It is not a sin to work hard and make money, particularly where the money is put to good use and shared. It is quite another thing to be motivated by greed.

A deeper understanding of "The Word", and an accompanying commitment to put this Word into practice, will lead to self–transformation. This transformation may begin with self–adjustment), with the deliberate shedding of excess baggage, of that which is holding us back from further development and from an increase in other–centred behaviour. This other–centred behaviour is also God–centred behaviour.

This sort of transformation is only possible through the exercise of divine grace. It is God's gift. It was this sort of behaviour that Jesus was referring to when he said to his disciples that their righteousness should exceed that of the Pharisees and the teachers of law. This behaviour, following from the teaching of the Word, involves the relinquishing of perverse desires daily.

第三章

为学者日益，闻道者日损

中国儒士说：活到老，学到老。通过经验获得普通的知识是没有止境的。求学分为小学、中学、高等教育。这是个不断积累的过程，知识的库存慢慢地填满了。这种学问的量日渐增加，学习的速度和知识的保存力也在加强。为了理解我们所学的、所看的，我们需要勤奋学习。否则，教了不理解，对老师有抵触情绪，那么，教了也是白教。中国有句俗话，叫对牛弹琴。然而"为学者日益"这句话是不无道理的。

相反，当我们进一步认识"道"的时候，我们也就不会为了贪欲而去牺牲了。有人说，要削除邪恶、贪求与私欲是个慢功夫。不懂的事还很多，这也是正常的。勤劳致富并非罪过，钱可以正用，可以施舍。如果动了贪念，那是另一回事。

进一步理解"讲道"，就把这道付诸实际，结果就是自身发生转变。这种转变起于"自均"---审慎地放弃多余的辎重，否则就会成为我们前进的障碍，阻碍他者为中心的行为进行下去。这种他人为中心的行为也就是以上帝为中心的行为。

这种转变只有通过神的恩惠才能实现。它是上帝的恩赐。这种行为就是耶稣对门徒所提出的关于他们的义必须高于法利塞人的义和文人的义。接受道以后，这种行为也就进入了闻道者日损的程序。

> In achieving understanding of The Word,
> one relinquishes perverse desires daily,

Lao Zi made a number of suggestions about getting rid of extraneous things so that they could be replaced by the intutions of the Dao. He argued that we should abandon extremities, do away with luxuries, and forgo indulgence or extravagance. He further argued that we should do everything in moderation instead of adopting extreme behaviours. There are many things that we can forego in our persuit of "The Word."

First of all, he contended, we should do away with luxuries, such as, "the multi-colours which may blind our eyes"; "the erotic music which may deafen our ears"; "the exotic flavours which may jade our tastes"; and "the over-excitement of games which may derange our hearts". The extreme experiences of our five senses are not necessarily good for our health. They may harm it. We should avoid these extermities as far as possible.

Secondly, we should forgo indulgance, such as "yearning for things that are difficult to obtain," and we should eat "to fill the stomach and not to please the eyes". We should reflect on what will meet our basic needs. Furthermore, he argued that we should not "hoard treasures in the house, for it will be difficult to protect them". In this, he cautioned against materialism. Those in government should not "over-tax the people so that they go hungry". This is a selfish abuse of power – enriching oneself at the expense of others.

Thirdly, we should not employ our cleverness to outwit others, where we seriously disadvantage them. The consequences of our actions will eventually catch up with us and pay us back. Nor should we play at one-up-manship, or blow our own trumpets. Such vanity, fuelled by a poor self-image, is like "trying to elevate oneself on a pile of ashes." Lao Zi put it even more succinctly when he contended that "those who try to stand on tip-toes will not sustain this position for long".

The Gospel according to Matthew records an encounter between Jesus of Nazareth and a rich young man. The rich young man asked Jesus what good things he must do in order to gain eternal life. Jesus told him that he must obey the commandments, and the young man innocently or otherwise, asked him which commandments. Jesus replied that he must not murder, must not commit adultry, must not steal, must not give false witness, must honour his parents and must love his neighbours as himself. And the young man replied that he had kept all these commandments, and asked what else he must do. Jesus answered that, if he wanted to be perfect, he had to sell all his possessions and give them to the poor. He would then be in a position to follow Jesus, a poor, wandering teacher. When the young man heard what Jesus said he went away sadly, because he had great wealth. This demonstrates how difficult it is to understand and accept the teaching of "The Word," Dao if one is not prepared to shed one's baggage.

In achieving understanding of The Word, one relinquishes perverse desires daily,

In understanding "The Word" one relinquishes perverse desires daily. The word "daily" suggests that this is a continuous process. Lao Zi emphasized the need to "keep on relinquishing". Jesus spoke of the need to deny oneself, take up one's cross and follow him. Following Jesus requires this sort of discipline.

The teaching of The Word, accepted by the heart, replaces human cleverness and worldly wisdom, which Lao Zi terms "false learning" (伪学 wei xue). In trusting ourselves to God, in faith, we are transformed into new, Christ-like people. Emperor Tang Gao Zong (613 C.E.), after conferring with all the religious leaders and scholars in the country, concluded that "the attainment of The Word makes one a saint". This parallels the comment of Apostle Paul that "when Christ is in you and you are in Christ, you are a new creation; the new has come and the old has gone."

It is relatively easy to "increase in academic knowledge daily". It is far more difficult to shed our covetuous desires day by day as we hear "The Word" of God.

"闻道者日损","日"这词就是不断的意思。老子强调"损了又损"。耶稣认为,人应该舍己,背起十字架跟着他,跟着耶稣要守这个纪律。

人接受"道",就可以代替老子所说的巧智和俗慧这样的伪学。信仰当中要依靠上帝,我们就会脱胎成为基督一样的新人唐高宗(公元613年)。招集国内各教派高僧和学者探讨后得出结论说:"人得道成圣,成圣为佛"。使徒保罗也说:"基督在你心里,你就在基督心里,你人是新的,新人来了,旧的去了"(《哥林多后书》5: 17)。

"为学者日益"不难理解,难的是"闻道者日损"。

CHAPTER FOUR
Do not live for oneself – live without selfish desires.

"Do not live for oneself" or "Do not live alone" is a behavioural objective of the Dao De Jing. Lao Zi expounded on this topic by talking about the nature of heaven and earth in chapter 51. He argued that "Heaven and earth are eternal and everlasting because they are indifferent and selfless". They do not exist for themselves, and have no self-interest. The sunshine and rain, the energy and refreshment the heavens offer are for the benefit of those sustained by them. The earth does the same, producing vegetables and minerals, which maintain life. Heaven and earth do not demand anything in return. Therefore, people, following the example of heavens and earth, should not abuse the power deriving from their intelligence and selfishly seek only their own good. They need to recognize that "no man is an island."

One example of those who did not live for themselves were the legendary emperors of ancient China, namely, Tang Yao and Yu Shun, who lived in the third millennium B. C. They were remembered for their kindness and benevolence to their subjects. Above all, they abdicated their thrones to the wise, young men who came after them. They did not keep their kingdoms within their families. They used their authority and power to serve others and did not dominate them. They lived by the maxim, "Do not live for yourself and avoid being captive to selfish desires".

Desire can be either good or bad, like a double edge sword. It is commendable if one's desire is to do good for others, to promote the welfare of others. On the other hand, if whatever one does is just for one's own sake, that is, only for himself, then it is detrimental to the well-being of society. The Dao De Jing suggests that it is better for us to adopt the policy of having "little private possession and negligible covetous desire".

In the hope of finding a positive balance between actions and consequences, Lao Zi suggested a number of maxims:

"The sage has no self-interst, but regards the interest of others as his own".

"I do not act against 'The Word" and the people transform themselves; I am fond of tranquility, and the people become righteous of their own accord (自正 zi zheng) ⋯ people become contented ⋯people take to simplicity.

第四章

不自生，无私欲

　　道德经的一个行为目标是"不自生"。老子引用天地的性格来阐述这个问题（第51章）。他认为，"天地之所以能长久者，以其不自生也"。它们存在不是为了自己，因为它们没有私利。天供给阳光、雨水、能量和滋养，使受到维系的事物得到利益。地也同样产生植物和矿物来滋养生命。天地从来不求报答。人民也以天地为榜样，但不要耍聪明自私地滥用职权。应该认清，"人并不是个孤岛"。

　　公元3000年，相传中国古代唐尧和虞舜就是"不自生"的榜样。他们和蔼、仁慈，受到人民的纪念。此外，他们禅位给年青贤达，没把皇位传给自家人。他们利用权势为人民服务而不奴役人民。他们遵守"不自生，无私欲"的格言（第51章）。

　　欲念好像双刃刀，有好也有坏的。如果人的欲念是行善，为他人谋福，就是可嘉的。如果只为自己，不想别人，就会有害社会。《道德经》上说，人应该"少私寡欲"（第63章）。

　　关于行为和结果怎么才能找个平衡，老子在《道德经》中有不少名言："圣人无恒心，以百姓之心为心"；"我无为而民自化"；"我好静而民自正"；"我无事而民自富"；"我欲不欲而民自朴"。

"… sages know their own abilities, but never praise themselves", and "they have self respect, but never treasure themselves". "If we are always talking about ourselves, we will not be recognized as distinguished"; "If we are given to self-display, we will not shine forth"; "If we boast about ourselves, it nullifies our merit"; "If we praise ourselves, we will not excel for long".

In Chapter 76 of Dao De Jing, Lao Zi argued that "if the rulers of the world can hold onto the teaching of 'The Word,' the people will find their proper place in society", "adjusting themselves to each other", and working in harmony.

Everyone of our actions precipitates a reaction on the part of others. If we are self-centred we will promote self-centredness in others.

We live in a delicately balanced ecosystem. Everything within the ecosystem has its usefulness, contributing to the health of the whole. This is illustrated by the usefulness of trees. We use timber for building shelters and furniture, and for paper etc. Trees refresh the air by using up carbon dioxide and giving back oxygen, providing clean air for us to breathe. This process by which the air is cleansed helps prevent global warming. The foliage of trees also retains water after a heavy downpour, reducing the likelihood of flooding. The leaves, when they fall, create compost that enriches the soil, promoting plant life.

It is said that after the bumper harvest in the 60s Chairman Mao Zedong thought it was a good idea for the country to rid itself of sparrows, which damaged the crops. He sent out an order to eliminate all sparrows. There were to be none left. With the sparrows gone, the trees were attacked by worms, which could do their work of destruction with impunity. Through the futile effort of ridding the country of sparrows, the Chinese realized the ecological usefulness of the sparrows. This lesson taught us that we should not concern ourselves exclusively with human interests.

The attitude of "not living selfishly" can not only make those adopting it generous, but it can assist others. In the words of Mo Zi, when "we make friends we benefit one another". He argued that "when righteous people govern the world, they intentionally bring benefits and eliminate disasters".

"圣人，自知而不自见"，"自爱而不自贵"（第37章）。"自视者不章"，"自见者不明"，"自伐者无功"，"自矜者不长"（第66章）。

老子在七十六章认为，如果统治者守道，人民"将自宾"、"自均"、和平共处。

每个人动起来，其它人就会有反应。如果你以自我为中心，他人也会以自我为中心。

我们生活在这个非常平衡的生态系统中，整个系统里面的一切都有它的用途，都有益于整体的健全。树木是有用的，便是个例子。木料用来建房子，做家具，造纸等等。树林吸收二氧化碳，释放氧气，来清新空气，供给人们呼吸。空气清洁的过程有助于避免全球变暖。暴雨过后，树叶存储雨水，减少了可能发生的洪灾。树叶落地，成为混合肥料，使土壤肥沃，促进了植物生长。

据说，在六十年代丰收以后，祸害农作物的麻雀政府要求务必除尽。麻雀是没了，虫子倒是无所顾忌地猖獗起来，啃起树来了。农村除雀失策了，中国人才意识到麻雀是有益于生态的。这是个教训，单考虑人类自己是不成的。

"不自生"的态度可以使大度起来，还可以达到助人的效果。墨子提倡"交相利"。他说："仁人之事者，必务求与天下之利，除天下之害"（《墨子新释，兼爱》142页）。

Thus, big countries will not attack smaller countries and large ethnic groups, communities, or families will not cause trouble to small ethnic groups, communities, or families. The strong will not oppress the weak, the majority will not dismiss the interests of minorities and the wise will not deceive the ignorant. People occupying high positions will not despise people of low status. He argued that "if you treat other people as you would treat yourself, you will not harm them." It is important for us to love others for themselves, and not because some benefit will acrue to us by our doing so. Mo Zi illustrates his argument by suggesting that: "just like the sun and moon, illuminate the earth without prejudice or personal motive". Living for others should be as natural an act as "fire burning upwards and water running downwards". [20]

In Judeo-Christianity:

The Covenant demands of Yahweh have consistently reminded people that they should not live for themselves alone. The Psalmist, in Psalm 24, argued that the earth and everything in it belonged to the Lord, who never held back anything from people. Heaven never hedges sunshine or hoards rain and the earth is ever ready to yield rich vegetation for all to enjoy. Therefore, it is against the Way of God for men to hoard possessions to themselves, a practice that amounts to selfishness, corruption and miserliness.

The Preacher wrote in Ecclesiastes: "Naked a man comes from his mother's womb, and as he comes, so he departs." (5:15).

It may be mythical, but the story of the temptations faced by Jesus of Nazareth indicates that early in his ministry, after spending forty days and nights fasting in the wilderness, Jesus was offered material wealth, authority, power and glory, which few would reject. Jesus was not moved, not distracted from his path. His mind was centred on God and the purpose God had for his life. This purpose was to preach truth and love. This illustrated the nature of the unselfishness to which Jesus called Christians.

Jesus' preaching drew large crowds. On one occasion, when he saw a crowd of about 5,000 following, and realized they had been without food for some time, he instructed his disciples to feed them. The problem was that they had nothing with which to feed the multitude. The disciples were at their wit's end. But there was a little boy in the crowd who had five loafs and two fishes. He was willing to share what he had. After the people had been asked to group in tens, Jesus blessed the food. He broke the bread and fish and distributed them. Five thousand people were fed. After the meal, the disciples gathered the remains into twelve baskets. What we share will go further than we realize.

以此推论，大国不会侵略小国，大民族、大族群或大家庭就不会找小民族、小族群或小家庭的麻烦。强不欺柔，大不压小，智不欺愚，贵不鄙贱（《墨子新释》143页）。他说：对待别人如同别人对待自己的话，那么，就不会欺凌他人了。（注：耶稣基督说："无论何事，你们愿意人怎样待你们，你们也要怎样待人[《马太福音》七章十二节]。"孔子说："己所不欲，勿施于人"）。重要的是要为爱他人而爱他人，而不是因为这样做自己会捞到好处。墨子模拟道："譬如日月兼照天下之无有私"。为他人活着，应当效法自然，"避之犹火之就上，水之就下也"（《墨子新释》167页）。

犹太和基督教：

耶和华圣约的规定不断提醒人们不要单为自己活着。作诗者在《诗篇》24中说："大地和其中的万事万物都属于主，主不在人面前从来不留任何东西。"天从来不遮蔽阳光，也不囤积雨水，地产出丰富的植物供人们享用。人如果私藏财富，是违反上帝的道，这种行为是自私，是败坏，是吝啬。

《传道书》是这样记载的："从母胎赤身而来，也照样赤身而去"。

这听起来挺神，耶稣开始布道的时候，就出现过这种诱惑。他在旷野40个日夜不吃不喝，人家给他送来了物质财富、权力、名位---这一切一般人很难拒绝，然而，耶稣却豪不动摇，依旧沿着他自己的路走下去。他的心只有上帝，他活着就是为了上帝，他的目的就是传播真理，播撒仁爱。这就是所说的无私本职，耶稣称之为基督（《路加福音》4：1-13）。

耶稣传道大批人围观。有一次，5000来人跟着他，他发现他们几天没吃饭了，就吩咐门徒给喂他们。问题是，人这么多，门徒们没有这么多的食物。茫然间，人群中有个小孩带了五块饼和两条鱼，他愿意与大家分享。人们十人一组，耶稣感谢了食物，分开饼和鱼，递给他们。五千人吃了。饭后，门徒收拾了12篮零碎。这个道理说的是，我们舍出去的往往超过我们所期望的。

Jesus did not live for himself, otherwise he would not have sacrificed himself for the world. He came to fulfill the will of God, bringing the Gospel of reconciliation and declaring God's forgiveness. As he explained to the Canaanite woman, God's love and forgiveness know no boundaries.

Jesus carried this purpose consistently through to the end. He could have avoided arrest in Gethsemane. When brought to both the Temple authority and the Roman governor he did not seek to defend himself. In a final moment of lucidity, on the cross, he said, "It is finished, " meaning his task had been accomplished.

Jesus of Nazareth could have lived to be a great teacher, like Confucius, with thousands of disciples and a comfortable life. Instead, he took upon himself a prophetic role, confronting the Pharisees, Saducees and Herodians. He was concerned, not with his own selfish interests, but with those of others. He humbled himself and was obedient to the will of God until death, death on the cross. No one in the history of mankind has surpassed the greatness of Jesus of Nazareth. Because of his humility, he was exalted to the highest.

In the early church, the disciples of Jesus lived a communal life, sharing their possessions. Those who had possessions sold their excess and gave to those in need. (21)This was an illustration of "not living for oneself, " or "not having selfish desires" . .Christians regard themselves as stewards of whatever wealth God has entrusted to them. They realize they do not even control their lives, let alone their material wealth. Both their lives and wealth are transitional. Both are temporary like the flowers and grass, which bloom one day but wither the next. Selfishness and covetousness are ultimately futile.

It is interesting to note that both the communes of the early church and those in China, nearly two thousand years apart, did not succeed as self-contained communities. Maybe both were too idealistic, though the intent was commendable. Perhaps the hearts of men have not changed a great deal in those thousands of years. People have always been self-centred, following the Way of Man.

The Apostle Peter, in his first letter to the Christians of Asia Minor, contended that Christians should "offer hospitality to one another without grumbling and each should use whatever gift he has received to serve others, faithfully administering God's grace in its various forms. If anyone serves, he should do as with the strength God provides, so that in all things God may be praised through Jesus Christ." (22)

耶稣没有为自己活着，否则就不会为世人牺牲自己了。他来到世上，是为了完成上帝的旨意，他带来和好的福音，传播上帝的怜悯。他向迦南女解释说，上帝的爱，上帝的宽恕，都是无疆的。

耶稣有始有终地担负起这个担子。他在客西马尼园可以躲过被捕。当他被带到圣殿公会和罗马总督前的时候，他不为自己辩护。头脑清晰的最后一刻，他在十字架上说道："结束了"（《约翰福音》19：30），指的是他的任务完成了。

耶稣可以像孔子一样，成为大师，收几千弟子，过上安逸的生活。相反，他担起先知的责任，与法利塞人、文士以及非律王的人对抗。他考虑的不是自己，而是他人。他自己卑微，直到死在十字架上，也服从上帝的意志。历史上没有人会超过耶稣的伟大。他之所以被抬到了最高处，是因为他谦逊（《腓立比书》二章）。

早期的教会，耶稣的门徒过着集体生活，共同分享财物。"有财产的人把多余的卖掉，分给需要的人"（《使徒行传》2：44-45）。这说明，他们"不自生，无私欲"。基督徒认为，自己是上帝赏赐财产的管家人。他们意识到，他们的性命他们做不了主，更不用说他们的物质财富了。他们的生命财产都是暂时的，好像花草一样，今天开了，明天凋了。自私自利终究一无所有。

早期教会和将近两千年后的中国公社作为自给自足的小区，都没有成功。两个制度都是可贺的，但过于理想。问题是，几千年来，人心没什么大的改变。人心向来追随"人之道"，永远是自我的。

使徒彼得在写给哥林斯人的第一封信里，认为基督徒"应该互相呵护，不发怨言，各人要按他所得的恩赐彼此服务，用不同形式来忠实地观照上帝的恩赐。如果有人服务，就要按着上帝所赐的力量服务，这样，凡事都通过耶稣基督使上帝得到赞美"（《彼得前书》4：9-11）。

Do not live for oneself – live without selfish desires.

    This hospitality refers to Christian love being extended to strangers or visitors from other places, who are in need of food and shelter.

    Many welfare organizations around the world have carried out this practice of hospitality. However, sometimes, this good work has been abused by both giving or receiving countries. This is acting against the Way of Heaven. [23]

    James, the brother of Jesus, commented in his letter that Christians should not be tempted by selfishness, greed, covetousness, which will lead them into sin and result in spiritual deadness. He argues that it is a sin for the rich to hoard things, which are corrupted by their disuse."[24]

    Paul, in writing to the Corinthians, commented : "Everything is possible but not everything is benefitial. Everything is permissible but not everything is constructive." [25]

    The Gospel of Thomas records Jesus saying, "If you have money, do not lend it at interest, but give it to one from whom you will not get it back."

这个呵护是指基督徒的爱施加给需要吃住的陌生人和远来的客人。

世界上许多福利机构都是呵护人的。但是，给予国也好，受益国也好，这种善事有时被滥用。这种行为是逆"天之道"。

耶稣的弟弟雅各布在书信中劝告基督徒受自私、贪婪的诱惑，那会使他们犯罪，致使灵魂消亡。他认为，富人囤积不用造成腐败，这是在犯罪。

保罗写给哥林斯人的信中说："凡事都有可能，但并非一切都是有益的。凡事都有道理"。

圣托马斯《福音》抄录了耶稣这样的语录："如果你有了钱，那么别放贷了，把钱送给不会偿还你的人吧"。

CHAPTER FIVE
Reduce the surplus and supplement the scarcity.

Lao Zi argued that the practice of "reducing the surplus and supplementing the scarcity" is the "Way of Heaven". At first, this could sound like "Rob Peter to pay Paul" or could appear to encourage heroic acts analogous to those of the outlawed Robin Hood of Sherwood Forest. What it does advocate is equality and basic human rights for all.

In the field of economics, the one who works harder may reap more, and it is only right and fair for this person to retain the surplus earned. The more you plant, the more you harvest. This is a universal and acceptable norm of everyday life. However, the Way of Heaven goes further, promoting generosity and encouraging the one with a surplus to share his surplus with those in need. To keep the excess is considered selfish, even greedy. This is in contrast to the "Way of Men", where retaining excess is considered normal. Lao Zi argued that we do not live solely for ourselves" and therefore, we should not keep the excess to satisfy our "selfish desire". To think of the interest of others before our own is fulfilling the Way of Heaven. The Dao suggests that "prosperity is being satisfied with whatever we have".

With effort and skill, these excess things are obtainable. To share the excess with others is easier said than done. Human selfishness thwarts our generosity. Confucian Chinese consider all "physical things to be outside their bodies" (身外物 shen wai wu), and these things are of less importance. Besides, all physical objects are regarded as "things that we did not bring to this world at birth and will not take away when we die". They belong to this world and they shall remain in this world. They are the things produced in this world for men to enjoy when alive. Therefore, excess is not what we need. It is the spare portion that we can give away without suffering want.

Why aren't others able to supply their needs? They are many reasons. They may be lazy, but this is by no means the only reason. Some countries are overpopulated, or have few resources. The people may have suffered war or famine. Poor leadership, or avarice on the part of leaders, may have bankrupted nations.

Lao Zi urged his fellow Chinese to exhibit superior integrity. He suggested they be generous, as water is generous, which refreshes without asking anything in return. Water always flows to the lowest places, filling them up to the level of those areas that are higher. Water is impartial, and has been used to measure levels. Water gives. It is generous.

第五章

损有余而补不足

老子说："损有余而补不足"天之道也。这句话好似西方俗语"抢保罗来给彼得"或是舍尔屋森林匪徒罗宾汉的行侠仗义。它所提倡的是人人平等和基本的人权。

从经济方面说，勤劳多获。把多余的收获储藏起来是正常的，没什么不公。多种多收获，这是日常生活普遍而又被大家接受的法则。可是，"天之道"进一步地说，就是大家慷慨些，把剩余的分给不足的。如把多余的留下来，就是自私甚至是贪婪。这是有誇"人之道"的，而把多余的存留下来在人们看来是理所当然的。老子认为，人应该"不自生"，把多余的留下来满足自己就是私欲。先为他人利益着想，然后在考虑自己，才是"天之道"。道提倡"知足者，富也"。

多余富足是勤奋加技能得来的，把多余的东西分给别人，说来容易做来难。人性自私超过慷慨之心。中国儒家认为，一切皆身外之物，是无所谓的。一切外物都是"生不带来，死不带去"。它们是世上的，应该留在世上。它们是人活着的时候来享用的，这样，富足的并不是我们所必需的。不需用的施舍出去，别人也就不至于匮乏了。

人为什么不让一下呢？原因很多，可能是由于懒惰，但这并不是唯一的原因。有的国家人口繁多，资源匮乏。人们遭受战争和饥荒之苦。领导人无能、贪婪，可能会把国家掏空。

老子要人们表现出高尚的德行，提倡"上善若水"，滋润万物而不求回报。水流往低处，直到一点点地灌满。水是公平的，所以做水平线用。水是给予，是慷慨无私。

Reduce the surplus and supplement the scarcity.

Does this saying advocate Communism? No, despite the fact that Communism, premised on an economic interpretation of history, is founded on the principle of eradicating inequality in wealth, unethical trade practices, invidious class distinctions and upholding human rights and social justice. Communism covers a much wider gambit of economic and social issues. Furthermore, the collapse of Communism in the Soviet Union and in Eastern Block countries revealed that the rhetoric hadn't worked out in practice. Scholars had earlier indicated that the philosophy itself was severely flawed, in spite of the insights, and was based on an erroneous historical analysis. It was an ideology, even a surrogate religion. It did not take sufficient account of the universality of the shadow side of individual and social reality. One economic group was demonized, while another was considered beyond corruption. It became obvious, over time, that no group was beyond corruption, and that philosophies of liberation could be used by those in power to enslave, and to justify sadistic slaughter. Xun Zi (313–238 B. C. E.) was right in commenting that there is an original perversity in the hearts of people. [26]

Lao Zi argued that "in serving the world", in following the Way of Heaven, a person will give away his excess to the needy. Yet very often you find the reverse is true. The rich, who pay one another compliments, scratching each other's backs, "trade flattery and honour their own kind with gifts". It is those people of high society who throw parties for one another and exchange exclusive and rare gifts. In ancient China, the ruling class taxed the poor and offered luxury presents to officials above them to gain favours from them. This is contrary to the Way of Heaven, for the officials "taxed the poor and needy commoners so as to supplement the surplus of the wealthy higher officials".

In Christianity:

In the Hebrew tradition there was a Covenant demand that one shares one's excess with the poor, the widow, the needy, and aliens residing in one's territory.[27] When you harvest your crop, you are neither to harvest to the edge of the field, nor to pick up the grains you have dropped on the ground. You are to leave something for the poor and needy to gather.

If someone living among you has become poor, you cannot lend him money with interest or sell him food at a profit. Neither can you make him work as a slave, but only as a hired worker, nor can you keep him or his family members as slaves after the year of Jubilee, which occurs after every forty-nine years. Indeed, on the Jubilee Year loans will be written off and slaves set free. This was the Israelite tradition, recognized more in default than in fulfillment.

这样的论调是在否赞同共产社会主义呢？不是的，共产主义的原则是消除贫富不均和不道德经营手段，消除不平等的阶级，支持人权和社会公正等等。共产主义涵盖更宽的经济与社会福利问题。共产主义在苏联和东欧国家集团崩溃说明，夸大其词难以成为现实。学者们早期的时候认为，共产主义哲学本身存在严重缺陷，它虽然具有洞察性，但却是以错误的历史观为基础的。这是一种意识形态，毋宁说是一种影子宗教。它对个人和社会现实所普遍存在的弱点考虑不足。一部分富起来的人被妖魔化，另一部分人的腐败到了不可收拾的地步。当然，从时间上来看，没有任何统治集团可以完全脱离腐败，统治者可以利用解放哲学来进行奴役，进行残暴的屠杀。荀子（公元前313-238正）认为，人性原本堕落，这是有道理的。

老子认为，要以遵"天之道"来"奉天下"，就要舍多余补不足。而实际上却恰恰相反。富人阶级常常互相恭维，互相利用，也就是"美言可以市，尊行可以贺人"。社会高层人士互相吃喝，贵礼往来。中国古代，统治阶级赋敛百姓，送礼邀宠。这是有违天道的，因为当官的是"损不足而奉有余"。

犹太和基督教传统中的"圣约要求"规定，把多余的施舍给住在本地的穷困、鳏寡和外乡人。收割庄稼的时候，不要割尽田角，也不要拾起掉在地上的颗粒，要留一些让穷苦人去拾。

你们中间如果有谁变成了穷人，那就把钱借给他们，但不可取利，也不要卖给他们食物去赚他们的钱。不要把人当奴隶使唤，他仅仅是个雇工，也不要像每四十九年的大禧之年的时候去把他或他的家人当奴仆。其实，大禧之年，欠债要一笔勾销，奴隶也要释放"（《利未记》25：35-41）。这便是以色列传统违约是大，守约是小。

Reduce the surplus and supplement the scarcity.

The Book of Proverbs states that if you are generous you will prosper, and if you hoard you will be cursed by the people.(28)

In the Hebrew Scriptures, it was emphasized that one must (1) fear the Lord, (2) obey his commandments (3) and walk in all his ways, (4) fasting. These were the Covenant demands of Yahweh, summarized in the two Great Commandments: "Love the Lord your God with all your heart and with all your soul and with all your strength" and "Love your neighbour as yourself." Jesus said that upon these two hung all that was written in the Laws and Prophets. For the Israelites there were Covenant duties to love one's neighbour as oneself. As the Prophet Isaiah argued, the true purpose of fasting was to humble oneself, and, above all, to loose the chains of injustice, to set the oppressed free, to share food with the hungry, to provide the poor wanderer with shelter and to clothe the naked. (29)That is to say, if one fears the Lord, one must be committed to social justice. Fasting covers the whole spectrum of the Second Great Commandment.

Jesus Christ warned people not to hoard surpluses solely to consume them on their own appetites. (30)

For the Christian, everything belongs to God. It is God who gives and who takes away. As such, our possessions are the gifts of God's grace. We are only the stewards of our wealth. Therefore, we should give without obligation and share our excess. This should be our underlying commercial motive.

The willingness to share will not only benefit those who receive and those who give, it will also promote political and economic harmony.

The unwillingness, on the part of individuals and nations, to share excess food, clothing etc, makes the rich richer and the poor poorer, a situation contrary to the Way of Heaven, to the Law of Moses, and to the ethic of Jesus.

Jesus of Nazareth is reported as saying that "it is more difficult for a rich man to enter the Kingdom of God than for a camel to pass through the eye of a needle." (31)He argued : "What will it benefit a man if he possesses everything in the world and loses his own soul." (32) Christians are taught that "it is more blessed to give than to receive." The Apostle Paul suggests to Timothy that he instruct the church "to do good deeds and to be generous and willing to share." In the letter of James, Christian are advised not to fatten themselves like animals awaiting slaughter, living in luxury and self-indulgence.

《箴言》11：24-25说："滋润人的，必得滋润，屯粮不卖的，民必咒诅。"

《旧约》是这样声明的：(1)要敬畏主，(2)遵守诫命，(3)遵行他的道，(4)禁食。就是耶和华立定的规约，归纳起来是两大诫命："你要尽心、尽性、尽意地爱你的上帝主"，"爱你的邻居如同爱你自己"。耶稣说，这两条诫命概括了律法和先知的一切思想。对于以色列人来讲，存在爱邻如爱己的规约义务。先知以塞亚说，禁食的真正目的是为了"先让自己低下去，松开不公的锁链，解放被压迫的人，把食物分给饥饿的人，给无家可归的人提供住的地方，让穿不上衣服的有衣可穿"（《以塞亚书》58章）。就是说，如果人敬畏神的话，就要匡扶社会正义。禁食包括两大诫命的全部内容。

耶稣基督警告人民不可囤积粮食来自己享受（《路加福音》12：15）。

耶稣徒认为，一切属于上帝，上帝能拿得出，也收得回。我们拥有的东西都是上帝恩典恩赐的。我们不过是财产的管家。我们没有施舍的义务，但我们可以把多余的施舍出去。这应该成为我们经营的动机。有福共享对施舍和被施舍双方都是有利的，有助于促进政治与经济和谐。

个人和国家如果不愿施舍多余的衣食用品，则富的更富，穷的更穷。这是有违天道的，有违摩西的律法的，有违耶稣观念的。

耶稣说："富人想进天堂，比骆驼穿过针眼儿还难呢"（《马可福音》10：23-25）。他说："如果人拥有全世界，但却失去了自己的灵魂，那还有什么意义呢"（《马可福音》8：36）？基督徒应该知晓："给予别人要比被别人给更有意义"。使徒保罗告诉提摩太，要让教会"行善事，讲慷慨，愿施舍"。《雅各布书》第五章劝告基督徒不要像牲口一样享尽荣华富贵，吃肥了等着挨宰。

Reduce the surplus and supplement the scarcity.

Some poor countries in Africa will remember that in 2000, the People's Republic of China, which has 1.3 billion people to feed, wiped off their national debt of US$1.2 billion. To some rich countries this would have been a pittance, but it represented "two very small copper coins that the poor widow, out of her poverty, could ill-afford." (33)It may also be true that there were political motives in this action!

Tax cuts for the rich, purportedly designed to promote greater employment opportunities, are not always in the best interest of the poor. In some instances, they may represent little more than a vote-catching ruse.

Democratic and Communist regimes are both of elitists, promoting special "relationships", "jobs for the boys." Both, in different ways, need to work at "reducing the surplus and supplementing the scarcity".

Proverbs 21:26b contended that "the righteous gives without sparing." On the other hand, as Ecclesiastes suggests, "Whoever loves money never has money enough; whoever loves wealth is never satisfied with his income. This, too, is meaningless." (5:10).

有些非洲穷国忘不了2000年中华人民共和国不顾自己十二亿人口的生活问题，免除了他们的十二亿美元国债。对于某些富国来说，这个数字微不足道，但是，"但对于无依无靠的穷寡妇来说，却是救人的两个铜板。"（《路加福音》21：1-4）当然，此举可能也带有政治目的。

富人减免税收，有意促进就业机会，最受益的并不总是穷人。有些情况下，可能是拉点儿选票而已。

民主制度也好，共产主义制度也好，都是上层人操纵关系，让"大家都有活干"。两者情况不同，都需要在"损有余补不足"上下点功夫。

《箴言》21：26论说："义人施舍不吝惜"。《传道书》也说："爱财的人总不知足，爱财富的人绝不满足收入，这么说也是没意义的"。

CHAPTER SIX

Wealth and Authority.

A Mansion full of Gold and Jade is not able to be defended.

When a government is deluded by power and authority,

What is normal becomes strange, and what is good turns to evil.

Lao Zi argued that "kind and generous people shall have no excessive possessions". It was his philosophy that men should live at a normal or basic level of comfort and should not hoard goods. People should give away excessive possessions, and should not seek things that are difficult to obtain. When rare objects are not valued as priceless treasures, people will not become thieves. It is difficult for one to defend a mansion full of gold and jade. Lao Zi criticized especially those leaders who taxed people excessively.

Lao Zi argued that people should neither live from hand to mouth at the minimum subsistence level, nor live at an over-luxurious level that amounted to waste. He suggested that people should live in a society that honoured both the individual and society, that is, what we would describe as the best of the capitalist and communist systems. In Chapter 56 of Dao De Jing, Lao Zi stresses the danger of "five colours that are likely to corrupt and blind one's eyes", and the glittering objects that stir up selfish desires and lead to greed and robbery. According to Dao Philosophy, if everyone lived for others, like heaven and earth do, there would be plenty of room for everyone in this world. Everyone would do his or her best in their occupations, giving away excess so that no one would need to worry about tomorrow.

The ideal would be a society in which there would be work for everyone to earn enough to support his family in comfort, and with a small saving for tomorrow or for rainy days. Like ancient Chinese society, the conscientious worker's big investment, alongside his small savings, would be his family and children, upon whom he would depend for his old age pension. He might not have a huge pension, but he would be contented and enjoy his retirement. A society would be benevolent enough to look after the welfare of those who were childless and could not support themselves. (In Japan, until the late 80s, big companies took care of their workers "from the womb to the tomb"). This ideal is more relevant to a simple agrarian community than to modern society, with its huge cities and sophisticated economies. There is need for those with the required knowledge and skills, as well as a commitment to Dao philosophy, to translate this rustic, rural ethic into the context of economically sophisticated contemporary modern society, as well as into a world order that is suffering from overpopulation and eulogistical devastation.

第六章

金玉满堂，莫之能守；正复为奇，善复为妖

　　老子认为，"善者不多"。他的思想是，人活着要平淡为安，不要积财。要把多余的财物施舍出去，难求的东西不要去求。"不贵难得之货，使民不为盗"，"金玉满堂，莫之能守"，老子尤其鞭挞统治者的暴敛行径。

　　老子认为，人民不应该生活在勉强糊口的最低水平，也不要铺张浪费。他认为，人们所生活的社会应该是个人和社会都有荣誉感，也就是我们所描绘的资本主义和共产主义制度达到的最高程度。在《道德经》第56章，老子强调了"五色令人目盲"的危急状态---明艳的物质激发起自私的欲念，导致贪婪和偷盗。道家哲学说，如果人为别人活着，正如天地为别人存在一样，则人在这个世界上的空间也就多了。大家努力工作，有所舍得，也就不会为来日担忧了。

　　理想社会就是人人有工作可做，挣的工资足以舒适地养家，小有积蓄以备不时之需。要像古代中国社会那样，除了自己少点储蓄，认真算起来，最大的投资就是家庭和子女，得靠他们养老。他的退休金可能不多，但是他可以满足平安地享受晚年。社会也应该搞慈善事业来关照无嗣、无助者的福利（直到八十年代末，日本大型企业职工的福利是一包到底）。这种理想在拥有大城市和复杂的经济结构的现代社会中还是比较贴近简单的农业社会的。对于具有专业知识和技能以及奉行道家哲学的人来说，有必要把这种土气的农村观念转变成为先进经济的当代社会的观念，使这个人口超载、在颂扬中走向毁灭的世界得以秩序化。

> Wealth and Authority.
> A Mansion full of Gold and Jade is not able to be defended.
> When a government is deluded by power and authority,
> What is normal becomes strange, and what is good turns to evil.

Businessmen should not scheme to control supply and demand so efficiently that they "corner" the whole market and dominate and unpoverish others. Nor should they charge excessive prices for their products so as to make exorbitant profits. If this happened there would be no expensive goods and whatever profits a businessman made would be used for investment and future trading.

Lao Zi also warned those in leadership not to be deluded by power and authority. Lao Zi argued that it would be "a waste of effort for a leader, who serves his or her selfish interest, to pretend to pray to god in heaven for blessing in his service of the people". When a leader begins enjoying authoritarian power, he often loses any sense of responsibility. Leaders in government, who are power hungry and greedy, have a tendency to corrupt what is essentially good, transforming it into evil. The power of such leaders is ultimately diminished by the cumulative consequences of their actions, which return to haunt them. It is for this reason that the Dao De Jing suggests that when "leaders act against the teaching of "The Word," it is difficult for them to rule the country". It is because of this dynamic that Lao Zi argued that people should have "few superfluous possessions, few covetous desires".

Dao Philosophy, refined by Lao Zi, can be summarized in two maxims: (1). "Do not act against the Way of Heaven", and (2). "Respect Dao and value integrity", which is roughly equivalent to Jesus: "Love the Lord your God, and love your neighbours as yourself" – Dao being the supernatural, undefineable, eternal Word.

Dao philosophy, no less than the teaching of Jesus, was occasionally corrupted. These corruptions found expression in numerous types of Dao religion, such a "Five Measures of Rice Dao", founded by Zhang Dao Ling, who demanded his followers contribute five measures of rice each to the leaders on admission as followers. Other, similar sects that sprung up were: "Peace Dao", "New Pope Dao", "Lou Guan Dao" (lou guan dao.– Lou Guan being the name of a town in Xianxi), "Tai Yi Dao or Supreme One Dao", "Real Big Dao". Some sects gave themselves to the search for the elixir of life and developed herbal medicines. These claimed that they would live forever, or else become saints and ascend to heaven without experiencing death.

商人不要操纵控制市场供求，也不可欺行霸市，不可高抬物价牟利。否则，货无好货，商人谋利所得就会用来投资贸易。

老子告诫执政者不要迷恋权位。他认为，"治人事天，莫若啬"。如果执政独裁，就会丧失责任感。政府的领导人如果贪权、恋权，往往会出现腐败，好人都会变坏的。此类领导天长日久，习以为常，终究有干不下去的时候。《道德经》有言："以其上之有为，是以不治"。因为如此，老子提出"少私寡欲"。

老子的经典之作《道德经》可以概括为两点：①无违天之道；②尊道而贵德。这基本上也就体现了耶稣的"爱你的主上帝吧，爱邻人如爱己"——这，也体现了"道，可道也，非恒道也"。

道学也和耶稣的教导一样，常被人歪曲。传道的方式有不少被人歪曲：如张道陵所创的五斗米道，入会要交五斗米。其他宗派如太平道、新天师道、楼观道、太一道、真大道等。有的宗派寻找长生不老药，配制药剂，声称可以长生不老，登仙成圣而不死。

> Wealth and Authority.
> A Mansion full of Gold and Jade is not able to be defended.
> When a government is deluded by power and authority,
> What is normal becomes strange, and what is good turns to evil.

Others claimed to have magical powers. Others, again, argued that they were descendents of "super men." These cults flourished because they appealed to self-centredness, and the quest for power and immortality. They claimed to be able to initiate people into the society of the immortals. Little wonder that Lao Zi argued that "What is normal becomes strange, and what is good turns to evil".

In 1851, Hong Xiuquan began a revolution, described as the greatest farmers' uprising in history. He intended wiping out the corrupt and weak Qing Dynasty and establishing a democratic, Christian form of government in China. His attempt to stamp out opium smoking gained popular support. However, it soon became obvious that Hong and his deputies aspired to imperial-style power, which undercut their democratic claims. Many factors contributed to the downfall of his government. Among these were the fact that he claimed to be the younger brother of Jesus Christ, which offended foreign missionaries. His anti-smoking reforms antagonized foreigners involved in the drug trade. Both groups of foreigners turned against him, cutting off the supply of funds and arms. In addition, he lacked administrative skills and was a poor strategist, leaving his army without supplies. Furthermore, his mistrust of his subordinates, and jealousy and in-fighting among his deputies loosened his grip of power. Hong's aim was commendable, and he began his reforms in good faith, but his ambition and administrative and strategic incompetence, together with the in-fighting of his deputies, and the fact that the foreign powers turned upon him, precipitated his downfall. Hong's revolution is a further illustration of "good turning to evil." (34)

有的人声称魔法，还有的人说他们是"超人"的后裔。这些异端之所以滋生，是因为他们自以为是，追求权力和不朽的声名。他们宣扬教人登仙。难怪老子批驳道："正复为奇，善复为妖"。

1851年，洪秀全领导了有史以来最大的农民革命。他志在推翻衰弱腐朽的清政府，在中国建立一个民主的、基督教式的政府。他铲除鸦片，受到人们的拥护。可惜，洪秀全及其所部企图掌握封建帝制的权柄，民主的呼声也就不存在了。他的政府垮台了，因素是多方面的：首先，他自称是耶稣的弟弟，这就冒犯了外国在中国的传教士。他禁烟之举，触犯了贩毒的洋鬼子的利益。这两伙洋人都反对他，切断了他的财路和武器供应。另外，他管理无能，缺乏谋略，使部队得不到保障。而且，对部下不信任，僚属之间妒忌、内讧，削弱了他的控制能力。洪秀全的想法固然可嘉，改革初始满怀信心，然而，他雄心有余，管理乏力，计谋不足，下属内乱，加上列强反目，这就加速了他的崩溃。洪秀全革命进一步说明了"正复为奇"。

Wealth and Authority.
A Mansion full of Gold and Jade is not able to be defended.
When a government is deluded by power and authority,
What is normal becomes strange, and what is good turns to evil.

Like other religions, philosophies, and contemplative traditions, Falun Gong suffers from disparities between what is claimed, and the behaviour of senior leadership. For example, while Li Hongzhi argues that by practicing Falun Gong exercises, followers do not need to seek medical treatment for illnesses, he himself underwent an operation on an acute festering appendix in July 1984. He also sought medical treatment for other illnesses. In view of what has been argued, it could be contended that Falun Gong is an example of the turning of good into evil.

In 2000, the Communist Government in China purged many of their commissars who were found corrupt in their dealings, men who build private "empires". Those who were corrupt had forgotten the basic principles of communism. They put themselves before the people. They could not resist the temptation of "glittering gold." This action was contrary to Party Disciplines, or, in Lao Zi's words, against the Way of Heaven. Mao Zedong used to encourage the cadets of his Party by using the story of the perseverance of " a stupid old man attempting to move a mountain". He argued that they should serve the people with perseverance as their first priority. When they did this the people would come to trust them and the party. Mao tried to put the teaching of the Dao into practice in this case that those wishing to lead the people must put their own interests last, "set an example themselves and serve the world as common servants" without seeking benefit for themselves.. Unfortunately, human greed and selfishness overpowered Party discipline. This was another example of turning good to evil.

The Christian Scriptures indicate that Jesus, before beginning his ministry, prayed and fasted in the wilderness for forty days and nights. As a consequence, he was hungry and weak. In this state he was vulnerable to temptation. The Scriptures depict his state of mind in terms of the mythology of the times. They portray him being tempted by the devil. The devil tested his integrity, asking him to turn stones into bread. Refusing to yield to self-interest, Jesus answered that it was written in the Scripture that people did not live on bread alone, but by every word that came from the mouth of God.

| 金玉满堂，莫之能守，正复为奇，善复为妖

　　法轮功也像其他宗教、哲学和反思的传统一样，其高级领导人的行径和所鼓吹的是有差距的。例如，李洪志认为，练习法轮功不需要求医问药，而他本人于1984年7月做了个急性阑尾炎手术。他得了别的什么并也照样去治疗（注：美国政府于2001年给予法轮功人员3000万美元的援助，这说明，法轮功是受外国指使、阴谋颠覆中国的邪教组织）。以此看来，法轮功就是"善复为妖"的典型例子。

　　2000年，中共政府揪出了许多建立私家"帝国"的腐败分子，他们贪污腐化，丢掉了共产主义的基本原则。他们把自己的利益放在人民利益之上，在"金灿灿的黄金"面前败下阵来。他们的所作所为违反了党的纪律，用老子的话说，就是"违反道"。毛泽东曾经用"愚公移山"的故事来鼓励党的干部，他说，要再接再厉，把为人民服务当作首要任务。只有为人民服务，人民才会信任党的领导。毛泽东努力实践道家之言："欲先民，必身后"，"以身作则"，"以身为天下牧"，"无私欲"。但是，贪婪自私的本性高过了党的纪律，这也证明了"善复为妖"的道理。

　　基督教《圣经》记载，耶稣传道之前，在野外禁食祷告40个日夜，结果，饥贫交加。此时是最容易诱惑的。《圣经》从当时神话的角度，描述了他的思想状态，形容耶稣在接受魔鬼的试探。魔鬼为了试探是否正直，叫他把石头变成面包。这个自私的行为被耶稣拒绝了，耶稣的回答是：《圣经》有言，人活着不单单只靠面包，还要靠上帝口里所说的每句话。

Wealth and Authority.
A Mansion full of Gold and Jade is not able to be defended.
When a government is deluded by power and authority,
What is normal becomes strange, and what is good turns to evil.

In the gospel of John, Jesus talks about three different types of leaders, or shepherds. First, there is the thief or robber, who climbs into the sheepfold to steal the sheep. Then there is the hired hand whose only concern is himself, who abandons the sheep when the wolf comes. The third type of shepherd is the good shepherd, who enters the fold by the gate and calls each sheep by its name and leads it to green pastures.

The first type of church leader is one who uses his position to advance his own interests. Members are pawns used to build numbers, influence or wealth. They are not cared for for their own sakes. They are used, exploited.

The Second type of church leader performs his role in a merely professional manner. They do what is expected of them. Their concern for those under their charge is minimal They avoid what is messy. They will not dirty their hands if they can help it

These first two styles of leadership have a tendency to transform "normal things into strange and good into evil". The third type of leader genuinely cares for those who are entrusted to his or her care.

在约翰《福音》里，耶稣谈到了三种不同类型的领导人，也叫牧羊人。首先是贼，爬进了羊圈偷羊。其次是，雇来的帮手只考虑自己，狼来了，扔下羊就跑了。第三类牧羊人还不错，开开门，进了羊圈，每只羊都叫出名来，领着羊到了青草地上。

从教会角度来看，第一种类型的领导人是以权谋私型的，属下只是个棋子，用来积累财富和名位的。他们不能为了自己，他们是被利用的，是被剥削的。

第二种类型的领导人干事只是尽尽责任而已，叫他们干什么他们干什么，不怎么考虑手下，杂事乱世一躲了之，即使可以帮上一把，也不愿脏了自己的手。

前两类领导的共同特点就是"正复为奇，善复为妖"。第三类领导却是真心关照所信任的人的。

CHAPTER SEVEN
The paradox of Softness and Hardness.

Lao Zi in his Dao De Jing highlighted a number of paradoxes to do with such notions as: "nothing and something" ; "yin/night and yang/day" ; "female and male" ; "benefit and harm; " "honoured and despised" ; "weak and strong" ; "high and low" ; "long and short" ; "quiet and motion" ; "heavy and light" ; "surplus and scarcity" and many others.

Chinese philosophy prefers "softness" or "gentleness" to "hardness" or "harshness" , believing that gentleness will overcome harshness. This principle is also adopted in marshall arts, like Tai ji and Judo, in which the defender makes use of the force exerted by the attacker, using the force of the attacker to overthrow him.

Lao Zi argued that softness and hardness represent the state of life and death respectively. Animals and plants appear tender and soft when they are young and growing, and they turn hard and dry when they become old and later die. When rice is cooked, the grains are soft and warm, and tend to stick to one another. They are not easily separable. But when they are frozen, they turn cold and hard and are easily separable. When a couple is loving and warm towards each other they enjoy each other's companionship. Wherever the husband goes the wife follows. When the relationship turns sour, they become cold and callous towards each other, and, even though they sleep in the same bed, they have different "dreams, " literally, . They begin living separate lives. Warmth and love are the opposites of cold and hatred.

Softness can overcome hardness. Rain-drops, over time, make depressions in stone pavements. The softness of water can penetrate even the hardness of stone.

Respecting the wise and conducting oneself with humility are two further elements of gentleness. There are many stories of the successful application of these two qualities.

第七章

柔胜刚

老子的《道德经》特别强调许多概念的矛盾性：无有、阴阳、雌雄、利害、贵贱、弱强、高下、长短、静动、重轻、盈亏等。

中国哲学倾向柔胜于刚，相信以柔克刚。这个道理也用在武术上，比如太极和柔道用的是借力使力打到对手。

老子认为，强弱代表生死。动植物年幼时是柔脆的，长大时坚硬，死亡时苦干。煮饭的时候，米粒温和柔软，粘在一起，不易分离。结冻时，就会变得冰冷坚硬，但却容易分开。夫妻彼此关爱体贴，心心相印，夫唱妇随。感情一旦恶化，便反目相向，同床异梦，分道扬镳。冷暖爱恨是一对矛盾体。

以柔克刚：一滴一滴的雨水久而久之能把人行道的石板击出坑来。水是柔弱的，会穿过坚硬的石头。温还有两个要素：谦贤、谦下---这两种品质印证了许多成功的故事。

The paradox of Softness and Hardness.

Emperor Shang Tang (b.c.1783 B.C.E. – death unknown) came to know about the ability of Yi Yin (b.c.1753 B.C.E. – death unknown), who was part of the dowry of Xin Shi's daughter. He intended to engage Yi Yin to work for him. He instructed the son of Peng to take him out in his carriage, without telling him where they were headed.

On the way, the son of Peng asked where the Emperor wanted to go. Shang Tang indicated that he wanted to engage the services of Yi Yin, who lived in a remote mountainous area. The son of Peng was puzzled. He told Shang Tang that Yi Yin was but an ordinary citizen, and if the emperor wanted to see him, he should summon him to the court. Shang Tang explained that a certain herb was an ordinary grass, yet ingesting the herb made one attentive and energetic.

Shang Tang exhibited a rare imperial humility. He treated wise men with gentleness and respect. He also knew that Yi Yin could be useful to him. Though he was the emperor and exercised considerable power and authority, he chose a gentle approach in inviting the wise man to his court. Through gentleness he won over the hearts of others, who served him with fidelity. As a consequence, his rule was efficient, popular and peaceful.(37)

This humane approach was also adopted by Liu Bei, one of the three warlords exercising power during the Period of the Three Kingdoms. He cordially and patiently invited Kong Ming to join his court in 207 C.E. He twice visited Kong Ming in his remote habitation with his two "brothers", but in vain. However, he did not give up hope. The third time he visited Kong Ming the wise man was having a nap. Liu Bei patiently waited for him to wake up before he mentioned the purpose of his visit. On this occasion, the War-lord persuaded Kong Ming to be his war-strategist. His patience and humility paid off, and Kong Ming helped him build a strong and sizeable kingdom. This is the famous story of "Three visits to the Reed Hut".(38)

It is said that many Catholics have visited St. Peter's Cathedral in Rome. They paid homage to Peter by kissing his toe of a huge bronze statue of the apostle. As years went by, the bronze toe was worn off. The soft lips of worshippers wore away hardened bronze.

Mohandas Karamchand Gandhi, better known as Mahatma Gandhi (1869–1948), after an apprenticeship in South Africa, developed forms of passive resistance – non-violent protests and hunger strikes –that resulted in Britain's withdrawal from India. Despite numerous imprisonments, nothing could deter him from achieving his goal.

皇帝商汤得悉陪嫁莘氏女的伊尹的才干，打算征用伊尹为他效劳，便指令彭的儿子带他出游，而没有告诉他的目的。

途中，彭的儿子问皇帝去什么地方，商汤说，去深山征用伊尹。彭的儿子很惊奇。他说伊尹不过是个草民，如果皇帝要见他，可以下诏进朝。商汤说，有一种草药和草没什么两样，但服了以后却提神健力。

商汤贵为皇室，却表现出了难得的谦逊。他待贤人以温顺和敬重，明知伊尹有用，身为帝王，可以使用权威，但是，他选择的是温厚的态度邀他来朝。温厚得人心，得人心者尽忠。因此，他政绩突出，受人爱戴，天下太平。

三国时代，三侯鼎立的刘备也采用温和的态度。公元207年，他耐心地恳请孔明进朝。他曾两度和两个把兄弟赶赴他荒野住处都没找到。但是，他并不罢休。第三次登门的时候，此位贤达在午间高卧。刘备耐心地等他起来，才告诉他造访的原因。这次，主公才说动孔明当他的军师。他的耐性和不耻下人的精神起了作用，孔明帮他建了一个强大的国家。这个故事就是著名的"三顾茅庐"。

据说，许多天主教徒去过罗马圣彼得大教堂，为了尊敬彼得，他们一一吻使徒铜像的大拇趾。一年又一年过去了，铜趾磨坏了。朝圣者柔软的嘴唇磨损了坚硬的铜。

莫汉达士卡拉南站特甘地（1869-1948）俗称圣雄甘地，在南非洲做短工以后，搞出了几种形式的消极抵抗，比如非暴力不抵抗运动和绝世运动，致使英国撤出了印度。虽然几次入狱，但没有什么能够阻止他实现目的的决心。

The paradox of Softness and Hardness.

Using a "soft" approach, he overcame the might of the British Empire in India. One of the images we have of Gandhi is of a bispectacled, soft-spoken, old man spinning his cotton yarn on a handloom. Britain granted independence to India in 1947. Non-violence and gentleness triumphed over colonial rule.

Nelson Mandela (1918 –), a native of South Africa, was sent to prison on an isolated island for twenty-seven years as a consequence of his fight to gain democracy, one-man-one-vote, for the black majority in South Africa. Under the pressure of world opinion, the then minority white government gave in and a general election was held, in which Mandela was elected president. Without resentment, Mandela began a reconciliation process to heal the hurts and wounds caused during the oppressive years of white-rule. The intent was to bring peace and stability to South Africa. Mandela exhibited integrity and a total lack of resentment for those twenty-seven years of imprisonment. Lao Zi argues that one with integrity should return resentment with goodness. It is only those without integrity who repay resentment with equally harsh and strong, vengeful measures. This is another example of softness overcoming hardness.

Hatred stirs up dissension, but love embraces all wrongs, as the Book of Proverbs (10: 12) so perceptively remarked.

A Story of Warm over Cold.

The Lord God made garments of skin for Adam and his wife and clothed them. And the Lord God said, "The man has now become like one of us, knowing good and evil. He must not be allowed to reach out his hand and take also from the tree of life and eat and live forever." So the Lord God banished him from the Garden of Eden to work the ground from which he had been taken. After he drove the man out, he placed on the east side of the Garden of Eden.Cherubin and a flaming sword flashing back and forth to guard the way leading to the tree of life.

Adam and his wife found themselves walking aimlessly along the bank of a big river. It was a beautiful day with blue sky and gentle sweet breeze of Spring. The meadow was of lushly green and the air was scented with enchanting fragrance of cherry blossom, and the sparrows danced from branch to branch, chipping love songs cheerfully. Fishes swam in the river with graceful movements and occasionally poped up their heads to have a glaze of Adam and Eve. Then they jumped out of the water and back, making a loud sound, "Tommm!" though Adam and Eve were kicked out of the Garden of Eden, the place where they landed was a pretty place except that they had to work for their living.

他用"软弱"的手段制服了大英帝国在印度的权威。甘地给人们的一个印象就是个织棉纱的老头儿，戴着个两用眼镜，说话柔声柔气。1947年，英国准许印度独立，非暴力的温和行动战胜了殖民统治。

纳尔逊·曼德拉（1918-）是个南非土著，为占南非多数的黑人取得一人一票民主选举权而奋斗，结果锒铛入狱27年。在世界舆论的压力下，少数白人政府被迫进行大选，结果，曼德拉当了总统。曼德拉无怨无悔，为弥补白人暴政期间所造成的创伤开始进行和解工作。他的目的是给南非带来和平和稳定。从曼德拉表现出的是正义，他对27年监禁的仇视完全不存在了。老子说，有德行的人要以德报怨，也就是有德司介，无德司撤。这也说明了什么是以弱克强。

《箴言书》十章十二节说："恨，能挑起争端；爱，能包容一切过错。"

温暖胜过冷酷的故事

耶和华神为亚当和妻子做了皮衣。耶和华说："人和与我们相似，知道善恶。现在他伸手去摘生命树的果子吃，想长生不老，这是不行的"。耶和华神把他撵出伊甸园自力更生去了。把他撵走后，在伊甸园东侧布置了基路伯，还有寒光四射的烈焰之剑，把守着通向生命之树的道路。

亚当和夏娃在大河岸边闲逛，美丽的蓝天，和畅的春风，葱翠的草甸，樱桃花的芬芳浸满了空气，麻雀舞枝，啁啾着爱的音符。河里的鱼自由翱翔，偶尔拱起头瞧瞧亚当、夏娃。鱼跃出水面，哗啦一声又翻了回去。

亚当和夏娃被逐出伊甸园，但他们住的是个非常美丽的地方，只是他们得自食其力。

The paradox of Softness and Hardness. |

Up in hevean, other gods were amazed that the Lord God chased Adam and Eve out of the Garden of Eden, dispite all the efforts creating such an ideal place with glorious environment for them to enjoy. It was obvious that the Lord God failed to make men obey his instructions. There were puzzling gaze among the gods.

Finally, there was a conscientious decision among the gods that anyone who could make men obey instructions would sit next to the Lord God. Wind-god had a grin on his face and proudly said, "I can!" Sun-god said mildly that he could too. Other gods looked at ane another, but were numbed with words as they didn't wish to jump into the arena.

So, the stage was set for the contest between Wind-god and Sun-god. All the gods in heaven gathered to watch the contest for the seat next to the Lord God. Some were jostling for a place to have a good view.

Wind-god appeared to be very confident and he suggested that he could start to show his might to make men obey. Sun-god did not object to the suggestion.

Adam and Eve did not know what took place in heaven. While on earth, there was peace, which was broken by the call of a swan looking for his mate. Eve stooped at the water's edge and stretched her hand to splash water on to the swan, which broke the serenity when it flapped the wings as it glided away. This was followed by a gash of wind.

But the wind became a little stronger. As the wind grew forceful, Adam quickly pulled Eve to his side. It was partly to protect her and partly to keep them warm. Wind-god was puzzled that with such considerable force of wind and the man didn't remove the garment from his body. Meanwhile, all the gods were watching attentively. With all the eyes of the gods looking at him, Wind-god became embarrassed, and needless to say, was annoyed. He thought he did not do with all his might yet. So in order to save his reputation and, most importantly, to win the contest, Wind-god blew very hard until his face turned red. The trees swayed, and leaves fell. Anything that was small flew all over the sky, which turned into frosted blue. Eve felt cold. She hugged Adam. And Adam held her closer. The wind was so strong that Adam and Eve took refuge under a gigantic tree. They squatted and held on to each other as hard as they could.

Wind-god was very furious, seeing all his efforts came to naught. Then he decided to give Adam and Eve a last blow. This, he thought, would not only tear Adam and Eve apart, but also would peel their clothes off. So, Wind-god repositioned himself, took aim at Adam and Eve, summoned all his might and directed his blow between Adam and Eve. He blew and blew, hoping that he could pry the earthlings apart. To his great disappointment, the damned earthlings held on to each other so hard that as if they were glued together.

天上的众神对上帝把亚当和夏娃逐出伊甸园之举表示惊奇，因为上帝费劲巴力地搞出了个理想之邦、荣华之所，目的就是让他们去享受。很明显，上帝无法迫使人们遵从他的诫命。众神们只好低声喃喃，疑顿地瞧着。

　　最后，经过慎重的商量，众神决定，听话的人可以坐在上帝身旁。风神一咧嘴，高傲地："我能"。太阳神温和地讲，他也能。其它神彼此相瞧了瞧，不想争个高低，也就默默无言了。

　　风神与太阳神相争的台子搭好了。天上的众神围过来观看这场争夺上帝座边席位的赛事。有的神挤到了视野开阔的地方。

　　风神踌躇满志，想先来它个下马威。太阳神对此并不反对。

　　亚当和夏娃不知道天上发生了什么。地上，一片宁静，只有天鹅寻偶的呱呱叫声。夏娃在水边弯下身去，撩水拨向天鹅去，天鹅扑棱棱展翅飞走了，这才打破原有的宁静。之后刮了一阵风。

　　风大了，风强了，亚当急忙把夏娃拉到身边，一来是保护她，二来可暖暖身子。让风神纳闷的是，风这么用劲，还没把那个人的衣服扒掉。众神全神贯注地瞧着，所有的眼睛都盯着他。风神难为情了，不用说也知道，他恼火了。他想，他还没把劲儿都使出来呢。为了挽回面子，更重要的是为了赢得比赛，风神卯劲儿地吹，吹得满脸通红。数摇晃起来，树叶吹掉了。凡是体积小的，都刮上了天，冷冰冰地融入了蓝天。夏娃冷了，抱着亚当。亚当把他抱紧了。风太大了，亚当和夏娃在一个大树下面避风。他们蹲下来，越抱越紧。

　　风神十分恼怒，他所做的一切都白搭了。于是，想给亚当和夏娃最后一吹。他以为，这不但可以拆开亚当和夏娃，而且还能把他们的衣服扒下来。风神重整旗鼓，对准亚当和夏娃，使出浑身力气，直奔亚当和夏娃的中间吹了过去。他吹呀吹，想把这地上的一对儿撬开。令他满心失望的是，这该死的人类挨得太紧了，好像胶在一起了似的。

The paradox of Softness and Hardness.

As all the gods agreed that Wind-god had failed to remove the clothes off Adam and Eve, they suggested that it was time for Sun-god to show his might. Wind-god stepped aside unwillingly, murmuring grudgingly. Then, Sun-god with his smiling round face came forward. He looked at Adam and Eve, two poor souls, squatting at the foot of the huge tree. He gave them a bit of warmth with a smile at first.

Adam and Eve realized that the cold wind had stopped and all the trees and plants stood erect. The leaves flapped and danced in the gentle breeze as they bathed in the sun. Butterflies and bees came out from their hidings, hovering over the flowers and greeting one another. Adam and Eve seemed much relieved as they stood up. They stretched their limbs and gave each other a smile, acknowledging that "What an ordeal; glad it's over!"

Sun-god smiled too. Nodding his head, he sent out more heat, just warm enough to melt the icicles that dripped down the cliff face in the distant snow-capped mountains.

The swan found its mate as they cruised across the river. Adam and Eve felt the warm too. They loosened the piece of tendril that was used to tie their clothes. They were much relaxed as they held hands, strolling down along the river bank. They came out of the woods into the beautiful meadow. All the flowers lifted their heads to greet the couple. The doe and the deer rubbed their heads on their left forelegs and then on their right. Then they lifted their legs and trotted round and round the meadow. They seemed to be rejoicing and celebrating the reappearance of sunshine.

Sun-god increased the heat a few degrees higher. Adam began to shake his coat in an attempt to allow a change of fresh air to cool down his sweaty body. Both Adam and Eve didn't mind a little bit of discomfort. As a matter of fact, they enjoyed the warmth radiated from Sun-god, as all other creatures did.

The contest between Wind-god and Sun-god had reached the most exciting moment that a decision had to be made. Sun-god was in no hurry. He just increased the heat gradually. By now, the warmth had changed from comfort to discomfort and now it was intolerance. Adam and Eve could not bear it anymore. They were too happy to bare their tops. So, they took off their top garments. They went down to the river to splash some water on them.

In heaven, there were shouts of jubilation. "Sun-god has won the contest!" Out came the announcement. There was no much discussion. They concluded that it was not "cold and strong force" but "warmth" that finally persuaded men to obey instructions. When the gods reported it to the Lord God the lesson that they all learnt, he smiled and nodded.

In the history of mankind, the Lord God in numerous ways and at numerous times through the prophets had tried to persuade mankind to obey his instructions. Not only men did not obey the Word, they persecuted the messengers. Despite all these, the Lord God continues to love men. The crux of the lesson is that the hard and cold, though powerful, will lose authority over the subjects. Only love and warmth will be able to win over the hearts of the world.

众神们认为，风神没能把亚当、夏娃的衣服脱下来，因此提议让太阳神来展示一下他的才艺。风神不情愿地站到一边，嘴里咕哝个不停。长着圆脸的太阳神乐呵呵地走过来。他看看蹲在树根的两个可怜虫亚当和夏娃，显示笑了一下，给他们一点温暖。

　　亚当和夏娃觉得冷风停了，树林和其它植物都挺起身来，树叶在阳光的沐浴下翩然舞动。避风的蝴蝶和蜜蜂飞出来，在花朵上盘旋着，互相打着招呼。亚当和夏娃站起身来，松了一口气。他们伸了一下四肢，彼此会意一笑，说道："好家伙，幸亏过去了！"

　　太阳神也笑了，点点头，发出了更多的热，热得足以溶化远方山巅上积雪流下悬崖的冰凌。

　　天鹅飞过河去寻偶，亚当和夏娃也温暖了。他们把系衣服的卷发抖开。他们的心情非常轻松，手挽着手，沿着河边散步。他们走出树林，来到美丽的草地，所有的花朵儿都抬头向他们问候，雌鹿和雄鹿用脖子擦擦左腿，又擦擦右腿，随后，撩起腿在草地上蹦着跳着。太阳又出来了，它们好像在欢欣雀跃。

　　太阳神调高了几分热度，亚当甩掉外罩，换一下新鲜空气，让浑身是汗的身体凉快一下。亚当和夏娃有点不舒服，但他们并不在乎。他们反而和其它生物一样，在享受着太阳神发出的温暖。

　　风神和太阳神比赛这场竞赛一决胜负的时刻到了。太阳神不慌不忙，只是在慢慢地增温。此刻，温度已经不那么让人舒服了，后来让人受不了了。亚当和夏娃再也受不住了。他们啥也不穿该多好哇，于是，他们脱下了上身，进了河里撩起水来。

　　天上欢声四起，公布道："太阳神胜了！"这是不争的事实。他们认为，让人服从命令，还得靠温暖，而不能靠冷酷，不能动硬的。众神把此事禀报上帝，上帝微笑点点头。

　　人类历史上，上帝屡屡通过先知来劝导人们遵从训谕。可是，人们非但不听，还要迫害使者。尽管如此，上帝还是爱人的。本节重点是讲冷酷、强硬的方法尽管有效，但在人们心目中是没有威望的，只有温和慈爱才得人心。

CHAPTER EIGHT
The paradox of "Nothing" and "Something"

"Nothing is the beginning of all things and Something is the mother of all creation", said Lao Zi. "Beginning" and "mother" are used synonymously here. Indeed, the Chinese character for "beginning" begins with the pictograph of a "woman". It is the female who gives birth to new life. In the life cycle, a woman bears and incubates the new life of the young, and female young grow into women and so the process of propagation is ensured.

In the Judaeo–Christian account of beginnings, the earth was described as "without form and void." Then God created the heavens and the earth, and all creatures in the waters, on land and in the sky. God brought "something" out of "nothing" through his Word. This "something" propagated and multiplied. Hence, "Something" is the "Mother" of all things.

Nothing and Something appear simultenously.

How do we understand the mystery of "nothing" and "something" appearing at the same time? That this can happen is illustrated by the simple example of a tea cup, where the vessel and the void in it appear at the same time when the cup is empty. We not only benefit from the structure of the vessel, but we also use the void in the vessel to contain the tea.

When we burn firewood to produce heat to warm our homes, the firewood diminishes as it burns, but the energy of the heat warms the air in the room. Though the firewood turns to ash, the energy it produces heats the area where it burns. Hence, nothing and something appear simultaneously. Today we would argue that matter is turned into energy.

Nothing and Something do co-exist.

The air, wind, and gases are good examples of "Nothing" and "Something" co-existing. They all appear to be "nothing," but we know they exist by our senses of smell, touch or taste.

At the North Pole during some days in summer there is no darkness, which means that day and night co-exist.

Lao Zi gave an excellent example of a bellows, which consisted of a simple pair of wooden planks with leather sides and a valve, fashioned with a nozzle to direct the air. When compressed, it drove a strong blast of air into the furnace. There may be "nothing" in the bellows, just empty space, but the air in the bellows is "something." This illustrates "nothing" and "something" can co-exist together. Musical instruments, such as accordions and organs, are good examples of this principle.

第八章

逆义的无和有

老子说:"无,名万物之始也,有,名万物之母也"。"始"与"母"是同义的,"始"字是先有"女"旁,母性生育新的生命。生命循环过程中,女性怀胎,孕育新的生命,姑娘出落成女人,生命就是这么繁殖下去的。

犹太-基督教《圣经》记载的太初是一片浑沌,后来,上帝创造天、地和水陆空里的一切生物。上帝用他的道"无"中生"有"。这个"有"成倍地繁衍,"有"便成了万物的本原。

无有同出:

怎么才能理解"无"和"有"同时存在呢?拿个茶杯来做个简单的比喻,当杯空是的时候,杯和杯里的空间就同时存在,杯体我们是可以使用的,杯里的空间是可以盛茶的。

我们烧柴取暖,木柴越烧越少,但是,热能温暖了室内空气。木柴即使烧成灰,所产生的热能使室内温暖。所以,"无"与"有"同时存在,也就是我们所说的物质转化成了能量。

无有相生:

最能证明"无"和"有"同时存在的是空气、风和气体。它们似乎不存在,然而,我们通过嗅觉、触觉和味觉证明了它们的存在。

北极的夏天有些日子没有黑夜,这证明昼夜是同时存在的。老子举了个风箱的例子,只用两块简单的木板,侧面钉上皮子,里面一个筏子来回导气。吹箱一推,一股强风就吹进火炉。风箱里面本是"无",不过空洞洞的,但是,风箱里"有"的是空气。这表明"有"和"无"是共存的。乐器中比如手提琴、风琴等也是这个道理。

The paradox of "Nothing" and "Something"

Zhuang Zi in Ren Jian Shi told the story of a carpenter by the name of Shi (石), and his disciple. One day the pair travelled to the county of Qi (齐) to look for timber. They came to a village where there was a big tree. It was so huge that it could shade a thousand cattle under its foliage. Carpenter Shi passed by it quickly without giving it a second look. His disciple was rather surprised that his master did not stop. So many people were standing around the tree, staring at it and admiring it. The trunk of the tree had a circumference of about thirty meters, and the branches reached out twenty-five meters, giving it a beautiful, straight trunk with spreading branches. It could provide enough timber to build ten boats.

The disciple was puzzled, and was eager to know the reason why his master had passed by the tree. Carpenter Shi told him that the quality of the timber of the huge tree was useless, saying, "Boats built from this timber would sink quickly; coffins would rot easily; articles would be damaged in no time; doors made from the tree would ooze oil; and beams would attract woodworms. Owing to its poor quality, the timber is useless to carpenters, which is why it has lasted so long without being cut down." (39)

Though the timber of the tree was useless, it could at least give shade to people and animals. Useless to one, but useful to the other is a good illustration that nothing and something can co-exist.

Consider there is Something in Nothing.

Lao Zi argued that we can regard "nothing" as "something," that is, make use of the void or empty space created and turn it to some purpose. He gave three examples:

1. The first concerns the thirty spokes in a wheel. It is the space between the axle and the wheel, or the length of the spokes that extends the circumference of the wheel, which contributes to the efficiency of the wheel. The void between the axle and the rim of the wheel, which is supported by the spokes, is designed to serve a certain purpose. The void serves a purpose.

2. When we put up four walls with a roof over them to make a room, it is the void within that we make use of as a room. When we cut an opening in the wall, it is the void of the opening in the wall that we make use of as a window or a door.

3. A cup is moulded from a lump of clay with a hollow space in the centre. We make use of the void in the cup to contain water and other things. We similarly use the space in the bellows.

逆义的无和有

庄子在"人世间"这章讲了个石木匠和徒弟的故事：

匠石之齐，至于曲辕，见栎社树。其大蔽数千牛，絜之百围，其高临山十仞而后有枝，其可以为舟者，旁十数。观者如市，匠伯不顾，遂行不辍。

弟子厌观之。走及匠石，曰："自吾执斧斤以随夫子，未尝见材如此其美也。先生不肯视，行不辍，何邪？"

曰："已矣，勿言之矣！散木也！以为舟则沉，以为棺椁则速腐，以为器则速毁，以为门户则液脂，以为柱则蠹。是不材之木也，无所可用，故能若是之寿。"

虽然是不材之木，至少也能为人畜遮荫。对一个人是没有的，但是对另一个人可有用的，这就很好地说明了有和无的关系。

当其无有

老子说，我们可以把无当做有，利用无或者是创造出无，来达到某种目的。他举了三个例子：

1. 第一是三十辐，共一毂，当其无，有车之用。埏埴以为器，当其无，有器之用。故有之以为利，无之以为用。
2. 凿户牖以为室；当其无，有室之用。
3. 泥团戳洞成杯，我们就用杯的中空来盛水盛物，风箱也是这个道理。

The paradox of "Nothing" and "Something"

The void in the above illustrations could be described as "nothing." But because of its benefit, we describe this "nothing" as "something." Therefore, Lao Zi argues that we should consider "nothing" as "something." This illustrates "nothing" and "something" can co-exist together.

We marvel at such profound wisdom, touching on common things in daily life that we take for granted. Few would have thought of the usefulness of "nothing." Such insight, though simple, must have seemed so revolutionary that it was taken to be nothing short of a revelation.

Most people want to be somebody, and want to avoid being considered nobodies. On the other hand, the few outstanding people who have graced human history have surmounted this need to be "somebody" and have served others with humility, people like Abraham Lincoln, Nelson Mandela and Mother Theresa. This is another illustration, a human illustration, of the way nothing and something co-exist.

Jesus Christ said that those who are humble shall be exalted and that those who deny themselves, take up their cross and follow him shall have eternal life. When we humble ourselves we empty ourselves of pride and arrogance, that is, we are willing to become "nothing" in the sense of not demanding respect from others because of our position or abilities. It is our "nothing", which, paradoxically, is truly "something", that is, of benefit to others. The paradox is even deeper than this, for it is impossible for us to be "nothing" unless we know ourselves to be "something", that is, unless we have sufficient self-esteem to deliberately relinquish any claim to be treated as special. It was because Jesus was in the form of Christ, and knew himself to be in the form of God, that he could empty himself. This "self-emptying" was not the deliberate ploy of a person who knew himself to be "superior", but the unselfconscious action of a person who was grounded in God, could respond spontaneously from that relationship.

逆义的无和有

上面说的无就是"无",我们习惯上把这个"无"称作"有"。老子认为,无即是有,无有同处。

日常生活中,我们接触的事物平平常常,却蕴含着深奥的智慧,我们对此感到惊异。几乎没有会考虑到"无"的用处,这种理解看似简单,实际上绝非简单,起码也能给人以启迪。

多数人想成名成家,不敢居于人下。然而,光耀人类历史的只是少数,他们不想当什么名人,有的只是谦和人下,林肯、纳尔逊曼德拉和圣母德雷莎就是这样。这说明,有和无是相生的。

耶稣基督说,谦卑的人必会被抬高,舍己的人要扛起十字架,跟着他得到永生。我们谦虚的时候,目空一切就远离了我们,也就是说,我们不要因为自己的名位而不去尊重别人,我们应该甘愿处于"无"的状态。这是我们的"无",才是辨证的"有",才能有利他人。这个矛盾体更深的还在于:如果我们不知道自己的"有",不充分地意识到必须放弃特权的话,那么,我们就不可能进入"无"的状态。耶稣是以基督形象出现的,自己知道是代表上帝的形象,他才会无我。这种"无我"不是刻意把自己打扮成尊贵的样子,而是胸怀上帝的自觉行为,这可以从人际关系中得到自觉的体现。

CHAPTER NINE
Retire after accomplishment or success

This is one of the major principles advocated in Dao Philosophy handed down from Yellow Emperor some 5,000 years ago. The principle was adhered to faithfully by the first two legendary emperors followed him. There are few extant, written historical records about these periods except some stories in the writings of the Spring and Autumn Warring States.[40]

The first legendary emperor was Tang Yao, who came to the throne c.2357 B.C.E. In his old age, he intended to abdicate his position to a younger, but wise man. He heard much of Xu You, whom he considered the most eligible candidate. Tang Yao invited Xu You to be his successor. The young man thought that the emperor had done so well for his kingdom and that he might not be able to do better. He did not have the courage to take up the challenge, turned down the offer, and went into hiding. The emperor admired his honesty and awarded Xu You with an area for his settlement. [41]The Emperor Tang Yao then appointed Yu Shun in 2255 B.C.E. to succeed him.

Zhuang Zi's Tian Dao recorded a conversation between them, in which Yu Shun asked Tang Yao about his policy as emperor. In his reply, Tang Yao said that he did not forsake the lonely and uncared-for people. He always helped the poor and needy, had sympathy for the dead, and was caring and compassionate to children and women.[42]Yu Shun followed the policy of Tang Yao and the country continued in peace and harmony. In 2205 B.C.E. he abdicated his throne to Xia Yu, a senior, trusted officer. Xia Yu was well-known for flood control. It was said that when he was on duty directing flood control, he passed his home three times, but never entered it.

Both Tang Yao and Yu Shun practised the principle of reliquishing their positions after successfully governing the country. They were not contentious and therefore there was no war. As Lao Zi put it, those who retreated after accomplishing their tasks acted according to the Way of Heaven. Unfortunately, the third legendary emperor did not follow the example set by his predecessors. Thereafter, authoritarian dynasties developed in China and periodic wars broke out among the warlords.

第九章

功遂身退

"功遂身退"是五千年前黄帝遗留下来的道学一大原则。这两位最早的传说中的皇帝坚守着这个原则,这段时期有文字的历史记载很少,流传下来的只有春秋战国时的一些传说。

第一个传说中的皇帝是唐尧,公元前2357年登基。他年迈的时候想把帝位传给年轻有为的人。他耳闻过许由,认为他是个接班最合适的人选。唐尧于是邀许继任。年轻人认为,皇帝把国家治理得这么有道,他是超不过了,就没敢接,谢绝以后藏了起来。皇帝感慕他的诚实,就赐给许由个地方让他安居。后来,尧帝任命虞舜继位(公元前2255)。

庄子在《天道》篇记录了他们的话,舜问尧为帝之道。尧回答说,孤寡无助者不弃,贫瘠者助,已故者悯,妇幼者恤。舜用尧的办法,国家持续平安和谐。公元前2205年,他把帝位禅位给近臣禹。禹治水有方,据说他抗洪时三过家门而不入。

尧虞舜都功遂身退。他们不争,所以没有战事。老子说,功遂身退,天之道也。不幸的是,传说中第三任皇帝没有效仿前任,伺候,独裁王朝在中国建立,诸侯混战时有发生。

The Dao philosophy suggests that people were created, like the heavens and the earth, to exist for each other. "Heaven and earth can be eternal and everlasting because they do not exist for themselves". Lao Zi argued that people should learn to live to serve others, just as water benefits all creatures and does not contend. Neither does water ask for rewards in return.

It was a common practice for those who had served the country well to be granted territory, as a reward, territory to which they could retire and where they could spend the rest of their lives peacefully. For example: Zhangjiajie, which is now a National Forest Conservational Area and a World Natural Heritage Area in the province of Hunan was granted to Zhang Liang and his clansmen by the founding emperor of the Han Dynasty about two thousand and two hundred years ago. Zhang Liang assisted Liu Bang, or Han Gaozu, to establish his kingdom. The territory with which he was rewarded was named "Zhang Family Territory," or Zhang Jiajie. Zhang Liang retired to this wide, scenic valley surrounded by beautiful slender mountains. He did the right thing in retreating to such a beautiful enclave after his accomplishments. This was consistent with the Way of Heaven.

Nelson Mandela is a very wise man. He spent twenty-seven years in an isolated island prison as a consequence of fighting for majority black rule in South Africa. When the minority white government gave way to international pressure, a democratic election was held under United Nations supervision and Nelson's African National Congress Party was voted into office. Nelson was the first black president of South Africa. Partly due to his advanced age (he was in his 80s) and partly owing to his wisdom, which had been maturated and mellowed during the long confinement, he retired after a few years in office. This is an excellent example of Lao Zi's contention that we should: "Retreat after accomplishment or success".

Few polititians are in touch with this Way of Heaven. They have not appreciated the wisdom of this sort of retreat, but have attempted to hold onto power, to their detriment and that of the countries they have sought to lead. For example, revolutional leaders like Jawahalah Nehru of India did not retreat after their accomplishments.

Prophets in Ancient Israel were not necessarily welcome. Unlike the philosophers of other traditions, they were not popular. They denounced evil and warned of a bleak future should leaders fail to heed their message. They were often opposed by the priests, who claimed that they were alarmist. A number of prophets met a sorry end.

道学认为，人被创造出来，好像天和地同存一样。"天地之所以能长久者，以其不自生也。"老子说，人们应该奉天下，若"水善利万物而不争。"水是不要求回报的。

　　在为国家效忠的功臣退休的时候，皇帝经常赐他一个地区，让他安度晚年。譬如，现在的国家森林自然保护区和世界自然遗产的张家界是2200多年前汉朝开国皇帝赏给张良和族人安居的。张良是汉高祖刘邦的建国功臣。这块地赏给他以后，命名为张家界。张良在这块秀峰林立、开阔美丽的深谷里隐退。他建功以后，隐居到这块美景之中是正确的选择，这符合"功遂身退，天之道"。

　　纳尔逊·曼德拉是个聪明人。他为南非多数黑人斗争，在孤岛坐了27年牢。少数白人政府在国际压力下，在联合国监督下举行民主选举，纳尔逊的非洲国大党当选上台。纳尔逊成了南非首任黑人总统。由于高龄（80多岁）的缘故，也由于长年监禁磨出来的练达，他当任几年后就退休了。这就是老子所说的"功成身退"，也遵守了"天之道"。

　　搞政治的很少有接触天道的。他们不欣赏这种引退的智慧，而是尽量抓权，印度革命领袖加瓦哈拉尼赫鲁就是功成不退。

　　古以色列先知们不一定受欢迎，不受拥戴，因为他们和其他传统哲学是不同的。他们斥责邪恶，警告领头的，如果不听他们的，是没有好下场的。他们经常遭到牧师们的反对，说他们造成了恐怖。几个先知都没得善终。

Jeremiah was stoned to death while living in exile in Egypt. Amos was kicked out of Israel and Hosea was thrown out of Judah. John the Baptist, who prepared the way for the coming of Jesus, excoriated King Herod for his sins and lost his head. While it was customary for prophets to retire from public life after delivering their messages, many did not have that apportunity, but were harried or cut down.

Jesus of Nazareth was also a prophet. Described by the Johannine Gospel as "The Word" became flesh, Jesus delivered a message of repentance, hope and love. Because his "gospel" challenged religious and political leaders, he was put to death. While he had no aspirations to political power, his enemies recognised that his message could unseat them. They felt they were left with no alternative but to have him put to death. Through his life, death, and consequent resurrection, Jesus, celebrated as the "Christ" or "Annointed One," has transformed the lives of generations of his followers.

It could be argued that Jesus also "retired" after accomplishing his task, a retirement albeit forced on him, but in which he acquiesed in spirit. He "retreated after compling his mission according to the Way of God". His "Kingdom", which took shape after he had gone, was not of this world.

The Apostle Paul described the attitude of Jesus, who voluntarily relinguished position and power, as the supreme example of humility. While in the form of God, he did not claim to be equal to God. He humbled himself like a servant and took human form; becoming obedient to the Will of God to the point of death, death on a cross. This, the greatest paradox in Christianity, is a supreme illustration of the Way of Heaven, of retreating after accomplishing the task to which one is called.

The proverb, "The fear of the Lord teaches a man wisdom, and humilty comes before honour" [43] can stand alongside the teaching of the Dao that we should retire after accomplishment, as it furnishes an effective reason for such retirement. One is also reminded of the passage from Isaiah, all men are like grass, and all their glory is like the flower of the field. The grass withers and the flowers fall, because the breath of the Lord blows on them. Surely the people are grass. The grass withers and the flowers fall, but The Word of our God stands forever. [44] Isaiah 40:6–8.

杰里迈亚放逐埃及,被用石头打死。阿摩司被赶出以色列,何西亚被抛出犹大。施洗的约翰筹备耶稣的来临,因为叱责希列王的罪行而被杀头。先知们按例应该是送完信以后就一退了之,然而,不少先知都没机会了,不是被蹂躏就是被砍倒。

耶稣也是先知。《约翰福音书》用哲理一样的语言说耶稣是道成肉身,他传的信息是悔改,是希望,是爱。他的福音和宗教、政治领袖发生冲突,所以他去死。他没有权欲,然而,他的敌人们认为,他的信息会推翻他们。他们别无选择,只好把他置于死地。耶稣在历尽生命、死亡和复活之后,被誉为基督,也叫受膏者,改变几代门徒的命运。

可以说,耶稣功成"身退"是被迫的,尽管他的灵魂是默许的。他遵守的是上帝的道,因此身退了。他的王国不在此世,而在他离开后的彼世。

使徒保罗描述耶稣时说,他自愿放弃了权位,是谦卑的楷模。他的形象是上帝,但不把自己等同于上帝。他虚己下人,变成人的模样,唯上帝是瞻,鞠躬尽瘁,死而后已。这也就是基督教的最大矛盾所说的功成身退乃天之道。

《箴言》说,"敬畏主教人智慧,谦虚在尊荣之前"。这句话可以和道训相提并论,也就是功遂身退,因为身退是有缘由的。《以西亚书》里有这样一段经文:"人好比草,荣誉好比地上的花。草有枯日,花有凋时,因为主吹到它们。百姓也是草,草要枯萎,花要凋零,惟有我们上帝之言永存。"

CHAPTER TEN
Superior goodness like that of water

Most ancient civilizations sprung up around water–courses. Water was a source of life, a necessary means of helping sustain life. Chinese civilization developed along the Huanghe and Chang Jiang. (45) The cradle of Indian civilization was in the Indus Valley. Mesopotamian civilization took shape along the Tigris and Euphrates rivers. Ancient Egypt was dependent on the Nile. In South America, before the Incas empire developed, villages were formed on the banks of a few rivers on the arid plateaus on the western flank of the Andes. All these civilizations survived because of water, which they drank and used to fertilize their fields.

The Eloist account of Creation in Genesis 1 argued that God first created a vast watery substance, only later creating land. This mythological and poetic celebration of creation highlighted the primacy of water for the sustaining of a myriad of life forms. Wells were of particular importance to desert nomads like the Hebrews. Wars were fought over them, and bargains struck. Genesis chapter 21 tells us a story about Abraham, an alien in Palestine, who complained to Abimelech, a chieftain who had prior claim to the area, that his soldiers had seized a well Abraham dug for his family and flock. After presenting sheep and cattle to Abimelech, as gifts, the Treaty of Beersheba was signed between them, granting Abraham and his descendants the right to use the well.

Water holes have been the popular spots, where animals congregate to quench their thirst, particularly in areas where there are no rivers or streams. Water holes and wells have become meeting places where social intercourse takes place. Many have developed into nerve centres of communication and trade.

The Greek philosopher, Thales (c, 624–547 B.C.E), thought water was the foundational element of the world. Certainly, without water life as we know it, our distinct biosphere would be unsustainable.

Water featured in Chinese philosophy from the beginning, because it is soft, tender, yielding. Ancient Chinese respected the gentle nature of water so much that they spoke of the "Integrity of Water" . The qualities of water were similar to the qualities of women. It is said that during the period of "Matriarchal Society, " some 8, 000 years ago, there was no fighting among different clans. War broke out when patriarchs took over the "management, " including the defence of society. The gentleness and yielding nature of water and women is said to be the origin of Dao Philosophy. (45)

第十章

上善若水

多数远古发源于江河流域。水是生命之源，是维持生命的重要元素。中华文明发源于黄河长江。印度文明的摇篮位于印度河谷。美索不达米亚文明是在底格里斯和幼发拉底两河流域。古埃及靠的是尼罗河。南美印加帝国出现之前，村落建在安第斯山脉西侧贫瘠高原上的几条河流区域。所有文明因水而生，水供他们饮用，灌溉他们的农田。

以罗欣人在《创世纪》说创造时认为，神最初创造了一大片水域，然后才创造了地。这则富有诗意的神话在欢庆造物的时候首先强调了养育万类的水。对于沙漠上的游牧部落比如希伯来人，水的重要性非同一般。因水而战，因水儿争。《创世记》二十一章讲了巴勒斯坦异族人亚伯拉罕的故事。他向占了地盘的部落首领亚比米勒控诉到，他的士兵霸占了他给自己的人畜挖的一口井。他把牛羊送给亚比勒后，他们就签了《别是巴合约》，允许亚伯拉罕和他的后裔使用这口井的权利。

没有河流溪涧的地方，水塘成了牲畜聚集涡饮的地方。水塘和水井成了社交集会的去处，这些地方很多都变成了交通和贸易的枢纽地带。

希腊哲学家塔耳氏（公元前624-547）认为，水是世界基本要素。没有水，独特的生物界是难以持久的。

中国哲学开篇便是水水的绵软、水的温柔、水的谦让。古代中国非常重视水的温柔本质，称之为水德。水性和女性有相似的特点。据说，8000年前的母系社会，部落间没有战争。父系接管社会以后，战事开始了，是说为了保卫氏族。水的柔软和谦让可说是道教的起源。

Lao Zi argued that water benefits all creatures, though it has never contended or asked anything in return. It exists for others, and not for its own sake, being completely unselfish. It is not resentful, nor contentious, and always flows to the lowest level, staying in humble places that others despise. It is accommodating and conforms to any environment, being generous and tolerant. It is always level, demonstrating justice, fairness, and a lack of favouritism. Though soft and yielding, water can penetrate the hardest things in the world, if given time. Lao Zi says that our goodness must be like that of water.

In Christianity, it is the sayings and doings of Jesus of Nazareth that are important to believers. It is through his words and deeds, which are the incarnation of The Word, or Dao, that Christ, or the Son of God, encouraged people to draw close to God. It was through his words and deeds that men came to know the grace and mercy of God, including, most important of all, God's agape, or divine love.

Jesus of Nazareth advocated a gentle, other-centred approach to life, or a flowing with life that avoided imposing burdens on others, as well as hypocritical self-righteousness. He welcomed and loved children who were brought to him.[47]He was the first to notice that a large crowd had followed him for many days and was hungry. He asked his disciples to feed the people.[48] Jesus was never self-righteous and told his disciples that their righteousness, or the quality of their lives, should surpass that of the Pharisees and teachers of law.[49]

There was no self-interest in what Jesus did for others. In fact, in helping them, he often drew down upon himself the ire of the authorities, who charged him with disregarding the Law. They were unwilling to countenance his healing of people on the Sabbath, or his reaching out to non-Jews. In healing the sick on the Sabbath Jesus expounded the essence of the Law, arguing that the Sabbath was made for man, and not man for the Sabbath. [50]He embraced people of all cultures, talking to the Samaritan woman at the well and healing the daughter of a Cannanite woman and the son of a centurion. [51]

Jesus was kind, compassionate and gentle. He was unafraid of associating with those who were socially ostracized, as well as those considered physically or ritually unclean. He was humble and sought to nurture humility in his followers. He disregarded the social etiquette of his time, mixing with those others regarded as the "wrong types." His mission was to reconcile sinners to God, whether Jews and non-Jews.[52]While he stood his ground, he was not contentious. He was generous with his time and abilities. Though he suggested to his followers that they needed to be perceptive and astute, he nevertheless advocated a generosity of spirit in relationship towards one's enemies.The Sermon on the Mount sums up the qualities of goodness that Jesus of Nazareth advocated, a goodness that embodied Universal Love. [53]

老子认为，水利万物而不争，水为人而不自利，完全是无私的。它不怨不争，流向低处，滞留在别人看不起的地方。水随遇而安，慨然有度。水公正无私，不偏不倚。水尽管软弱、柔顺，但却能穿透世上最坚硬的东西。老子说，我们要学水的善良。

基督教中，耶稣身体力行对于信徒来说是重要的。通过他的言行，也就是道的化身，基督，这位上帝的儿子，鼓励人们靠近上帝。通过他的言行，人们才能认识上帝的恩惠和慈悲，最重要的是，还有上帝之爱，也叫圣爱。

耶稣倡导温良，多他人考虑，生活顺其自然，不给别人增加负担，也不要装出伪善的样子宣扬自己的正义。带到他那里的孩子他都欢迎，都喜欢。他头一个发觉，大伙儿跟了几天饿了，便吩咐门徒给他们东西吃。耶稣从来不自以为是，他告诉门徒做事要公道，人活着，不要虚伪，不要僵化。

耶稣为别人做事从不考虑自己。为了帮助他人，他常常把当局的怒气揽到自己身上，结果被控违法。他们不愿意见到他在安息日给人医病，不愿意见到他和非犹太人来往。安息日医治病人的时候，耶稣道出了法律的灵魂，认为安息日是为人设立的，而不是人为安息日而生的。他接受各种文化的人们，他和撒玛利亚女人在井边谈话，治疗迦南妇女的女儿和百人队长的儿子。

耶稣仁慈，体恤，温和。他敢于接触被社会排斥的人们，敢于接触被认为身体和仪态不洁的人们。他谦卑，也要门徒们谦卑。他无视当时的社会礼仪，而同"罪人们"混在一起。他的使命是帮罪人们，犹太也好，非犹太人也好，皈依上帝。他的立场就是不争，为此，他愿意出人出力。他认为，门徒要机敏、精明，以大度应对敌手。《登山宝训》是这样总结的：耶稣所体现的优良品质包含着博爱。

CHAPTER ELEVEN
The Heart is Buddha.

Jesus told the Samaritan woman at Jacob's well that "God is Spirit, and worshippers must worship God in spirit and in truth." Jesus Christ said this to encourage the woman to distinguish between the physical and spiritual realms. It is important that we appreciate that there are two realms, the physical and the less observable spiritual world.

What do Chinese know about Fo or buddha? The Chinese character for "buddha" consists of two parts, namely: "man" and "no". This can be interpreted as "a man with no self" or a "selfless person." Any selfless person, who walks in the Way, may attain "The Word of God." Whoever has attained "The Word" is honoured as a "saint" in the West and as a "buddha" by the Chinese.

Thus, the definition of Fo is one who has attained "The Word" of God. For example, Siddartha Gautama is an "Enlightened One" and is called Buddha or Fo in Chinese. Lao Zi is venerated by some Daoists as one of the "Enlightened Ones," or Fo and Confucius as a great teacher.

The Emperor Tang Gao Zu (Tang Gaozu or Li Yuan, the first emperor of theTang Dynasty) in 618 C.E., after summoning Daoist, Confucian and Buddhist leaders for a discussion, decreed that "the Dao can produce a buddha, buddha is the product of Dao, Dao is the master of the Buddha, and Buddha is the disciple of the Dao". [54]

It is important to differentiate buddha, from God, or the Lord-on-High. This is what the Tang Emperor concluded, as is obvious from his comment that "when a person who has been enlightened or when a man has attained Dao, he is a saint", or in Chinese an "immortal". And "a saint is venerated as a buddha". [55] God and Dao do not belong to this physical world. They are spiritual entities. That is why God, and his "Word," or Dao, cannot be described. [56]

第十一章

心即是佛

　　耶稣在雅各井边告诉撒玛利亚妇女："上帝就是神灵，必须用心灵和诚实来崇拜上帝"。耶稣这样说，是为了鼓励这个女人把肉体和精神区分开来。我们认为，这是两个领域，即肉体世界的和看不到的心灵世界。

　　佛字是什么？"佛"字有两个部分：人和弗。这可以解释为"一个人没有自我"或者是"一个没有私欲的人"。 人无私心，便可得道，得上帝之道。得道者西方为"圣人"，中国为"佛"。

　　"佛"可以说是得了上帝之道者。比例：释迦摩尼是位"领悟的人"，中文叫做"佛"。道家尊老子为"领悟的人"或是"佛"，而孔子被称为大师。

　　唐高祖李渊（*唐朝开国皇帝*）公元618年宣诏全国儒释道领袖召开法会，颁布"道能生佛，佛由道成，道是佛的师父，佛是道的弟子"。

　　佛、神和上帝怎么分辨，这是要紧的。唐高祖是这样总结的："人得道成圣"，"人成圣为佛"佛。上帝和道不属于这个物质世界，它们的本质是灵。因此，上帝及其训谕（也称道）是不可言喻的。

The Heart is Buddha.

Chinese culture embrace Confucian teaching and they honour the following qualities in a person: patriotism, propriety, benevolence, love, faithfulness and peace. They cultivate these ideal ideas in the young minds of their children in primary schools. Around the country, they built temples or pavilions to commemorate and venerate persons with qualities mentioned above.

For example: Yue Fei (1103-1141 C.E.) is venerated for his patriotism. In Hangzhou, tourists are brought to visit the temple and grave of Yue Fei, where the history of Yue Fei is told. In fact, figures of those, who betrayed him, were curved in stone, kneeling before his grave. Chinese today deep-fry two long strips of dough, representing his enemies and call it "Deep-fried Kwai", Kwai being the name of his enemy.

Qu Yuan was a patriotic officer in the state of Chu in the 3rd Century B.C.E. His patriotism and poetry have inspired the Chinese for generations. In fact, the Chinese commemorate his death on the 5th day of the 5th month of the Lunar Calender, when dragon boat racing take place and bamboo leaves wrapped dumplings are eaten. The story goes like this: Qu Yuan convinced the emperor of his sincerity and patriotism for the state by committing suicide in the river. Realising his mistake the emperor ordered people to save him from the river. Owing to long hours working in the boat, the wives of those boatmen wrapped up some rice in the bamboo leaves for their husbands' tiffin. It is a festival even today.

Legendary heroes or righteous persons, like Guan Yin, Ma Zu and Guan Gong, have been unofficially canonized as Fo. However, they were good human beings. They earn veneration, but do not deserved to be worshipped. We do not worship people who are canonized by other people as saints or fo. We venerate them for their great deeds, such as where we speak of Guan Yin's benevolent heart or Guan Gong's righteousness.

Ma Zu was a fisherman's daughter named Lin Mo, who lived in the Song Dynasty. She helped fishermen in distress. After her death, whenever a fisherman was in trouble, and saw the image of Lin Mo, he was saved. That is why people along the coastal regions of China worshipped her.

Guan Gong was a great warrior named Guan Yu, in the period of Three Kingdoms, which succeeded the Han Dynasty. People worshipped him for his bravery and faithfulness. In Kaifen City in Henan Province there is a huge temple and a gigantic burial ground in rememberance of him.

People became Fo or "buddhas" because of their benevolent hearts. It is the quality of the heart that qualifies people for sainthood.

中华文化接受儒家教育，重视以下品格的培养：忠信仁爱和善。小学生的头脑里灌输的就是这些理想观念。全国各地到处修建廊庙，祭祀具有上述品德的人。

岳飞（公元1103-1141年）就是一例，因为尽忠报国而得到敬仰。杭州的游客们到岳王庙和岳飞墓去听人讲述岳飞史。还要把害死他的人雕成石像，跪在坟前。今天，中国人油炸成两股，代表敌人，起名叫"油炸粿（与桧同音）"，秦桧就是这个敌人。

屈原是公元前三世纪楚忠臣。他的爱国诗篇激励着历代中国人。农历五月初五，中国人都要纪念他，赛龙舟，吃粽子。据传说，屈原为向怀王表白自己尽忠，投河殉国。怀王醒悟后知错，下令人们去捞他。打捞作业时间因为工作久了，船夫家眷用竹叶包上米饭，给丈夫送来当午餐。这个风俗流传至今。

传说的英雄义士，如观音、妈祖和关公等都被民间尊称为佛。他们都是好人，值得尊敬，但还不至于崇拜。成圣成佛的人我们不必崇拜。我们尊敬他们的伟业，比如说观音的慈悲或关公的义气。

妈祖是明朝一个渔夫的女儿，名叫林漠。她帮助渔民出苦难。她死后，渔民遇难的时候，就会看到林漠，就会得救。所以，中国沿海地区的人都崇拜她。

汉末三国时期的关公（也称关羽或关云长）是一位英雄。人民敬仰他的勇气和信义。河南省开封市有个巨大的关帝庙，还有一个大型的关林墓园，都是为了纪念他。人因为心慈而成佛，因为心善而成圣。

The Heart is Buddha.

When Confucians say that the heart is buddha, they are referring to those who have kind hearts. No wonder Confucius emphasized the "benevolent heart," as the heart is the source of integrity. It is little surprise that Jesus of Nazareth commented: "Blessed are the pure in heart for they shall see God." The heart is the citadel of one's attitudes and motives. It is important that the heart should be pure, so as to produce the right attitude, which is then expressed in behaviour. If the heart is pure, and the attitude is right, the behaviour will be righteous. As a consequence, one will be just and blameless in the sight of God. Such Christ-like persons are justifiably called "saints," or "enlightened ones" or "buddhas," or "fo." This explains why the benevolent heart is as good as a buddha, fo, to the Confucian Chinese. However, buddha, fo, is not God, but someone who has attained "The Word" of God, or Dao. Such a person is still human and will decay after death.

Interestingly enough, the Chinese word for buddha, Fo is also representative of the selfless person. Father Matthew Ricci, after prolonged study of Chinese customs and culture, went as far as to refer to Confucius as "St. Confucius." The Apostle Paul said that if anyone was in Christ (or Dao), and Christ was in him, he was a new creation. Those considered that Christ-like new creations are the enlightened ones, or saints, or buddhas, or fo. Chinese Buddhism, besides featuring statues of Gautama Buddha with Chinese facial features, also celebrated other legendary heroes and heroines, persons who had done great and good deeds. It also included mythological figures.

The heart in Confucian teaching is "the kind or benevolent heart". It is the seat of our attitudes, which generates our actions and behaviour. A kind heart produces kind thoughts, which are expressed in kind behaviour.

The heart in the Judaeo-Christian tradition played a major role in human history from the creation onward. It was a disobedient and unfaithful heart that led to the downfall of Adam and Eve in the creation story in Genesis 2 and 3, and has forever blighted humankind. The Hebrew Scriptures repeatedly mention how the Lord was frustrated by the unfaithful hearts of his chosen people. In Jeremiah 4:4 the Lord said: "Circumcise yourself to the Lord, circumcise your hearts, you men of Judah and people of Jerusalem ⋯" and in 31:33b "I will put my law in their minds and write it on their hearts, I will be their God ⋯"

Proverbs: A heart at peace gives life to the body (14:30).

A happy heart makes the face cheerful (15:13).

Heart of righteous weigh its answer (15:28).

A cheerful heart is good medicine (17:22).

Be wise and keep your heart on the right path (23:19)

A man's heart reflects the man (27:19).

儒家认为，心即是佛，他们指的是仁爱之心。难怪孔子强调"仁心"，因为心是正直之本。也不怪耶稣如是有言："清心的人有福了，因为他们将要见到上帝"。心是态度和动机的堡垒。心必须清静，这样，才能端正态度，表现行动。如果心清了，态度端正了，行为必定是正直的。在上帝面前，人应该走得端，行得正。基督一类的人可称得上是圣人、悟者或是佛。这说明，在儒家看来，仁心即是佛心。然而，佛并不是上帝，有的人却成了圣，得了道。此类人实际上还是人，死后就会烂掉。

有意思的是，汉语中的"佛"代表不自私的人。神父雷马太经过长期研究中国风俗文化，把孔子叫做"孔圣人"。使徒保罗说，谁能走进基督，基督也就走进谁，谁就会换了一个人。有人认为，新生的基督徒是悟者、圣者、是佛。汉传佛教在释迦摩尼佛像上贴上中国人的面孔，同时也祝福传说中的其它英雄豪杰。其中也包括捏造的人物。

儒家所说的心是个仁心。世人都认为，态度决定行为举止，仁心产生善良思辨，通过善行得以表现。

在犹太和基督教的传统中，心自古以来起着主导作用。在《创世纪》第二、三章里的创世故事中，不忠之心和叛逆之心导致了亚当和夏娃的堕落。希伯来《圣经》重申上帝对选民的悖逆之心是多么的失望。《杰里迈亚书》第四章第四节记载："犹太和耶路撒冷的居民啊，你们当自行割礼，归耶和华，将心里的污垢除掉..。"第三十一章第35节记载，"我要将我的法律灌进他们的脑海，写在他们的心上，我要作他们的上帝..。"

《箴言》：
平和之心给肉体以生命（14：30）
欢乐之心面带笑容（15：13）
正直之心必为通达（16：21）
愉悦之心乃是良药（17：22）
智慧之心正道直行（23：19）
人心就是人（27：19）

The Heart is Buddha.

In the New Testament:

Treasure is where your heart will be (Mt. 6:21).

Out of the mouth comes from the heart (Mt. 15:18).

For out of the heart come evil thoughts ⋯ (Mt.15:19).

For those with a nobble and good heart ⋯ (Lk. 8:15)

Doing the will of God from your heart ⋯ (Eph. 6:6).

The good of this command is love, which comes from a pure heart (1 Tim.1:5).

Only when our hearts submit to "The Word" of God, and become Christ-like, and full of love, and when Christ lives in our hearts, we will become selfless saints. In such circumstances we can truly say that "the heart is buddha."

Jesus Christ said that the Kingdom of Heaven is within you. In other words, your heart is the powerhouse of your own happiness.

《新约》如是有言：
你的财宝在哪里，你的心也在哪里（6：21）
脱口而出的，是心里发出来的（15：18）
从心里发出来的，有恶念（15：19）
诚实善良之心的人们……（8：15）
从心里遵行上帝的旨意（6：6）
命令的优点就是爱，爱来自纯净的心灵（1：5）
　　唯有当我们的心完全信服上帝的道，像基督一样充满爱心，把基督装在我们心中，我们就可成为一个无私的圣人。在这种情形下，我们才可以说句真心话："心即是佛"。耶稣说，天国就在你的心中。换句话说，你的心是你自己幸福的动力之源。

第十二章

人之道

　　人类智慧增加了,作出决定的正确与否来自经验和判断。有的决定是主观的。根据人自身的观点或为了自身的利益作出的判断被称为"人之道"。只有为他人利益的才符合"天之道"。然而,我们所做的并不都符合"神之道",因为我们所做的往往带着很强主观色彩。

　　墨子的爱和管教邻居孩子的人之道:

　　春秋、战国时期,鲁阳文君将攻郑,子墨子闻而止之,谓阳文君曰:"今使鲁四境之内,大都攻其小都,大家伐其小家,杀其人民,取其牛马狗豕布帛米粟货财,则何若?"

　　鲁阳文君曰:"鲁四境之内,皆寡人之臣也。今大都攻其小都,大家伐其小家,则寡人必将厚罚之。"

　　墨子曰:"夫天之兼有天下也,亦犹君之有四境之内也。今举兵将以攻郑,天诛亓不至乎?"鲁阳文君曰:"先生何止我攻郑也?我攻郑,顺于天之志。郑人三世杀其父,天加诛焉,使三年不全。我将助天诛也。"

　　墨子曰:"郑人三世杀其父而天加诛焉,使三年不全。天诛足矣,今又举兵将以攻郑,曰'吾攻郑也,顺于天之志'。譬有人于此,其子强梁不材,故其父笞之,其邻家之父举木而击之,曰:'吾击之也,顺于其父之志',则岂不悖哉?"

And he then went on, "Attacking your neighbouring kingdom, killing their people, robing their animals, grains and properties, and then writing up the history of your exploits or engraving it on plagues, telling future generations that none will surpass your victories. Is this a proper thing to do?"

Lu Yang Wenjun said, "According to what you have just said, whatever the world permits to do may not necessarily be the right measure."

Mo Zi commented, "Most world rulers understand petty things and neglect major issues. Now, someone steals a pig or a dog, and people consider him unloving. But when a powerful country overruns another country to annexe a region, everyone regards it as righteous. Again, a tiny man looks at a white object and says that it is white. But a huge man comes and looks at the white object and says it is black. This is why the rulers of the world understand petty things but don't understand big issues, just as they cannot differentiate white from black." (57)

Lu Yang Wenjun was presumptuous, thinking he could teach the Zheng Kingdom a lesson by flexing his military muscle. He saw his action as just and righteous, and considered he was doing the Zheng Kingdom a great favour. Unfortunately, this was merely his approach to the problem, and his way of solving the problem. This was not acceptable to a sage like Mo Zi. No one should take the law into his own hand and beat others with a big stick.

Mo Zi succeeded in persuading Lu Yang Wenjun not to wage war against a rogue state, as he was a great advocate of love and peace. Hence, he avoided unnecessary slaughter, plunder and destruction of property. He argued that "you must love others more, doubling your love for them" and "you must benefit others more by communicating and negotiating with them". Waging war may not be the best method of teaching "love and peace." Because of his philosophy of "love and benefit the world", (58)Mo Zi was honoured as the "Father of the God of Love". Agape is the Way of God.

The fable detailing the contest between the Sun-god and the Wind-god, mentioned in chapter 10, illustrates how tenderness and warmth overcome harshness and cold. It is not the cold and hard measure that wins the heart of the people. In fact, every action has a direct and opposite reaction. When our response is tit for tat, both parties suffer loss. An "eye for an eye" produces two blind men. It is not a win-win situation. Even the strongest power in the world may not come out unscratched. On the other hand, Lao Zi says that "If people do not fear death, what is the purpose of threatening to kill them?". Unfortunately, the Way of Men is preferred to the Way of Heaven by men.

墨子谓鲁阳文君曰:"今攻其邻家,杀其人民,取其狗豕食粮衣裘,亦书之竹帛,以为铭於席豆,以遗后世子孙曰:'莫若我多。'亓可乎?"

鲁阳文君曰:"然吾以子之言观之,则天下之所谓可者,未必然也。"

墨子曰:"世俗之君子,皆知小物而不知大物。今有人于此,窃一犬一彘则谓之不仁,窃一国一都则以为义。譬犹小视白谓之白,大视白则谓之黑。是故世俗之君子,知小物而不知大物者,此若言之谓也。"

鲁阳文君专横跋扈,想以武力来教训郑国,认为自己正义之举,也以为是替郑国干了件好事。不幸的恰恰在于他解决问题的方法。这是圣人墨子所接受不了的,打着法律的旗号大打出手是不应该的。

墨子劝告鲁阳文君,对野蛮之邦,应该非攻,因为他是非常爱好和平的。这样,他便制止了一场不必要的屠杀、抢劫和毁灭。他主张"兼相爱"和"交相利",认为讨伐并非仁和的上上之举。墨子被尊崇为"爱神之父"——友爱者,神之道。

第十章里,举了个太阳神和风神之争的寓言,证明温柔和热情可以克服坚强和冷酷,也就是以柔克刚。冷酷和强硬的手段是不得人心的。客观上,每个举动都会产生直接的或相反的反应。如果我们的反应是针锋相对,那么就会两败俱损。"以眼还眼",结果是四眼皆瞎。这么做是不会双赢的。世界上最强权的也不可能一点伤也不带。老子说:"民不畏死,奈何以杀戮之也。"不幸的是,人之道胜于天之道。

Should the superpowers punish or intimidate the small states?

Zhu Geliang's crafty Way of Men, accompanied by love and compassion won the day.

During the period of the Three Kingdoms, at the beginning of the Third Century, Zhu Geliang, the prime minister and war strategist of the Shu Kingdom, wanted to fortify boundaries and make peace with the minority tribes on the fringes. He came to the north-west and met Qiang Wei, a great warrior of the Qiang tribe, who held the strategic pass between the Tibetan Highlands and the plain of Sichuan. Zhu Geliang's generals could not fight with Qiang Wei, as they lost to him one by one. Qiang Wei refused to negotiate with Zhu Geliang, and yet held his fort. Zhu Geliang was out of his wits. Finally, he thought of a plan. He sent out spies to spread the rumour that another fort of Qiang was falling, and meanwhile he had his army climb over and around the mountains to the other side of Qiang's fort. When Qiang Wei led his army out to rescue the fort under seize, Zhu Geliang took over his fort from behind. A few days later, after a trip, Qiang returned to his fort. On arrival, he found the gate was wide open and noticed a welcoming party. To his amazement, he saw at the forefront a grand carriage with his mother sitting beside Zhu Geliang. He was puzzled. Then he heard his mother calling out to him, saying that Zhu Geliang was a wise and kind gentleman, and a respectful leader. She said that the Shu army had never hurt the Qiang people, but gave them plenty of food and clothing, and helped them in many other things as well. She convinced Qiang Wei that Zhu Geliang was a good and loving leader, who could be trusted and was trustworthy. Qiang Wei agreed, and joined the Shu forces. Qiang Wei won many battles, and was one of the best generals in the period of Three Kingdom. (59)

This story demonstrates how Zhu Geliang could use love and kindness (and, of course, his astuteness) to win over the hearts of the Qiang people, and its leader, without shooting an arrow. Zhu Geliang could have destroyed the fort and killed all the people, but he would eventually lose, by forfeiting their hearts and support. Love overcomes fear.

Should humanitarian aids be used to unite the world in peace and harmony?

The Way of Man as in the Tibetan feudal system:

Background:

On the quieter side in the "Lost Horizon", hidden away in the highlands foreigners called "Shangri-La", "Utopia", a feudal serf system had been established for hundreds of years.

人之道

超级大国该惩罚或威胁小国吗?

诸葛亮的诈人之道、悯爱之心赢了。

公元三世纪初的三国时代,蜀国丞相兼军师诸葛亮,为巩固边防,与边境少数民族和好。他来到西北地区,遇到羌族猛将姜维,把守西藏高原和四川平原的要塞。诸葛亮的大将们一个一个都败在姜维手下。姜维拒绝与诸葛亮讲和,坚守要塞。诸葛亮束手无计。最后,他想到一个对策。他派奸细散布谣言,姜维的另一个要塞要被攻下来了,此时,诸葛亮排军兵翻山绕到姜维要塞的侧部。当姜维带兵出城解救被围要塞时,诸葛亮乘机从后面占领了要塞。几天后,姜维空跑一场返回要塞。抵达要塞的时候,发现城门大开,见到迎接队伍。令他吃惊的是,他看到母亲和诸葛亮坐在前面的大车上。他一时摸不到头脑。此时,他听见母亲说,诸葛亮如何如何贤明慈善,尊重别人。她说,蜀军不但没有伤害羌民,反而给他们许多衣食,也帮了他们不少忙。她说,诸葛亮这个领导温和、慈善,是可靠的,是可信的。姜维同意归顺蜀军。姜维打了不少胜仗,是三国时代的一位猛将。

这则故事说的是诸葛亮用仁爱之心加上机敏,没费弓弩之力,就赢得了羌族人及其头人的心。诸葛亮本来可以摧毁要塞,赶尽杀绝,但是,那样做就会丧失人心,失去支持,什么也得不到。

人道主义援助能够促进世界和平、和谐吗?

西藏封建制度下的人之道:

背景:

在高原深处静悄悄的"失去的地平线"那边,也就是洋人叫做"香格里拉"或"乌托邦"的地方,有个建立了几百年的封建农奴制度。

When the Mongols conquered Northern China in 1227, occupying Western Xia Region and the Tibetan tribes in Hehuang and Taomin, before the establishment of Yuan Dynasty (1271–1368 C.E.), they confiscated much land. In 1239, the Mongol Prince Godan sent troops to Lhasa, and, in 1244, summoned the Sagya Sect's supreme leader, Gonggar Gyaincain and his nephews, Pagba and Qana Doje to Langzhou for negotiations. The issue was the terms of Tibet's submission to the Mongols, who later appointed Tibetan temporal and secular leaders as government officials. The Mongols distributed land to members of the Mongol aristocracy and to Buddhist establishments. The statistics taken in 1959 showed that out of 3.3 million ke, (which is equal to 220, 000 hectres,) of cultivated land: the government had 1.2837 milliom ke, or 38.9%; aristocates, 79790, 000 ke, 24%; monasteries and upper class lamas, 1.2144 million ke, 36.8% and owner-peasants, 9, 900 ke, or 0.3%. This means 5% of the total population of Tibet, composing of goernment officials, aristocrates and lamas, owned 99.7% of cultivated land, which made 95% of the population serfs and slaves. The heavy taxation introduced by the Mongols brought about improvishment of the poor peasants, as well as the artisans.

Government officials, aristocrates and lamas were the feudal lords of Tibet from the beginning of 13th century. Tibetan Lamaism was the most contaminated form of Buddhism, containing elements of shamanism and sorcery. The pontiff of this Yellow Sect, the Dalai Lama, instituted an authoritarian theocracy. The dictatorship of the aristocrats and the lamas integrated politics and religion. [60]The feudal serf system and slave society before 1959 was more cruel and inhuman than the serfdom prevailing in Europe in the Middle Ages and in Russia before the 1917 October Revolution.

The Serf system:

Serfs were of two classes, chapa and tuichiung, and the slaves were the langsheng. Chapa serfs were the property of their feudal lords. They were granted a piece of land to till and in return they had to perform compulsory labour, including tilling the land for the landowners. They did not enjoy personal freedom, and were at the owners' disposal. They had to pay taxes and various rents out of the produce from the granted land. 60% to 70% of all serfs were chapa serfs.

Tuichiung serfs were of low caste, and were poorer than chapa serfs. They could rent a small amount of land to till on condition that they provide free labour to till the land for feudal lords. Normally the produce from the small amount of land was hardly sufficient to support life. The tuichiung craftsmen sold their skills, and the labourers their labour. They formed 30 to 40% of the serfs.

The serfs, who were raised at home were langsheng, and were actually slaves. They had no means of livelihood, no personal rights, and no freedom and were under the strict control of their owners. Even their children did not belong to them. They were barely able to support themselves. Their feudal lords could give them away as gifts, transfer, mortgage, or sell them. Langsheng could be handed down from generation to generation.

公元1227年，元朝建立之前，蒙古人征服中国北方，占领西夏地区和西藏河防和道明的西藏部落，没收了许多土地。公元1239年，蒙古王子哥丹派兵进驻拉萨，1244年，命召塞雅派最高首领贡卡该因堪和他的侄子伯巴和差那多杰赴兰州谈判。谈判的主题是西藏归服蒙古，委任西藏宗教和世俗首领执政。蒙古人把土地分给蒙古贵族和佛教机构。据1959年统计，共有330顷耕地：政府占128.37万顷（38.9%），贵族占79万顷（24%），佛寺和高僧占121.44万顷（36.8%），农民为9900顷（0.3%）。这意味着，西藏总人口的5%，包括政府官员、贵族和高僧，拥有99.7%的耕地，其它0.3%的耕地才属于占人口95%的农奴。蒙古繁重的赋税使贫穷的农工苦上加苦。

13世纪初期开始，政府官员、贵族和高僧都是西藏的封建主。西藏喇嘛教是最不纯的佛教，掺杂着萨满术和巫术。黄教的主教达赖喇嘛设立了独裁的神权政治。独裁的贵族和喇嘛政教合一。1959年以前，封建农奴制度和奴隶社会惨无人道，其程度甚于欧洲中世纪和俄罗斯1917年十月革命前的俄罗斯。

农奴制：

农奴有两种，"查巴"和"堆张"；奴隶叫做"浪圣"。农奴"查巴"是封建主人的私有财产。他们有一块土地耕种，但必须强制劳工，给地主种地。他们没有个人自由，命运听凭主人摆布。他们得从赏赐的地产中缴纳苛捐杂税。"查巴"占农奴的60%到70%。

最底层的是"堆张"，比"查巴"还穷。他们租一小块农田，但是，租赁的条件是无偿给封建主种地。正常情况下，一小块土地生产的作物是难维持生计的。"堆张"中的工匠卖手艺，工人卖劳工。他们占农奴的30%到40%。

家养的农奴叫"浪圣"，实际上是奴隶。他们没有别的谋生手段，没有人权，没有自由，受主人严厉的管制。连他们的子女也不属于他们。他们勉强地活着。封建主可以把他们当做礼物送人、转让、抵押或出卖。"浪圣"一代又一代就是这么传下来的。

The heavy taxation system exploited the serfs, which plunged them deeper into debts. Serfs could commit Children-Grandchildren Debts or Hereditary Debts and Jointly Garanteed Debts. They were perpetually in debt. The debts of a serf stayed with him when he was sold or given away. When a serf died, his family members, or children, were responsible for his debts. When all the members in a family died, the new serf, who took over the granted land, inherited the debts of the previous serf. After 1959, when the 14th Dalai Lama, together with a number of lamas and aristocrates fled the country, the serf and slave system was abolished. This brought an end to the evil feudal system.

Dalai Lamas of all periods set up departments to lend money and grain at exorbitant rates of 30% and 20% respectively. The monasteries accounted for the greatest amount of usury, which made them immensely wealthy. No wonder the male children aspired to be monks, and consequently, the population of Tibetans dwindled. The human misery in Tibet before 1959 was intolerable, and yet no one raised a voice to highlight the injustice. Yet today, the Dalai Lama is considered a champion of freedom and independence!

Gautama Buddha argued that people should avoid the extremes of "Self-indulgence" and "Self-denial," and discover the "Middle Path". The route to this "Middle Path is through the "Noble Eight-Fold Path," which consists of (1) Right View, (2) Right Thought, (3) Right Speech, (4) Right Action, (5) Right Mode of Living, (6) Right Endeavour, (7) Right Mindfulness, and (8) Right Concentration. Following this Eight-Fold Path, it was argued, would lead to liberation from desire and craving, and the attainment of the state of No-Self.

Dalai Lamas are supposed to be "Living Buddhas." However, they departed from the teaching of the Buddha. They were the pontiffs of their religion and politics and perpetuated the evil feudal serf system, exploiting helpless serfs, condeming them to a form of slavery.

In 2004 November, the author went to visit "Shangrila" on the Tibetan Plateau in Yunnan, with a group of friends. After enjoying the beauty of the ancient town, Lijiang, we traveled northwestwards, climbing up higher and deeper into the Tibetan Plateau. We came to a village. We were taken to visit the oldest Tibetan house of the village, where an old serf in his late 70s stayed. The old man described the miserable life he led under the serf system. Besides hunger, he had never lifted his head, walking on the street until after the liberation. It was not just the poverty but also the loss of human dignity.

In September 2007, I visited Tibet with a friend. We landed in Lhasa. As the air was thin, we took it easy on the first day. However, on our way from the airport, we stopped at a Tibetan house by the roadside. It was a casual visit.

繁重的税务制度剥削农奴，使他们债上背债。托付债，遗留债，联保债，农奴的债子子孙孙永世负债。农奴被卖了或被送出去以后，债得跟着走。一个农奴死了，他的债得由家人或子女担着。农奴和全家都死了，承接这块土地的新来的农奴得把前任农奴的债背起来。1959年，达赖14世及其喇嘛、贵族们逃遁，农奴制被废除，结束了万恶的封建制度。

几代达赖喇嘛设立机构，放钱放粮，高息分别达到30%和20%。寺院的高利贷最大，因此也极其富有。男孩渴望着出家也就不足为怪了，这也说明了西藏人口减少的原因。1959年以前，西藏人民的苦难是无法忍受的，然而，没有谁站出来讲一句公道话。今天，达赖喇嘛却被当作是自由和独立的卫士！

高达玛佛陀认为，人不要过分"放纵自己"和"否认自己"，要"中庸"。同乡"中庸"的途中要经过"八条正路"：1、正观点之路，2、正思想之路，3、正言论之路，4、正行动之路，5、正生活之路，6、正奋斗之路，7、正认真之路，8、正专心之路。据说，沿着这八路走下去，能消除人欲，达到"无我"的境界。

达赖喇嘛说是"活佛"，但是，他们离佛教太远了。他们是自己教派的教皇和政治上的君主，他们永远存留着邪恶的封建农奴制，剥削无助的农奴，把他们变成奴隶。

2004年11月，作者和几个朋友去了滇藏高原的"香格里拉"。赏完美丽的丽江以后，我们向西北一路游过去，翻过高山，迈进深谷，进入西藏高原。我们到了一个村子，村民带着我们到了藏式最旧的屋子里，见到了一位七、八十岁的老奴。老人说，解放前，他一辈子在农奴制下过着悲惨的生活，且不说挨饿，就是走在路上，也抬不起头来。这不单单是贫穷，连做人的一点尊严都没了。

2007年9月，我和一位朋友到了西藏。我们在拉萨着陆，因为空气稀薄，头一天自由活动。离开机场的途中，我们在路旁的一个藏族农户停了下来，偶然进去瞧瞧。

The Way of Man

The planning of the house is similar to that of other ethnic groups in Yunnan. The house is of two storeys and has a courtyard surrounded by rooms. The entrance, which is located at the middle of the property wall, leads to a courtyard and the main lounge is at the end of it on the left. On the left flank of the lounge are the dining, kitchen and a grain store. To my curiosity, I opened the door of the store and found bags of grains, such as barley and wheat, piled up to the ceiling. The rooms on the right frank of the lounge are smaller sitting rooms and guest rooms. On the first floor, right on top of the lounge is the family sitting room. The bedrooms are all equipped with beds, both Tibetan and modern ones. I get the impression that the family has a comfortable life style. The old lady showed us around saying that the young folks were at work in the fields. They all own their own farms, as the serf system is now abolished in Tibet.

Word Play in the Way of Men:

A good example of the cunning Way of Men was the prompting by the last British governor of Hongkong, in 1994, to put more democratic institutions in place before Communist China resumed ownership in 1997. At first glance, you will think that it would be a noble idea to further democracy in Hongkong. However, it can be argued that Hongkong had no democratic institutions during the last 160 years, a fact symbolized by a placard at the entrance of the Country Club at Mid-Level, Hongkong, stating that "Chinese and dogs are not allowed!"

Another illustration of the way we play with words is revealed in the contrast between the two sentences, which refer to the return of territories to China. The first read: "After the Chinese took over Hongkong in 1997 ⋯" while the second began "The former Portugese colony (Macau), which reverted to Chinese sovereignty in1999 ⋯" Both Hongkong and Macau were leased, the first to Britain and the second to Portugal after the Opium War of 1842. Why should it be stated that Hongkong after the expiration of the lease, "was taken over" by the Chinese, while Macau "reverted" to the Chinese?" Says a lot! It is The Way of Men again.

When the Uygurs throw bombs in Xinjiang, the West called them "freedom fighters". However, when 300 Uygurs were rounded up in Afganistan and were taken away and locked up in detention camps in Guantanmara Bay in Cuba, and when China Government asked for their return as they are Chinese nationals, [64]the U.S. said they were terrorists, and not "freedom fighters".

War criminals are normally the losers from war, such as the German Nazis of World War II, and recently, Slobadan Milosevic of Yugoslavia, who was accused of killing defenceless civilians. What about the Japanese general who was in charge of the Nanjing masacres and the general of Unit 731, who conducted biological research and germ warfare on Chinese civilians?[65]

房屋的设计类似云南少数民族的风格。房子是个两层阁楼，两侧厢房中间是个院子。大门在院墙中间，直通院子。大堂在左侧最里面，大堂左侧有餐厅、厨房和粮食仓子。我好奇地推开仓房门，发现一袋袋大麦、小麦等堆到棚顶。大堂右侧有个小客厅和客房。一楼大堂的上边是起居室，卧房里都是床，有藏式的，也有现代的。这个家庭给我的印象是他们是个小康家庭。老太太带我们看她的家，又说，年轻的都下地去了。他们有自己的农田，因为西藏农奴制度早已废除了。

人之道之道

英国最后一任港督于1994年耍了个人道的花招，就是个例子，在中国1997年收回香港以前，运作了许多民主机构。最初，你会以为，香港会更加民主了。然而，有人认为，过去160年，香港没有民主机构，半坡村俱乐部门前闯个牌子，上面写道："中国人和狗不准入内"，这恰恰说明了他们的伪善。

还有个人之道的例子，说的是领土回归的两种表达方式。第一个句子是"1997年，中国接管香港以后……"，第二个句子是"前葡萄牙殖民地（澳门）1999年回归中国主权后……。"香港和澳门都是1842年鸦片战争后租给英国和葡萄牙的。为什么香港到租期已满，是被中国接管（或拿过去），而澳门是回归中国呢？其中的说法太多了！这又是"人之道"。

当新疆乌格族人投炸弹的时候，西方称他们是"自由战士"。但是，当300多乌格人在阿富汗被抓，被送到古巴关坛马拉湾扣留营的时候，因为他们是中国公民，中国政府遣返他们，而美国说他们是恐怖主义者，不是自由战士。

战败者通常成为战犯，如第二次世界大战后的纳粹和最近南斯拉夫的史罗巴旦米罗社维被控告杀害没有防卫能力的平民。指挥南京大屠杀的日本军官是不是战犯呢？用中国人来做细菌战生化试验的七三一部队是不是战犯呢？

The Japanese generals were protected from prosecution because Japan not only surrendered all the biological and chemical research to the US, but also could play a significant role in the U.S. containment of Communist Rusisa, China and North Korea.

When civilians are accidentally killed by U.S. indiscrimate bombings, this is described as collateral damage.

In Time magazine of May, 7, 2001, Johanna McGeary and Karen Tumulty reported in "The Fog of War" that the decorated U.S. Navy Lieuternant, Robert Kerrey confessed that one night 32 years ago in Vietnam he murdered a score of unarmed civilians, mainly women and children. Those who took part in the raid said the killing was a deliberate execution. Robert Kerrey was decorated with the Bronze Star. He took part in politics and became a senator. The massacre was excuseable because it took place in the fog of war.

Former President of Chile, Allende, was murdered on the street in Santiago. The documentary film, The Kissinger Case, reported that approval for the killing was given by the US Defence Department, which insisted that there was a gunfight. However, the son of Allende witnessed the incident, saying that there was no exchange of gunfire. (66)

Wealth, Power and Authority as the Way of Men:

James 4:1 reads "What causes fights and quarrels among you? Don't they come from the desires that battle within you?" People lust after wealth, power and glory. This comment describes the Way of Men.

Confucius could not understand the Dao. He went to meet Lao Zi, and asked how he could obtain it. This is what Lao Zi told Confucius about those who lacked contact with the Dao, and who followed the Way of Men. (67):

"Those who think only of their own prosperity will not share their wealth with others;

Those who think much of their own honour will not appreciate others' good reputation;

Those who are corrupted by power and authority will not delegate power to others.

They are fearful of holding them (wealth, power and glory), yet are disconsolate when they discard them.

Not knowing sufficiently their benefits and disadvantages, they pursue earnestly wealth, power and honour like those under punishment.

这些日本将领没有受到审判，因为日本不但把所有生化研究成果交给了美国，而且在美国遏制中、苏和北韩共产党过程中扮演了重要角色。

美国在越南狂轰滥炸，百姓遭到涂炭，这种创伤被称为是随带着的，是无意的，是无罪的。

2001年5月7日，美国《时报》报导了约翰那麦格里和卡兰杜姆儿在《战争烟雾》一书里的内容：美国海军上尉罗伯特克里承认32年前一个晚上，在越南杀害十几个没有武器的平民，主要是妇女儿童。同袭者说，此次屠杀是有意的。克里获得了铜星勋章。他参加了选举，当了参议。那次屠杀是可以宽恕的，因为那是战争。

前智利总统阿伦得在首都圣地亚哥街上被暗杀。纪录片《基辛格事件》说，美国国防部致使这次暗杀行动，但强调说，是在枪战中死亡的。不过，阿伦得的儿子目击了该事件，说当时并没有交火。

人之道的富裕、权利和权柄

《雅各布书》第四章一节说："你们中间争争吵吵，是为了哪般呢？难道不是你们内心的争夺欲造成的吗？"人们贪图的是名利。这说的就是人之道。

孔子不识道，去老子那里问道。老子给孔子讲了失道和从《天运》的故事：

以富为是者，不能让禄；

以显为是者，不能让名；

亲权者，不能与人柄。

操之则栗，舍之则悲。

而一无所鉴，以窥其所不休者，是天之戮民也。

The Way of Man

Resentment, grace, receiving, giving, reprimanding, instructing, letting live and killing are the eight methods of correction in the world. Only those who abide in the Way of Heaven, and are not obstinate, will apply them with ease.

This is the reason why it is said that: 'Those who are upright themselves shall be able to correct others..

The Way of Heaven shall not be revealed to those who are not right in their hearts. (68)

Lao Zi argued that "Overcoming others is strength, but it is might that overcomes one's self". This is true if one encounters and surrenders to the Way or Dao of God.

Confucius argued that "Gentlemen, who are amicable and uninfluenced by the characters of rascals, are powerful". This is the Way of Moderation.

Sun Zi, a war strategist, and contemporary of Confucius, argued that "It is not the best of skills for a general to win 100 victories in 100 battles, but it is the acme of skill for a general to subdue enemies without a fight". (69)

It is not might that always wins wars. The Way of Men is to monopolize the possession of weapons of mass destruction, and to dominate other nations, militarily and economically. Lao Zi argued, in De Jing that "A large state must act with humility and lowliness … If it lowers itself to the level of the small state, it can win over the support of the small state…",

人之道

怨，恩，取，与，谏，教，生，杀，八者，正之器也。惟循大变无所演者为能用也。

故口，止者，正也。其心以为不然者，天门弗开矣。

老子说："胜人者，有力也；自胜者，强也。"人如果近道、服道，这句话也就应验了。

孔子说："君子和而不流，强哉矫"。这就是中庸之道。

孔子同时代的兵法家孙子说："是敌百战百胜，非善之善者也，不战而屈人之兵，善之善者也。" 赢得战争的胜利凭借的不总是武力。人之道是拥有大规模杀伤性武器，在军事上和经济上制约别国。老子在《道德经》里说："大邦者，小流也。大邦以下小邦，则取小邦。"

According to the Way of Men, it is natural for people to be tempted with wealth, power and authority. The message in the Gospel according to Luke suggested that before Jesus began his ministry he had to forsake wealth, power and authority. [70]

It is up to the leaders of superpowers to conduct themselves in the Way of God. Sad to say, most often it is the American people, and not their leaders, who suggest that foreign policies should be conducted morally. [71]Will the superpowers stop selling antiquated weapons to third world countries to kill one another? Will the developed and wealthy nations use globalization and free trade to erase poverty, hunger and diseases from poor nations?

Might is Right as the Way of Man in the 20th. Century:

The Mighty says, "Whatever I do is right, and whatever you do what I did is wrong".

"The Axis of Evil".

The terrorists of the world.

Mo Zi in Jian Ai argues that "The people of the world must love one another. Then the world can be governed in peace. When relationships between people is bad, there will be chaos in the world".[72]He maintains that if there is love in the world, countries will not attack one another, and families will not fight with one another, and there will be no thieves …

Jesus argued, in the Sermon on the Mount, that people should replace the maxim "An Eye for an eye and a tooth for a tooth," with "Love your enemy and pray for those who persecute you." "If someone hits you on the right cheek, turn your left cheek also." "If someone wants you to walk a mile, walk with him three miles." Is it not a reciprocal blow for blow, which perpetuates hatred? The Way of Heaven is the reverse to the Way of Man. It is warmth and love that conquer cold and hatred. It is universal love without discrimination of nationality, race or colour, religion or creed. This universal love recognizes a person as being made in the image of God, and penetrates the physical features of the person to the inner beautiful soul given by God. It is God that love sees in a man.

人之道

依照人之道，人们自然会受名利的诱惑。《路加福音书》上说，耶稣开始传道之前，他得放弃名利。

遵从神之道，要靠强国的领导人。可惜，提出外交政策要讲道德的，常常是美国人民，而不是美国领导人。强国应不应该不再把老式武器卖给第三世界国家来自相残杀？富裕发达应不应该利用全球化自由贸易来消除贫困、饥饿和疾病？

二十世纪的人之道：强权就是公理：

强权者说，我做的是对的，你做我做过的是不对的。强权者可以任意指定谁是：

"邪恶的轴"和"世界的恐怖主义者"。

墨子在《兼爱》篇说："故天下兼相爱则治，交相恶则乱。" 他说，如果世界有爱，国家间不会彼此交战，家庭间不会吵架，也就会不有贼……。

耶稣在《登山宝训》中说，人们要"爱你的敌人，并为迫害你的人祈祷吧"，而不要"以眼还眼，以牙还牙"；"如果有人打你的右脸，那么把左脸也转过去让他打吧"；"如果有人逼你走一里路，你就同他走三里。"如果以拳还拳的话，不是加重了仇恨了吗？天之道是人之道的反面。温暖和热爱可以征服冷酷和仇恨。不要歧视国别、种族、肤色、宗教或信仰，这才是博爱。博爱认可的人是上帝的形象，穿过人的体貌特征，渗透到上帝所赋予的最美妙的灵魂深处。爱一个人，人见到的是上帝。

Jesus went on to comment:

Be careful not to do your 'acts of righteousness', like giving alms, to evoke acclaim. Do not let your left hand know what your right hand is doing. You should not announce it with a triumpet when you give to the poor and needy. Do it in secret and do not expect honour from others. (73)

"Seek and you shall find, and ask you shall be given …" This is the teaching of the Christian Scripture, which represents the Way of God.

If Christians lived this way, developed countries would not dominate the economies of smaller countries. What has often happened, however, is that the economies of smaller countries have been cripled. This has enabled more powerful countries to buy all the cheap produce of the land with their devalued currency, (cheap beef from Argentina, coffee beans from Brazil and cheap oil from small Arab sheikhdoms and Venezuela etc.). These smaller debtors are then given loans with a string of conditions attached. "Free Trade Zones" and the negative effects of globalisation collapse the economies of vulnerable countries. It was Mexico and now it is Argentina. The IMF and World Bank have been accused of collusion in this process.(74)

The Prophet Isaiah argued that true fasting meant to loose the chains of injustice and untie the cords of the yoke, to set the oppressed free and break every yoke? Is it not to share your food with the hungry and to provide the poor wanderer with shelter when you see the naked clothe him, and do not turn away from your own flesh and blood?" (75)

Paul in Colossians argued, "See to it that no one takes you captive through hollow and deceptive philosophy, which depend on human tradition and the basic principles of this world rather than on Christ." (76)

James similarly contended: "Religion that God our Father accepts as pure and faultless is this: to look after orphans and widows in their distress and to keep oneself from being polluted by the world." (77)

耶稣还说："你们施舍，做了好事，要注意，不要为了博得赞扬。不要让你的左手知道右手所做的事。施舍穷困者的时候，不要吹喇叭，要在暗中进行，不望想得到人家的赞美。"

代表神之道《圣经》说："寻找的就会发现，有所求的就有所得......。"

如果基督徒以这种方式生活，那么，发达国家绝不会控制小国的经济。而现实常见的是，小国的经济已经无法恢复。这就使强国贬值的货币购买该国出产的一切廉价产品，比如阿根廷的廉价牛肉、巴西的廉价咖啡豆、阿拉伯酋长国和委内瑞拉的廉价石油等。这些小额债务国于是得到贷款，但是，附加条件是不少的。"自由贸易区"和全球化经营摧毁了脆弱国家的经济。过去是墨西哥，现在是阿根廷。国际货币基金组织和世界银行被指控为在此过程中相互勾结。

先知以赛亚说，真正的禁食松开的是不公的锁链，解开的是轭上的枷锁，使被欺压者得到自由，挣脱条条锁链。是这样吗？把你的食物分给饥饿的人，给无家可归的人找个窝住，见到穿不上衣服的，就让他遮体，你的同胞你不要一走了之。难道不是这样吗？

保罗在《歌罗西书》说，"空洞和欺诈的哲学来自人类传统和基本的处世原则，而不是基督；但是要注意，谁也不会用这种哲学俘虏你的。"

《雅各布书》也认为，上帝，我们的主所接受的是纯净无疵无暇的：照顾患难中的孤儿寡妇吧，不要被世俗所玷污。

2001年8月17日，《金融时代》发表了菲利普斯蒂芬的文章《全球化的穷困为例》。他引用世界银行前副总裁的话说，自由贸易可以使大家都过得不错，但是并不意味着大家过得都不错。

CHAPTER THIRTEEN
Return to the origin

"Life Cycle" is a term in common usage today. Why is it that life is viewed as a cycle, rather than a linear progression, beginning with birth and ending with death? It is a cycle because, when life reaches maturity, an animal reproduces, and a plant leaves "something" behind in the form of a seed or a sapling or a shoot, which repeats the same process of growth and propagation as the previous entity did. The animal or the plant dies, decomposes, and returns to the earth as humus, which nourishes future plants. All forms of life end in death, or return to their origins. Water, too, follows this cycle. Rain falls on to the earth from rain cloud in the sky. The earth collects the water and channels it into rivers, which run into the sea. Water evaporates from the sea and rises into the sky as rain cloud, and so on.

Lao Zi mentions five different cycles, saying that: "one shall return to insight" (Dao De Jing ch.15); "everything returns to its root of origin" (ch.60); "return to the innocent state of a new-born babe"; "return to the original wholeness"; and "return to extreme nothingness". (Chapter72).

Return to insight.

Lao Zi argues that we should not be conceited, presumptuous and self-centred in whatever we do. For example, when we learn something new, we make sure that the knowledge we have acquired is accurate and specific. We should also test the knowledge for its usefulness, that is, put it into practice to make sure it will benefit ourselves and others. We also need to check out consequences. The process is circular. We learn something. We put it into practice. We evaluate the practice and thus add further to our knowledge.

The theme of Lao Zi's writing is based on "knowing" and "using". First of all, we must know the teaching of "The Word" of God. To know it really well we must respect "The Word". Then we must put it to use in our daily life. The degree to which we practice what we know depends on how we "value our integrity". In evaluating our actions, we can determine the degree to which we are encorporating the teaching of "The Word". Evaluation will also help us determine whether we have acted contrary to "The Word." By not "acting against" the teaching of "The Word" we gain "insight into The Word" and understand it more thoroughly.

第十三章

复 归

"生命周期"是今天常用的名词。为什么生命被看成周期，而不被看成从生到死的线性过程呢？它是个循环，因为生命成熟了，动物繁殖了，植物留下了"东西"---种子啦，树苗儿啦，树芽儿啦--又重新开始了新一轮的生长和繁殖。动植物死后分解，回归泥土，变成腐殖质，滋养新的植物。所有种类的生命终有一死，复归于原本状态。水也一样地循环。雨水从天空的雨云中落到地上。地上积水，汇成沟渠，流入河道，流入海洋。水从海面蒸发，升到天空，变成雨云，依序往复。

老子说，复归有五：复归其明，复归于其根，复归于婴，复归于朴，复归于无极。

复归其明：

老子说，不管做什么，决不能自负，决不能自以为是，决不能只顾自己。例如：学习新知识的时候，我们要拿准，我们所获得的知识是准确的、有特定意义的。我们要考察这种知识是不是有用，通过实践大观察它是否有利于自己，有利于他人。我们要检验结果。这个过程是环状的：我们学习，我们实践，我们在实践中进行鉴别，进而充实我们的知识。

老子言论的主题依据是"知"和"用"。首先，我们要识道，而识道的前提是尊道，然后是在日常生活中行德。行德的程度取决于我们如何"宝贵德行"。评价我们的行为，我们可以确定遵道的程度。评价也会有助于确定我们的行为是否违道。如果我们守道了，我们便"明道"了，甚至是通道了。

Jesus said something similar in arguing that whoever knows the "Word" of God and puts it into practice is his sister, his brothers, or his mother, (78) that is, they were in a close master-disciple relationship with him.

Everything returns to its root, its origin. This applies, not only to physical things, but to many other areas as well. It has application to metaphysics, which deals, among other things, with first principles. For example, take Lao Zi's advice about "knowing The Word" and "putting it to practice." "Knowing" is the foundation from which we proceed to practice. This knowing is not superficial, not something merely theoretical. It is an experiencing of the essence of that which we claim to know. It is in this way that we go to the root of the whole process of knowing.

Jesus Christ criticized the Pharisees and teachers of the law with setting aside the commands of God to observe their man-made traditions, or to pursue their selfish desires. (78)They were often making use of the law to subvert the ethical intention behind the law. The oral tradition that grew up alongside the Ten Commandments rendered many of the commandments ineffectual. They sometimes crippled the lives of ordinary people. For example, the Pharisees disapproved of the healing of the sick on the Sabbath day, arguing that healing amounts to "work," which they contended contradicted the commandment to keep the Sabbath "holy." Jesus pointedly reminded the Pharisees that: "the Sabbath is made for people, not people for the Sabbath."

Return to the innocent state of a newborn babe; return to the original wholeness; and return to the "extreme nothingness".

These sayings related to the question: "Respect The Word and Value Integrity." In order to carry through on this advice, we should return to the original state of our humanity, what the Buddhists call our "original face," that is, our essential humanity with all its potentiality. It is in this sense that it could be argued that we should return to the innocent potentiality of newborn infants.

John's gospel depicts Jesus indicating to Nicodemus, a Pharisee, that to see the kingdom of God, to understand what Jesus was talking about, he needed to be born again. It is of course impossible for someone, who is old, like Nicodemus, to be born again. What Jesus meant was that the knowledge that Nicodemus had acquired had so structured his thinking that he could not see things as they really were. All he looked out upon was pushed into a preconceived mold formed by an accumulation of inherited opinions.

耶稣也说过类似的话：不管是谁知道了道，而且行了道，就是他的兄弟姐妹，就是他的母亲，就是说，他们和他的关系像师徒一样亲密。

各复归于其根：这不仅指物化的东西，而且也指其他领域的事物。它应用到形而上学的时候，就也涉及了一些首要的要则。比如说，老子说了的识道和行道。识道是行道的基础，识道不是表面上的，也不只是理论上的，而是我们称之为认识事物本质的一种体验。只有这样，我们才能深入到整个认识过程的根源。

耶稣基督批评伪君子作风，批评教条做法，认为他们不顾上帝的诫命而去奉行人为的传统或者是追求私欲。他们利用法律来颠覆法律背后的伦理观念，这是常有的事。出现十诫的同时，也产生了口口相传的习俗，使许多诫命发挥不了作用。有时，就要了平民百姓的命。比如：法利赛人不许安息日治病，因为治病等于工作，这是违反安息日守圣的诫命的。耶稣尖锐地告诫法利赛人：安息日是为人设的，人不是为安息日造的。

复归于婴、复归于朴和复归于无极：与这些格言相关的是尊道而贵德。为了实践这种忠告，我们应该复归人性的原本，就是佛家所说的"本色"。换句话说，我们基本的人性都是有潜力的。这意思是说。我们应该回归到新生儿天真的潜在状态。

《约翰福音》说，耶稣指示法利赛人尼哥底玛：要看到天国，要理解耶稣所说的话，那么，他就得再生一次。当然，像尼哥底玛这么大年龄的人是无法再生的。耶稣的意思是说，尼哥底玛所得到的知识解构了他的思维，使他无法认清事物的真面目。他所能见到的都被层层累计起来的、流传下来的观念事先给框定了。

He had to start over again, to learn to look at life in a new way. He needed to become as impressionable as a new-born baby. (80)On another occasion, Jesus told his disciples that anyone who would not receive the kingdom of God like a little child would never enter it.(81)

In a society where there are class distinctions, or where specific functions are honoured above others, people will either be honoured or despised, and their accomplishments will be regarded either as glorious or disgraced. This state of affairs, which is almost universal, is a sad departure from the givenness of human potentiality, with its capacity to respect and honour all people in a society in which differences are recognized and celebrated. Our problem is that we have become accustomed to thinking in dichotomies. Lao Zi argues that it is because "people acknowledge beauty that they contrast it with ugliness". "In honouring the learned they despise the ignorant". "In not desiring rare things that are difficult to obtain people will not become thieves". This dichotomous thinking, this "either/or" thinking, this dualistic thinking is contrary to the teaching of "The Word". Pristine human potentiality, in its more positive aspects, is good, generous, humble and replete with integrity. It is wholesome, like an original block of wood, uncut and unpolished. Therefore, it is considered vital to promote "good integrity" among all people, so that all can contribute towards the building of a peaceful and harmonious society. This is why we must discover the original image, the positive aspects, of our God-given human potential. (82)

Return to "Extreme nothingness."

According to Confucian Philosopher, Zhou Dunyi (1017–1073), who was the first to study "Metaphysical Thought" in China, (1) "Wu Ji" is the highest level in the universe is empty or absolutely nothing. It is beyond the "beginning." The second level (2) is "Tai Ji", which is the very extreme, representing the "beginning." This is followed by (3) "Yin Yang", which includes heavenly bodies or astronomy. The fourth level is (4) "Wu Xing", which consists of metal, wood, water, fire and earth.

他得从头再来，用新的视角看待人生。他得像新生婴儿那样敏感。有一次，耶稣告诉门徒，谁不接受天国，就像小孩儿进不了天国一样。

在阶级分明、等级严明的社会，人们或贵或贱，或荣或辱。这种情势几乎普遍存在，人类舍己为人的可能性成为过去---舍是能动，是社会明显意识到了差异的时候，人们舍出来，让所有的人尊重和自豪。问题是，我们习惯了用两分法进行思维。老子说："天下皆知美为其美，恶已"；"不尚贤，使民不争"；"不贵难得之货，是民不为盗。"这种或者/或者的两分法思维（也叫二元思维），是违反道的。从比较积极的方面看，人之初，性本善，本慷慨，本谦卑，本正义，好比原木一样没有被雕琢，没有被刨子光。因此，必需在全体人民中间提倡"善行"，这样才有助于建设平安、和谐社会。为此，我们应该发现上帝赐予人类潜能的原始形象和积极方面。

复归于无极：根据中国首位研究玄学的儒家周敦颐（公元1017年1073年）的观点，无极是宇宙最高境界，是虚无，绝对的虚无。它超出了"太初"。第二层是很极端的太极，代表"太初"。接着是阴阳，包括各种天体。第四层是五行，包含金、木、水、火、土。

The lowest, or fifth level is (5) "Wan Wu", which includes all creatures.(83)

The expression of "Wu Ji" is the source of energy for "Tai Ji." This theory suggests that "something" comes from "nothing," and that "something" will return to "nothing," when it is decomposed. Lao Zi argued that this "nothing" represents potentially the genesis of all creation.

The Hebrew Scriptures, using anthropomorphic language, argue that when God created man, he took a lump of clay and shaped it in his own image –a relational rather than a plastic image. Then he breathed into it and it received life from God. When the man grew old and later died, his/her body returned to the earth, and his/her soul or spirit, which was the breath of God, returned to God.

However, as Lao Zi contended, while man lived on earth, his/her spiritual task was to "respect The Word of God and value his/her integrity". Drawing upon both traditions, it could be argued that, when we are alive, we should love the Lord our God and love our neighbours, and thus put "The Word" into practice. Thus, when we die, our bodies will return to dust, and our spirits will return to God.

Fu Gui, "return to the origin" reminds us of the importance of following "The Word." Both Lao Zi and Jesus emphasized the importance of discerning and following the Word. Christians believes that men shall die, but their souls shall return to the Creator God in heaven. The return to God is a return to "Extreme emptiness." Fu gui yu wu ji, the nothingness of a potentiality replete with energy and life, out of which everything arose.

最底层也就是第五层，是万物。

无极是太极的能动之源。这个理论认为，"有"出自"无"，"有"分解后复归于无。老子说，万物就是从"无"中产生出来的。

希伯来经文使用赋予人性的语言认为，上帝造人的时候，用一团泥土塑成自己的形象这一点具有关联性，而不是可塑性。后来，上帝朝它吹了一口气，它就得到了上帝给予它的生命。人长大，老死了，身体回到了泥土，他的灵魂既然是上帝的呼吸，就回到了上帝那里。

老子则认为，当人在世的时候，他的灵魂是要"尊道而贵德"。从中西传统来讲，可以说，我们活着的时候，我们应该热爱上帝，我们的主，热爱我们的邻居，这就是行道。我们死后，身体归于尘土，我们的灵魂复归于上帝。

复归向我们指明了尊道的重要性。老子和耶稣识道和随道的意义。基督徒相信，人死了，他们的灵魂会回归天上的造物之神那里。复归于神就是"复归于无极"，潜在的"无"充满着万物生长的能量和生命。

The Ethics of Confucius

What you do not wish for yourself,

Do not do to others.

孔子的伦理

己所不欲，勿施於人。

CHAPTER FOURTEEN
What is his name?
The Lord-on-high) or Heaven and Yahweh, The Lord.

Chinese Beliefs:

At least since the time written records began to be made, in the 18th Century B. C. E. Chinese worshipped the Lord-on-high (上帝 Shang Di). This Lord was the supreme Lord, the Lord of all creation, which included spirits and ghosts. The ruling family of Shang Dynasty prayed to the Lord-on-high, as well as to their ancestors, seeking consultations and requesting blessings. (Shang Zhao c. 1766-1122 B. C. E.)

The expression "Lord-on-high" was replaced by the word "Heaven" in the Zhou Dynasty (Zhou Zhao c. 1122-256 B. C. E.). It would appear that "Lord-on-high, " which evoked the presence of this Lord, was too sacred a name to be mentioned. This Being could no longer be addressed in this way. "Heaven, " the abode of the Lord-on-high, began to be used as a synonym for God.

The Chinese, in later years, worshipped other deities besides the Lord-on-high. These others were natural deities, such as the sun, moon, wind, rain, earth, trees, grains, mountains and rivers etc. The spirits they worshipped were the high spirits, like Huang Di and Yan Di, the half brother of the Yellow Emperor. All Chinese are regarded as the "descendants of Yan-Huang". Later generations also worshipped other royal personages, as well as a number of aristocrats. It was thought that those who were in authority might have the power to bestow divine blessings and power. The lower spiritual beings, worshipped in anticipation of blessings and protection, were the souls of ancestors. They also sought to appease ghosts so that the latter would not harm them.

Lord-on-high (上帝Shang Di):

Lao Zi (b. 568 BC.) could not put his finger on this mysterious supreme Being, the Lord-on-high, who could not be seen, heard, or touched. Yet this Being was everywhere, in all creation. It was omnipresent and omnipotent. It was the source of all creation. It had no name. Lao Zi, however, referred to it as "Word". He wondered whose offspring this Dao was, and whether the Dao existed before the Lord. There is clear indication that Lao Zi acknowledged the existence of this supreme "Lord".

第十四章

上帝、天、耶和华或主

中国信仰：

自有历史记载以来，公元前18世纪，中国人就崇拜上帝。这个主就是至高的神，创造神鬼在内的万物的神。商朝的统治阶层（公元前1766-1122年）崇拜上帝，祭祀祖先，卜卦求福。

上帝这个称谓至周朝（公元前1122-256年）被"天"字取代。上帝这个称谓怕招来主的下凡，所以连提都不敢提了，不敢叫了。天，本来是上帝的居所，开始用来称呼上帝。

后来，中国人除了崇拜上帝以外，也崇拜别的神明，都是自然神，比如有日、月、风、雨、土地、树、五谷、山河等。他们崇拜的上神，如炎黄。所有中国人都认自己是"炎黄子孙"。后来，也崇拜皇族和贵族。人们以为，掌权的有权赐予神圣的权位。他们也崇拜下神——自己的祖神，求他们攘灾祈福。他们还敬鬼消灾。

上帝：

老子（公元前568年生）无法染指这神秘至高的上帝——上帝是看不到的，是听不到的，是摸不到的。然而，上帝存在于万物的每个角落。上帝是全能的，是无所不在的，是万物之源。上帝没有名字，老子给他取名为"道"。他不晓得这"道"的先人是谁，也不晓得是否"象帝之先"。但是，老子认为，至高的上帝是存在的，这是毫无疑问的。

What is his name?
The Lord-on-high) or Heaven and Yahweh, The Lord.

What he argued was that the message of this "Lord", or ever present but invisible essence, should also be acknowledged as "Word", or Dao. Lao Zi advised people "not to act against" the teaching of the "Word," or the "Way of Heaven". This reverence for the teaching of the "Word", coupled with appropriate action "implementing integrity", was wholesome. A cogent argument can be advanced to suggest that, for Lao Zi, "Heaven" meant Lord, or the Lord of Heaven. (84)

Confucius (b. 551 B. C. E.) considered that Heaven was a personal God, who rewarded good and punished evil. By the time he reached the age of fifty, he was arguing that he reverenced the Will of Heaven. As Heaven was intangible, he preferred not to talk about it, and chose, instead, to teach people how to act towards one another with integrity. Confucian philosophy, with its strongly humanist bent, its emphasis on poetry, books, propriety (or ritual) and music was favoured, not only by Zhou emperors, but also by the ruling classes of subsequent dynasties.(85)In spite of his almost exclusive ethical focus, Confucius posited a supreme God. He believed in the power and protection of "Heaven." In Shi Jing, Confucius used three nouns, "Lord", "Lord-on-high", and "Heaven" as synonyms for God. These terms were used in the following ways in the classics:

In Huang Yi "The Lord-on-high is almighty and gracious, overseeing all on the earth, protecting and blessing the people with peace"; "The Lord declared to Emperor Wen: 'Do not use your might without restraint; do not desire merits, but seek a good reputation in settling disputes'".

In Da Ming: "Only Emperor Wen cautiously and diligently obeyed the will of the Lord-on-high and received blessings abundantly".

In Xiao Min: "The wrath of Heaven falls on all the earth because of the misdeeds of the emperor and his court. When will they stop doing wrong?".

他所说的是，"主"这个信息虽然存在，但实际上是看不见的，应该叫做"道"。老子劝人们不要违"道"，不要违"天道"。遵道贵德方为完人。由此可以确切的推证，老子所说的"天"，是指"主"或"上天之主"。

孔子（公元前551年生）认为，"天"是赏善罚恶的个体之神。他到五十岁的时候，还说尊天意。因为天是不可捉摸的，所以宁可不提它，而是教导人们怎样行德。儒学大力倡导人道，重视诗、书、礼、乐。这些不但为周朝历代皇帝所推崇，而且也被后代的历朝统治阶级所推崇。孔子主要专注伦理，但他断定有一位至高的神。他相信神权和天佑。孔子在《诗经》里用过三个名称：帝、上帝、天，这些都是上帝的同义词。上述用语见于下列典籍：

《皇矣》篇："皇矣上帝，临下有赫，监观四方，求民者莫。"上帝很伟大又光明，垂见天下人间很显明，观察四方的事情，又庇佑人民得到平安宁静。

"帝谓文王：无然畔援，无然歆羡，诞先登于岸。"上帝告诉文王，不要无限制地发挥权威，也不要尽量贪欲争功劳，只要追求和事诉讼来的名望。

《大明》篇："维此文王：小心翼翼，昭事上帝，聿怀多福"。就是说这位周文王，他很小心又仔细谨慎，他知道敬畏服侍上帝，便得到许多上帝的祝福。

《小旻》篇："旻天疾威，敷于下土，谋由回遹，何日斯沮？"上天震怒得很厉害，遍及全地，这都是朝廷多次错误谋事，这样要到何年何日才会停止呢？

What is his name?
The Lord-on-high) or Heaven and Yahweh, The Lord.

In Zheng Min: "Heaven created all people and all things systematically. The people obey and love integrity".

Such passages support the contention that Confucius did acknowledge the existence of God, even though he avoided discussing anything about God. By way of justification for not speaking about the Supreme Being, he argued that, "If you cannot serve men, how do you serve ghosts?". He considered it was better not to talk about things one could not see.[86]

Mo Zi (b. 490 B. C. E.) in Tian Zhi argued that "Heaven" has human-like characteristics and is lord over all creation. He classified these characteristics thus:

1. Heaven is omnipresent and omnipotent, observing all things and knowing all that happens. Normally, if you offend your parents, you can hide for a time in the homes of your relatives, who will advise you to reconsider your behaviour and refrain from committing the offence again. If you offend the ruler of the country, you can hide in a neighbouring country. In this case, your parents, relatives and friends will advise you to repent and avoid committing the offence again. However, "if you offend Heaven, you can neither hide in the thick forest, nor in the deep and uninhabited valley. 'Heaven' can clearly discern your whereabouts".

2. Heaven is the source of righteousness. There were many examples in the past of wise and righteous emperors, who brought peace and prosperity to the country. Both righteousness and wisdom came from Heaven. "When there is righteousness in the world, there is life, and without it, death. When there is righteousness, there is prosperity, and without it, poverty. When there is righteousness, there is security, and without it, chaos".

3. Heaven is in control of the universe. "Emperors cannot govern in whatever way they please, because Heaven will govern and judge them". This is why an emperor has to set a good example for his officials, and his officials for the people under them. "Heaven is honourable and wise, and this is why it is said that righteousness comes from Heaven".

《烝民》篇："天生烝民，有物有则，民之秉彝，好是懿德。"上天创造人民和万物都是依照规则，人民都顺从诫命，也都爱好美德行善。

以上几段可以证实，孔子虽然他避而不谈论上帝的事，但承认上帝的存在。可以证实他不提上帝的理由是："不能事人，岂能事鬼"。他认为，人看不见的事物最好不要去说。

墨子（公元前490年生）在《天志》中说："天"有人的性格，主宰着万物。他把这些性格分为以下几个方面：

1. "天"无所不在，无所不能，无所不知，审视万物。平时，如果你冒犯了家长，可以到亲属家躲一阵子。亲属会劝你考虑考虑自己是怎么做的，错了就别再犯了。如果你冒犯一国之主，你可以跑到邻国去。这时，你的父母，你的亲戚和你的朋友都会建议你悔过，不要再犯错误了。如果你得罪了"天"，你就无处藏身了，"大不可为林谷幽门无人，明必见之"。得罪上帝的，世上是没有地方可以隐藏的。

2. "天"是义的发源处。过去有许多贤明而正义的国王，他们为国家带来太平昌盛。公义和智慧来自上天。"天下有义则生、无义则死；有义则富，无义则贫；有义则治，无义则乱。"

3. 上天匡正和统治宇宙。"天子未得次之己而为政，有天政之"。皇上也得在百官面前以身作则，百官则为治下的百姓以身作则。"天为贵，天为知而己矣，然则义果出自天矣。"

Heaven desires righteousness, and dislikes unrighteousness." " Heaven rectifies the behaviour of men with righteousness". As there is only one Will of Heaven, everyone has to keep in line, even emperors, who are not above this Will of Heaven.

4. Heaven loves all people. "I know Heaven loves all men in the world very much". For our survival and enjoyment, Heaven created the sun, moon, stars and constellations, which regulate day and night, the four seasons, and the sunshine and rain that sustain and nourish the creation. The earth provides mountains and valleys, forests and rivers, and all kinds of minerals resources. Mo Zi uses all these reasons to argue that Heaven, the Lord, loves people.

5. Heaven rewards goodness and punishes evil. To comply with the Will of Heaven, a big country will not attack a small country, a big clan will not bully a small clan, the wise will not despise the ignorant, and the rich will not look down upon the poor. "In order to obey the wishes of Heaven, men must live to love and benefit others." "If the son-of-Heaven, that is, the emperor, is kind, Heaven will reward him, and if the son-of-Heaven blunders, Heaven will punish him". (87)

Mo Zi's Heaven, is a supernatural being, the creator God. Mo Zi used the term "Lord-on-high" in a passage in Tian Zhi that reads "… as sacrifice to the Lord-on-high, ghosts and gods", indicating that he considered Heaven, Tian as a synonym for Shang Di, the Lord-on-high.

Zhuang Zi (b. 369 B. C. E.), a follower of Lao Zi, in Yang Sheng Zi, wrote about Di, the Lord: "If a man regards life and death as normal and natural, then sadness and happiness will not enter his heart. The ancient saying describes this as 'the Lord released someone from hanging". (88)

An offering made at the time of the Shang Dynasty was taken seriously. The domesticated animal – cow, sheep, pig or chicken – had to be perfect, without any defect. The animal had to be fed with the best grains, and kept separately from other animals. Some of these details are described in the writings of Mo Zi. (89)

"天欲义而恶不义"，"天以义匡人。" 世上只有一个天意，甚至连国王也要顺从天意，不能凌驾于天意之上。

4. 上天爱所有的人。"且吾所以知，天之爱民之厚者"。为了人们的生存和愉悦，上天创造了宇宙、日、月、星辰，掌控着滋润万物的昼夜、四季、阳光和雨水。陆地有高山、深谷、树林和河流，以及各种矿物。墨子由此证明，上帝是爱人的。

5. 上天赏善罚恶。顺从天意，大国不会进犯小国，大族不会欺凌小族，智者不会藐视愚者，富人不会傲视穷人。"顺从天意，爱人利人"，"天子有善，天能赏之，天子有过，天能罚之。"

墨子的"天"是超自然的，是创造之神。墨子在《天志》文中也使用了"上帝"一词："……祭祀上帝鬼神。"墨子认为，"天"就是上帝。

庄子（公元前369年生）是老子的弟子，在《养生子》一文中也写到"帝"："安时而处顺，哀乐不能入也，古时谓是帝之县解。"如果一个人认为生和死是很普通，很自然的，那么悲哀和欢乐就不能侵入他的心。上古有句话说：上帝替他解开上梁绳子。

商代祭祀是很严肃的，牲礼牛、羊、猪、鸡等务必完美，不能出任何纰漏。这些牲礼必须和其他动物分开豢养，并用最好的谷米喂食。《墨子》中对某些情节有详细描述。

What is his name?
The Lord-on-high) or Heaven and Yahweh, The Lord.

In another classic, Gu Wen Guan Zhi – a recorded conversation between the warlord Yu Gong and his adviser, Gong Zhiji in 656 B. C. E.– mentioned the righteousness of Heaven. Yu Gong said, "When I make an offering, the things that I sacrifice must be plentiful, clean and sumptuous. When this is the case God will surely protect me." But Gong Zhiji replied,

"According to what my humble-self has heard, while gods and ghosts treat everyone the same, they only help those who have integrity, and that is why the Book of Zhou argued that 'Heaven is impartial, and only helps those who have integrity.'" He continued, insisting,

"It is not the offerings themselves that have fragrance. It is the persons making the offerings, who have integrity, and that gives the offerings fragrance" [90]This story clearly illustrates that it was common to believe in gods and ghosts. What is more, the sincerity that was spoken about was a type of openness or faith.

In visiting the Temple of Heaven in Beijing today, [91]one can see evidence, in the structure of the prayer platform, or altar, and in the Temple itself, of the worship of Heaven, or of the Lord-on-high. There is no trace of an idol in the Temple precinct. The altar is merely a raised granite platform, situated in the open. At the center is a circular slab, where the emperor, the "Son of Heaven", stood to offer his annual thanksgiving, praying to the Lord-on-high, with all the officials kneeling in the surrounding area. That represented the official worship. They prayed to the Lord-on-high in Heaven.

Today, among Chinese, especially those who received a Confucian education, it is still common to use the term "Heaven" in place of God. For example: when someone commits an evil deed, another would warn him, saying, "Heaven will punish you". To encourage someone not to be disappointed with the good they have done, they are told that "Heaven will not disappoint good people".

Since the beginning of their written history, the Chinese have worshipped one god. This was the creator God, who was in control of the universe. Later, they created more and more gods by canonizing righteous people, often great teachers, like Lao Zi and Kong Zi or

"Confucius", affording them the status of gods. Confucian teaching argues that "men after attaining Dao shall become saints, and becoming saints will be regarded as buddhas, or gods". These so-called gods, or buddhas, are not supernatural beings like the Creator God.

另一部典籍《古文观止》记载了虞公和军师宫之奇（公元前656年）关于天义的对话。公曰："吾享祀丰洁，神必据我。"对曰："臣闻之，鬼神非人实亲，维德是依，故周书曰：'皇天无亲，惟德是辅'。又曰：'黍稷非馨，明德惟馨。'" 这段话清楚地说明当时的人们普遍信鬼信神，所说的诚信就是一种虔诚或信仰。

如今，去北京天坛的时候，从祭天台的构造、祭拜上天或上帝的天坛本身来看，就可以得到证实。整个天坛四周，没有一个偶像。祭台是用花岗岩在空场上砌成的。天子每年要站在中央的石台上向上帝祈祷，祭献牲物，文武官员跪在周围。这是官方的崇拜，他们崇拜在大的上帝。

现代的中国人，尤其是受过儒学教育的，时常用"天"这个词来代替"上帝"。比如说，有人干了事，别人会警告他："不怕遭天谴吗！"对于做了善事的人不要失望，可以安慰他们说："天不负忠良"。

有史以来，中国人就崇拜上帝。他就是主宰宇宙的造物之神。后来，他们又造更多的神，把正义之人比如说老子、孔子确立为大师，奉若神明。儒家认为，"人得道成圣，成圣为佛。"然而，圣也好，佛也罢，都不是造物之主这样的超自然之神。

What is his name?
The Lord-on-high) or Heaven and Yahweh, The Lord.

Missionaries working in China in the late sixteenth and early seventeenth centuries, in particular, Francis Xavier and Matteo Ricci, decided that the Chinese expression "Shang Di", the Lord-on-high, or "Tian", Heaven, which was regarded as equivalent to the Lord in Heaven by Protestants, or Tian Zhu, which was the preferred Catholic term for God, were roughly equivalent, and could be adopted by Chinese Christians. (92)

Christian Belief:

Christianity had its roots in Israelite history. The Israelites of the patriarchal era addressed their God in a number of ways. These differences reflected their prehistoric roots. In some passages, God was referred to as "Elohim, " a plural noun. Later passages used the term "Yahweh." The Yahwist strand tended to be more anthropomorphic. Overtime, "Yahweh" won out over "Elohim." "Yahweh" meant "The Lord." Towards the close of the period covered by the Hebrew Scriptures, expression like "The word" (memre) of God were substituted for Yahweh. In the Gospel of Thomas, Salome was decribed as wondering aloud whether Jesus was from "The One". In using this expression, she was obviously avoiding the use of the word "Yahweh".

The patriarchs gave God many names. In the Book of Genesis, it was recorded that the king of Salem, Melchizedek, who was a priest of "God Most High", blessed Abraham. In doing so, he used the name "God Most High, Creator of heaven and earth" (14:18). God was reported to have appeared to Abimelech, king of Gerar, in a dream, and to have conversed with him (20:3). Both instances suggest that, at least for the author of Genesis, this Creator God was worshipped by other nations beside Israel.

Abram addressed God as "Sovereign Lord" (15:2). When God changed the name of Abraham, from Abram to Abraham, after he was found to be righteous and blameless, he introduced himself as "God Almighty" (17:1). After the establishing of the Treaty of Beersheba, Abraham planted a tamarisk tree and worshipped the Lord, "the Eternal God" (21:33).

When Jacob wrestled with God he asked for the name of his adversory, but was not given any (33:29). After Jacob ran away from his father-in-law, and returned from Paddan Aram, he bought a piece of land outside the city of Shechem, where he set up an altar which he called "El Elohe Israel", meaning "God, the God of Israel" (33:20). When Jacob moved to Bethel, he set up an altar and named it "El Bethel" or "God of Bethel" (35:7). At the time when God changed the names of Abram (Abraham) and Jacob (Israel) he told them that he was "God Almighty" or "El Shadai" (17:1 and 35:11).

When Moses asked the voice in the burning bush to identify itself, the reply was, "I SHALL BE WHAT I SHALL BE." As a consequence, the Israelites referred to God as Yahweh, that is, "The Lord." The Psalmist described God as "Shepherd" in Psalm 23, while the prophet Jeremiah described him as "Potter." (92)

16世纪末17世纪初，在中国的传教士，尤其是法兰斯士蕯维尔和马蒂奥墨西认为，中国所说的上帝或"上天"等同于基督教中的"主"，天主教称之为天主。他们是物同异名吧。

基督教

基督教起源于以色列，在以色列父系氏族时期，上帝的称谓是很多的。这说明，这些称谓史前就存在了。上帝被称作"以罗欣"，是个复数名词。后来，一些典籍中用了"耶和华"这个术语。耶和华派更加赋予人性化，之后，"耶和华"这个称谓就彻底取替了"以罗欣派"。"耶和华"的意思是"主"。后来，希伯来《圣经》便用上帝的"道"来代替耶和华。《多马福音》书所描写莎罗米猜测耶稣是不是来自"那个'一'的"。之所以使这个表达方式，显然是避免使用耶和华这个词。

父系氏族使用了许多名称。《创世记》记载，沙林王麦基洗德自称是至高的上帝的仆人，他用至高的上帝的名称祝福的亚伯拉罕。他所使用的名字是"至高的上帝，创造天地的主"（14: 18）。据记载，上帝在基拉耳王亚比米勒的梦中出现，与他进行了对话（20: 3）。这两个例子说明，《创世记》的作者至少认为，这位创世之神除了以色列以外，还被许多国家所崇拜。

埃布尔兰管上帝叫"最高的主"（15: 2）。当上帝因埃布尔兰公正无私而替他改名亚伯拉罕的时候，上帝自称为"全能的上帝"（17: 1）。签订别是巴合约以后，亚伯拉罕栽了一棵垂柳，把这位主拜称为"永恒的上帝"（21: 33）。

雅各布和上帝较劲儿的时候，问对方叫什么，但是没有得到回复。后来，雅各布逃离岳父，回到巴旦亚兰，在示剑城外买了一块地，搭了一个坛子，起名叫"伊利伊罗伊以色列"，意思是"上帝，以色列上帝"（33.20）。雅各布搬到伯特利时，建了个坛子，起名叫"伊勒伯特利"或"伯特利的神"（35: 7）。上帝替埃布尔兰和雅各布改名的时候，告诉他们，祂的名字叫"全能的上帝"（17: 1，35: 11）。

摩西对着燃不跨的荆棘里发出的声音问它叫什么的时候，得到的回答是："我就是我。"结果，以色列人称他为耶和华，意思是"主"。《诗篇》作者在第二十三篇中比喻他为"牧者"，先知雅利米亚则描写他为"窑匠"。

What is his name?
The Lord-on-high) or Heaven and Yahweh, The Lord.

In the Gospel of Matthew, written for a community of Jewish Christians, Jesus was depicted as proclaiming the "Kingdom of heaven," rather than the "Kingdom of God," which one finds in the Gospel of Luke. Even in Luke, however, in the parable of the lost son, the prodigal is depicted as rehearsing a confession in which he admits to having sinned against "Heaven" and against his father (Luke 15:18). Here, as well, the word "Heaven" was used as a synonym for "God".

When the Israelites settled in Palestine, they were influenced by the people they eventually conquered. In the light of this it is hardly surprising that they worshipped other gods besides Elohim/Yahweh. In the story of Jacob's flight from Laban, his father-in-law, his wife Rachel stole her father's household gods (Genesis. 31:19). The worship of the gods of the indigenes was a constant temptation, particularly as they were more visible than "Yahweh." The Israelites were frequently chastised by the prophets for worshipping the Canaanite god "Baal."

In the early days the Israelites worshipped the "God of the Fathers", that is, the God worshipped by the patriarchal chieftains, Abraham, Isaac, and Jacob. This god was a tribal god. Other tribes had their gods. Tribal clashes were seen as clashes between gods. In time, the Hebrews came to regard their God, not only as one among many gods, but as the God who ruled all peoples. The deities of other tribes were seen as no more than idols, in spite of the fact that many Israelites were seduced by them. In the two centuries prior to the advent of Christ, the sense of Yahweh's universality increased. It was argued that he would draw worshippers from all nations to Jerusalem – Mount Zion – to worship.

Following Jewish tradition, the Christian God was seen as the creator of heaven and earth, whose rule was universal. He was the creator and sustainer of all reality. He was righteous and faithful, full of love and mercy. Though he punished sinners, he forgave those who repented and trusted themselves to him. The perception of this God as a God of forgiveness, mercy and love, which was present in the experience of the Hebrews, was intensified. It was these aspects that Jesus highlighted in his Sermon on the Mount.

Jesus embodied the love of God, bringing God closer to people. As a consequence, the followers of Jesus ceased to regard God as distant and aloof. The intimate way in which Jesus referred to God, as "Abba" or Daddy," lightened the sternness of the divine image for his disciples. Jesus, in teaching his disciples to pray, encouraged them to begin with, "Our Father in heaven …"

Unfortunately, Christianity, over time, divided into various denominations and sects. Many mainland Chinese believed that Protestants and Catholics worshipped two different gods. The Protestants prayed to the Lord-on-high and were seen as followers of Ji Du Jiao that is, the "religion of Christus," and the Catholics prayed to the Lord of Heaven and were considered to belong to Tian Zhu Jiao, the "religion of the Lord of Heaven." To add to this confusion, Catholic churches displayed figures of Mary and a range of saints. They prayed to Mary as "Mother of God," regarding her as an intermediary between humankind and God. Patron saints further confused the issue.

《马太福音》是为犹太基督徒们撰写的，书中说，耶稣宣称的是"天国"，而不是《路加福音》中所说的"上帝之国"。然而，在《路加福音》里失子的比喻中，描写浪子惭悔的时候，承认他得罪了"天"（15：18）。这里的"天"是上帝的代名词。

以色列人定居在巴勒斯坦的时候，受到了他们后来所征服的人们的影响。从这点上说，他们拜耶和华或者是其他以罗欣以外的神，也是正常的。在雅各布逃离岳父拉班的时候，妻子拉结偷了父亲家中的神像（创世记31：19）。崇拜土著的神像常常是抵不住的诱惑，主要理由是"耶和华"是看不见的，他们是看得见的。以色列人因为崇拜迦南地的巴力神经常受到先知们咒骂。

早些时候，以色列人崇拜"祖先的上帝"，就是父系族长亚伯拉罕、艾萨克和雅各布所崇拜的上帝。这个上帝是部落之神。其他部落也有他们的神，部落冲突可以看作是神之间的冲突。有时，希伯来人拜自己的上帝，不仅因为这个上帝是众神中的一位，而且是因为这个上帝统治万民。其它部落的神不过是个偶像，许多以色列人却被这个偶像诱惑了。基督降临前的两个世纪，耶和华就越来越感到应该进行普世了。先知们说，祂会把所有国家的崇拜者吸引耶路撒冷的锡安山来朝拜。

根据犹太的风俗，基督徒的上帝是创造天地，统治宇宙的神。他是创造者，也是一切现实的扶助者。他正义，诚实，悲天悯人。他虽然罚恶，也宽恕和相信悔罪的人。体认这个上帝，就是体认悲悯宽恕之帝，希伯来人所经历的则证实了这点。耶稣在《登山宝训》中所强调的恰恰是这些内容。

耶稣体现了上帝的爱，让上帝走进的人民。耶稣的追溯者们也就不再把上帝看得遐不可及了。耶稣指认上帝为"阿巴"或"爹爹"，这种亲昵的方式使弟子在神圣形象的肃穆气氛中放松了。耶稣教弟子们祈祷，鼓励他们开场时这么说："我们的天父……。"不幸的是，基督教后来派系林立。中国大陆不少人认为，清教徒和天主教徒信的神不同。清教徒祈祷上帝，比如说基督教徒祈祷的是基督教；天主教徒祈祷天主，因此属于天主教。天主教堂为了混淆耳目，推出了玛丽和一排圣徒的形象。他们祈祷玛丽，称之为"圣母"，把他看作是人神之间的纽带。"守护神"则乱上添乱。

In addition, Catholics and Protestants used two different Bibles and professed different doctrines and creeds.

In spite of these differences and accretions, it can be argued that the essence of Christianity is simple. It advocates worshipping God as "Spirit and Truth, " at least according to the Jesus of the Johannine Gospel. While Christianity necessarily focuses on the "words and deeds" of Jesus of Nazareth, and argues that he uniquely incarnated this Spirit, it does not disallow the possibility of other incarnations. In fact, the whole of creation is redolent with the divine Spirit. Furthermore, all peoples are made in the image of God, and incarnate this Spirit. Some are more transparent to this Spirit than others. However, these saints, or buddhas, who finally attained the stature of Christ, or Dao, or Enlightenment, are not regarded as supernatural beings. They are not elevated to the status of gods, or worshipped by their followers.

While it is inappropriate for us to consider saints and buddhas to be on a par with God, they were, nevertheless, messengers, who went a considerable way towards incarnating the "message" they brought. This "message" was not something external. The Creator, the Ultimate Reality, the Spirit, found expression through them. They were transparent to that Reality, that Spirit. Worship afforded by those best able to judge their worth was offered, not to their idiosyncratic humanity, but to the Spirit alive within them. This Spirit, this Creator God, was described as the Alpha and Omega, that is, the First and the Last, the one who is, and was, and who shall ever be, the Everlasting, the Almighty. The ancient Chinese Lord-on-high was nothing less than this Creator God, the God of all nations.

此外，天主教徒和基督教徒使用两种圣经，信奉不同的教义和信条。

尽管存在上述差异，增加了一些问题，实际上，基督教的要义并不复杂。它主张用"心灵和诚实"来拜上帝，这是《约翰福音》里耶稣所提倡的。基督教特别关注耶稣的"言行"，认为，他是圣灵的唯一化身，此外不可能有其他的化身。然而，整个创世充满着圣灵的芬芳，全人类都是依照上帝的形像创造出来的，是这个圣灵的化身。只是有的化身更显明一些罢了。但是，圣也好，佛也好，最终达到了基督（也称为道或教化）的境界，而不再被看作是超自然存在了。他们不会登仙成神，也不会用追随者崇拜。

我们如果把圣和佛与上帝并列考虑，这是不妥当的。他们不过还是使者，想把他们带来的"信息"具体化，还有相当长的路要走。这种"信息"不是外在的，是造物主、终极的现实和圣灵（圣父、圣子、圣灵）通过它们得以体现。在现实和圣灵面前，他们是彰显的。能够最好评价他们价值的办法，就是他们所表现出来的崇拜之心，崇拜的不是特质的人性，而是活在他们体内的圣灵。这位圣灵，这位创世之主，是创始成终的，是昔在，是今在，是以后永在，是长久不息，是全能。中国古人的上帝不是别人，正是这位创世的上帝，这位万邦之神。

CHAPTER FIFTEEN
What is the son of God?

Let us know the God in Christianity first before we talk about the "Son of God".

Christianity believes in monotheism, the Creator God.

1. God has no physical image.

Whatever has image is a creature. The Book of Genesis states that God made man according to his image (1:20). Regarded as the first man, Adam had not seen God, even though he followed God in the Garden of Eden, and heard his calling, but he never said God's image is like his own.

Jaccob wrestled with a man in his dream. Guess it was a spiritual struggle and not a bodily struggle. He asked the man for his name, but the man retaliated, saying, "Why do you ask for my name?" (32:24) This story narrated a physical struggle in a dream at night, but this cannot prove that God has physical body and image.

Moses went up to Mount Senai. He heard the voice came out of the burning bush, that was never being destroyed. But he didn't see God. Moses was the first prophet chosen by God. He walked with God all his life. They often talked, but Moses never saw God. (Ex.3:3)

Job innocently lost his family and properties in the gamble between God and Satan. He suffered painful sores all over his body. He earnestly hoped that he could face God sometime so as to allow him to pour out his complains. However, he did not have his wish.

All the prophets in the Old Testament and all the great priests in the inner part of the holy temple had not seen how God actually look like.

Lao Zi described the image of God as "following without seeing its back, and approaching without seeing its face."

More than 5,000 years ago, Chinese worshipped the God in heaven and called it "the most High Lord in Heaven". There was no image and neither the Chinese carved any idol.

2. God is spirit.

This Creator God is spirit, which transcends the world of nature. As God has no image, man can only communicate with God in spirit and in heart. Confucius said that man must "fast" their hearts in order to obtain the words of God.

Jeremiah just sat quietly in the council of the Lord to wait for the revelation of God. That was the communication of spirits. It did not actually involved physical actions

第十五章

什么是神的儿子？

让我们先认识神，然后才讲祂的儿子。基督教相信上帝造物的一神教。

1. 神没有外在的形象

凡有形象的都是造出来的。《创世纪》说，上帝依照祂的形象造了人（1：26）。认为人类始祖亚当从来没见过上帝，尽管他跟着上帝进了伊甸园，听到了祂的呼唤，但是，他从来没有说过上帝长得和他一样。

雅各布梦见和摔跤，猜想是精神的格斗，而不是肉体的较力。他问那个人叫什么，那个人回答："何必问我的名字？"（32：29）夜里做梦这个故事描述了肉体格斗，但是，这证明不了上帝是有肉体的，有形象的。

摩西上了西乃山，听到燃烧不灭的荆棘中传出来声音，却看不见上帝。摩西是上帝选择的第一个先知，与上帝同行了一辈子，他们经常说话，但摩西从来没有见到过上帝（《出埃及记》3：3）。

约伯在上帝和撒旦赌输赢的时候家破人离，够冤枉的了。他浑身伤痛，渴望能够见上帝一面，好让他诉诉苦，但是，这个冤枉做不到。

《旧约》里的一切先知们以及至圣所里的大祭司们从来没有见到过上帝究竟长什么样子。

老子所描绘的上帝的形象是："随而不见其后，迎而不见其首"。

5000多年以前，中国人崇拜上帝，称之为"昊天上帝"。上帝没有影像，中国人也没有雕刻任何偶像。

2. 上帝是灵

造物的上帝是灵，超越了自然界。由于上帝是无形的，人类只能用心灵和上帝沟通。孔子说，人要用"心斋"才能得道。

杰里迈亚先知静静地坐在会堂里，等候上帝的启示。这是灵与灵的沟通，并不一定非要肉体接触。

Body is the temporary residence of the spirit. The bodies of all creatures can be destroyed. All animals and plants grow and die in their life cycle. Spirit has no image or sex.

Jeremiah described bodies of men as pots made out of clay. Apostle Paul in his profession described the bodies of men as tents.

3. God has no name.

God, the Creator, has no name. All creatures have names. It is the Creator, who names his creation. Only the name of God is eternal.

The Book of Genesis mentioned about Enoch, who walked with God for 300 years. (5:22) With such long relationship, Enoch did not know what the name of God was.

Abram obeyed the words of God and for his faith, he was righteous. (15:6). He addressed God as "the Lord, God most High, creator of heaven and earth." (14:22). When he was 99 year old, "God appeared to him", saying he was the Almighty God. (17:1). The Bible does not mention in what image or form God appeared to Abraham. Neither did God tell his name. Yet God changed the name of Abram to Abraham.

Since the beginning of the Jewish history, God has no name, because he was not being created. All the idols created by man have names. So are the saints who are venerated and given their titles. All these are not universal and eternal.

Because God is spirit, he has neither images no name. Spiritual realm is beyond the world of nature and is imaginative. Lao Zi said that "look and it can not be seen, listen and it can not be heard, and catch and it can not be held." Corinthians 4:18 says that those can be seen are temporary and those that can not be seen are eternal.

The Word of God is likewise imaginative. Not the slightest thing of it that man can catch or hold it in their both hands and show to others. That is the reason why men feel both God and his Word are far away and imaginative to cause them immediate concern. Besides, their demands are difficult to fulfill. Even for worldly authorities, when they are too far away, it becomes ineffective, as the saying on the occasion goes: "the mountains are too high and the emperor is far away". As such, men push the demands of God aside and follow the worldly trend, worshipping the idols such as wealth, authority and reputation etc.

肉体是灵魂的临时居所，一切生物的肉体都会毁灭，一切动植物在生命循环中生长和消亡。灵没有形象，没有性别。

雅利米亚认为，人体是泥土制的罐子，保罗用他的行话说，人体是帐篷。

3. 神没有名字。

造物的上帝没有名字。万物都有名字，是造物主命名的。只是造物主的名字是永存的。

《创世纪》说，以诺和上帝同行300年（5：22），这么久的关系，以诺却不知道上帝叫什么。

亚伯兰遵从上帝的教导，因为守信，被称为义人（15：6）。他把上帝叫做"主，至高至圣的主，创造天地的主"。他99岁的时候，上帝向他显圣，自称是"全能的上帝"（17：1）。虽然圣经说"上帝向他显圣"，但是没有一字描述上帝的形象，上帝也没有说出自己的名字。后来，上帝把亚伯兰改名为亚伯拉罕。

犹太有史以来，上帝没有名字，因为祂不是被创造的。人所造出的偶像都有名字。被供起来的圣人也有尊称，但是，他们不是普世，不是永恒的。

上帝是灵，所以，没有形象，没有名字。灵界是超越大自然的，是很抽象的。老子说："视之而弗见，听之而弗闻，揩之而弗得"。《哥林多后书》说："所见的是暂时的，所不见的是永恒的"（4：18）。

上帝的道也同样地抽象。没有丝毫可以让世人抓到或捧着展示给别人。因此，世人感觉到上帝及其道是遥远的，抽象的，是不可及的。他们的要求是难以满足的。对于世上的权力机构来说，遥不可及的就是无效的。正如俗语所说的那样：山高皇帝远。结果，索性把上帝扔一边去，人云亦云，去崇拜名利等偶像去了。

Lao Zi said, "Word that can be discussed is not the eternal Word, and Name that can be named is not the eternal Name".

4. The Word is the tool of creation.

With his word God created heaven and earth. Both the Old and New Testaments recorded thus. The word "bereshidth", in Hebrew, means "through his first fruit". So, God created heaven and earth with his words, or through his first fruit, or by his first product.

God's word is surely his own word that was with him in the beginning. Because God's word came out of his mouth is his product. The prelude in the Gospel of John introduced that all things were made through his word and without his word nothing was made that has been made. Lao Zi said that this word seemed to be the beginning of all things and existed in all things.

This Word is the first fruit produced by God. It is spiritual, having the same essence as God, "HOMOOUSIOS". The early church used this term to explain about the Trinity God. The Latin Church used "Una Substantia" to describe "One person".

The word of a person is often used to represent the person. "My word is my honour" as a saying goes. The same goes with a Chinese saying, "once the words come out of a gentleman, speeding horses can't catch up with it". An honourable man speaks what he means. His word is his promise, which reprents him. Simply, his word is him.

Philo of Alexandria, Egypt (born c. 10–15 BCE) was a Jewish philosopher, well-educated in Greek. He was the first to analyse the understandable part of God's existence and the mysterious characteristics of God. He reckoned that God planted his love in the hearts of men and wanted them to reflect that love in order to express the nature of God.

During his time, Christian doctrine and theology were underdevelopment. Philo led the recognition of "LOGOS" as the mediator between men and God, and as the "first born of God" or the alternate god, or even the "second god". Theologians took a step further and called that "the word incarnated in Christ".

Incidententedly, Philo's explanation coincided with the Chinese thought on Dao, or, the Word. In 600 C.E. the first Tang Emperor Li Yan concluded that "men become saints after attaining the Word (Logos), and the saints are buddhas, or gods". In other words, when men obtained the Word, they became saints, who were full of the loving characters of God.

Apostle Paul said in 2 Corinthians 5:17 that "whoever is in Christ, he is a new man."

老子说:"道,可道也,非恒道也。名,可名也,非恒名也。"

4. 道是造物的工具

上帝用道创造了天地,圣经《新约》和《旧约》都是这样记载。希伯来文BERESHIDTH的意思是"借着祂第一颗果实"。《创世纪》第一章第一节也可以翻译成"上帝用自己的话,用自己的第一颗果实,第一个产品,创造了天地"。

上帝的话就是祂自己的话,当然与祂同在。上帝的"话"出自上帝之口,是上帝的作品。《约翰福音》前序说,"万物都是用上帝的道造出来的,凡被造出来的,没有一样不是用道造的"。老子说,道"似万物之宗",存在于万物之中。

道是上帝的"第一颗果实",是属灵的,与上帝同质(HOMOOUSIOS)。早期的教会使用这个术语来解释三位一体。拉丁教会使用拉丁文UNA SUBSTANTIA来描述"一体"。

一个人说的"话"常常代表说话的人。有一句谚语说:"我的话就是我的名誉"。中国人也有句谚语:"大丈夫一言既出,驷马难追"。讲究的人说了就做。他的话就是他的诺言,代表着他。简单说,他的话就是他。

埃及亚历山大费罗(生於公元前10-15年)是受过希腊教育的犹太人哲学家。他头一个认为,神的存在和神的神秘性是可以理解的。他认为,神先把祂的慈爱放在人的心里,使他们对那种爱作出反应,从而传达上帝的本质。

当时,基督教教义和神学还没发展起来,费罗首先认为"道"(LOGOS)是神与人之间的介体,是神的长子,是神的替身,甚至是第二位神。神学家们进一步把它称之为"化身于基督的道"。无独有偶,费罗的说明也符合中国的道教思想。唐高祖李渊(公元618即位)说:"人得道成圣,成圣为佛"。换句话说,人得道成圣,因为圣人充满了上帝的慈爱。

《哥林多后书》(5:17)说,"走进基督,他就脱胎换骨了"。

What is the son of God?

5. The meaning of Christus.

The word Christus in Greek means "the anointed one", a title conferred on kings, high priests and prophets, according to Jewish tradition. Before the distinction of the tribe of Israelites, such tradition had already existed in the Middle East. The ointment was used as medition and cosmetic, representing power and glory. At the close of the Old Testament era, the Jewish tribe was yearning for a Messiah to release them from the external conquering rulers.

The New Dictionary of Christian Theology expresses different theory and explanation on Jesus of Nazareth and the faith in Christ. The original Christian faith was very simple, just as Jesus said that believers must "love God with all their hearts, with all their souls and with all their minds", and "love others as themselves". All the laws of Moses and the teachings of the prophets are hung on these two commandments.

Similarly, as a comparison here, Lao Zi advised the world to "respect the Word (Dao) and value integrity", which is in unison with the two commandments mentioned above.

The Gospel of John introduced that "this Word was with God in the beginning and this Word is God". Then, he described philosophically that this "Word became flesh and lived among men". As God is spirit and is unseen, it is only through the expression in words and actions that we can see the grace and truth of God. It is only through this "word in action" that it is called "the one and only begotten son". The author of the Epistle to the Hebrew described this "word in action" in the creation of the world as the "first born". The mission of Jesus of Nazareth was to preach repentance of sins and to call people to obey the commandments of God. This is the work of a "Messiah" that the Jewish nation had been waiting for. For this Jesus is called Christ.

6. Son of God.

There are many references in the Bible where Pais in Greek means Son or Servant.

The Jews claim to be the chosen people of God and address God as their Heavenly Father. Though they reckon that they are God's children, they regard God as extremely holy and they simply address God as Lord or Yahweh and they don't even pronounce it. When they copied the scriptures in those old days and when they came to the word Lord, they had to wash their hands before they could proceed copying the word "Lord". As such they were very far away from God. Jesus taught his disciples in their prayer to address God as "Father", which brought them close to God and made them feel the intimacy and love of God.

Psalm 2:5–7

2 Samuel 7:4–14

Exodus 4:22

Psalm 89:20, 26–27

5. 基督的含义

基督（CHRISTUS）这个词是希腊语，意思是"受膏者"。根据犹太的习惯，受膏只有国君、祭司和先知。以色列这个部落还不存在的时候，中东就已经有了这个传统。油膏用于医药和化妆品，代表力量和荣耀。《旧约》末期，犹太部落渴望出个"救星"，把他们从外侵者的手中解放出来。

《基督教神学新词典》认为，新约所记载的耶稣和基督信仰的理论和见解不同。原来的基督教信仰是非常简单的，正如耶稣所说，信徒"要尽心、尽性、尽意"，要"爱人如己"。摩西的所有律令和先知的教诲都体现在这两个诫命当中。

比较而言，老子也劝世人"尊道而贵德"，和这两条诫命是相吻合的。

《约翰福音》认为，"道开始与上帝同在，道就是上帝"。从生理上讲，"道变成肉身，生活在人中间"。上帝是灵，是不可见的，只有通过言行，才能认识上帝的惠真。只有通过"行言"，才称之为"唯一而独生的儿子"。《使徒书》的作者向希伯来人描写了这个"行言"，称之为创世时的"长子"。耶稣的使命是劝人们悔罪，服从上帝的诫命。这个"救星"的使命是犹太国一直在寻觅着的。为此，耶稣被称作基督。

6. 上帝之子

《圣经》里有许多引文，希腊语里的Pais意思就是儿子或仆人。

犹太人自称是上帝的选民，称上帝为天父。他们虽然认为是上帝的儿子，可是他们认为，上帝是异神，把祂叫做"主"、"耶和华"，甚至这个称呼也不是随便说的。过去，他们抄写《圣经》的时候，如果抄到"主"字，必须先洗净手，然后才写这个"主"字，尽管他们离上帝甚远。耶稣教门徒祈祷的时候，把上帝叫做"父亲"，使他们贴近了上帝，感受到了上帝的亲密和慈爱。

What is the son of God?

The Word of God was with God in the beginning and was God. So, the Word is Christ, which is full of grace and truth and which made the love of God known.

Historically, Christian faith is like the shifting sand, with endless development. It is because the Church has shifted away from the 1st Century Christianity and has drifted according to the Way of Man instead of the Way of Heaven. Let us, systematically, analyse the Word of God.

First of all, the Word was with God in the beginning before anything that has been created. Then, with his Word, God created the universe. This Word was the first born of God.

Then, God made a Covenant with his people. But the Covenant demands were not faithfully kept. So, God gave Moses the Ten Commandments. Besides, God through his prophets in many times and many ways instructed our ancestors. And in the end time, God spoke to us through his Son, the Logos, or Word incarnated in Jesus Christ. This Word was the Christ of faith of the 1st Century Christianity.

"Faith is what we hope for and certain of what we do not see" (Hebrew 11:1). Someone once said that if we can read the whole Bible in one single breath, he will sum it up in the Two Great Commandments. Then, where do we place Jesus in our faith? As Evangelist John put it that Jesus was "Word became flesh". The importance in our faith is the "Word" rather than the "flesh". It is mentioned above that the Word is the "tool" of God in creation, or the "instructions" of God he gave to our ancestors through the prophets, or the "laws" of Moses. (Hebrew 1:1)

Again, the Word is the "words and deeds" of Jesus in his mission according to God's plan for the salvation of the mankind. According to the Jewish explanation, Jesus was the postsman who delivered the message of the Heavenly Father to mankind.

In Old Testament, God was the Saviour. God called Moses to act on his behalf to save his people. The story of Exodus described how difficult Moses had sacrificed himself in order to bring the people of Israel out of Egypt physically. He acted under the instruction of God. Moses not only brought Israelites out of Egypt physically, but also gave them the Creator God and the Ten Commandments for their spirituality. Moses was not accredited the honour of a "saviour". He was a prophet and a servant of God. In the Old Testament, there are 27 times God reminded his people that he was their only Lord God and their Saviour.

In New Testament, God is still the Saviour. Jesus of Nazareth was given the mission to save people of the world from sin. The words and deeds of Jesus had fully expressed the Truth and Grace of God, that John the Evangelist described Jesus philosophically as "Word became flesh."

什么是神的儿子？

太初，上帝的道与上帝同在。道是上帝，是基督，充满了惠真，把上帝的爱彰显出来。从历史的角度讲，基督教的信仰好像过沙子，不停地动。

教会一世纪就离基督教而去了，原因是"人之道"，而非"天之道"。下面详细地说说上帝之道。

首先，太初还没有创造之前，道就与上帝同在。有了道，上帝创造的宇宙。这道便是上帝的长子。

后来，上帝和他的子民立了个约定，所立的约没有被信守。所以，上帝给摩西十诫。上帝也通过众先知屡次多方"晓谕"列祖（1：1）。末世的时候，上帝过祂的"儿子"，耶稣基督化身的道来晓谕我们（1：2）。道就是一世纪基督教的信仰基督。

"信仰是我们所希望的，却是我们肯定看不见的"（11：1）。有人说过，如果一口气把全本《圣经》读完，就可以在两大诫命中总结出信仰。那么，我们信仰中的耶稣在哪里呢？福音传道者约翰认为，耶稣是"道的肉身"。我们的信仰主要是道，而不是肉身。上面说过，道是上帝创造世界的工具，道是上帝通过先知、摩西的律令来晓谕列祖的。

而且，道是耶稣执行上帝拯救人类的使命时的"言行"。根据犹太的说法，耶稣是个信使，把天父的信息传给了人类。

在《旧约》中，上帝是救世主。上帝叫摩西代表他去拯救黎民。《出埃及》记述了摩西牺牲自己、带领以色列人出埃及的故事。他按照上帝的旨意行事。摩西不仅把以色列人领出了埃及，而且从精神上带给了他们造物主和十诫。摩西并没有因此被称为救世主，他只是个先知或神的使者。《旧约》上帝27次提醒黎民，他是独一的主，他们的救星。

《新约》里，上帝仍然是救星。耶稣肩负的使命是拯救世人于罪恶。耶稣的言行充分地传达了上帝的惠真，福音传道者约翰从哲学上认为，耶稣是道的化身。

Christians believe that all mankind is the son of God. From the genealogy, Jesus was a son of Joseph, according to Jewish custom, and it can be traced back to their forefather Adam. The Gospel according to Luke 3:37 states that Adam is the son of God. So, Jesus is the son of God and likewise we are also sons of God through faith.

基督教徒相信，所有的人类都是上帝之子。从谱系来看，耶稣（跟据犹太人的风俗）是约瑟的儿子，是始祖亚当的后裔。路加福音3：37认为，亚当是上帝的儿子。这样，耶稣是上帝的儿子，通过信仰，我们也是上帝的儿子。

CHAPTER SIXTEEN
Christians before Christ

Christians are those who follow the teaching of Christ, the Word. They were first called in Antioch before the martyrdom of Paul c. A.D. 67.

"Then, Barnabas went to Tarsus look for Saul, and when he found him, he brought him to Antioch. So for a whole year Barnabas and Saul met with the church and taught great numbers of people. The disciples were called Christians first at Antioch". (Acts 11:25–26)

As a new religion, Christianity did not have the book called "The Holy Bible" as yet, and the doctrines were drifting around the travelling preachers. Gnosticism forced the issue about the Truth and the overall purposes of God. Justin Martyr (c. 100–165 A.D.) was among the group of apologists, who were mostly philosophers and were well versed with the Greek inquiry into mythology, cosmology, philosophy and pagan religions at those days. Justin considered Christianity as the True Philosophy and began to propagate his new religious philosophy. He was denounced as subversive and condemned to death.

Append below here is a page, showing the definition of Christians by Justin Martyr:

"But lest some should, without reason, and for the perversion of what we teach, maintain that we say that Christ was born one hundred and fifty years ago under Quirinius, and taught what we say. He taught subsequently in the time of Pontius Pilate; and should urge against us as though all men who were born before Him were irresponsible, let us anticipate and solve the difficulty. We have been taught that Christ is the first-born of God, and we have declared above that He is the Word of whom every race of men were partakers; and those who lived with reason are Christians, even though they were thought atheists; as, among the Greeks, Socrates and Heraclitus, and men like them; and among the barbarians, Abraham, and Ananias, and Azarias, and Misael, and Elisa, and many others whose actions and names we decline for the present to recount, because we know it would be tedious.

Eusebius, the Church historian, held the view that "teaching of Christianity was neither new nor strange. What was new was the Church, the race of Christians. Their corporate existence, their general piety, and their increasing influence were indeed new, but their teaching was not. It had been followed centuries before them by Abraham and Moses and the later prophets; and the religion of the patriarchs was identical with that of the Christians.

第十六章

基督以前的基督徒

保罗受难之前（公元67年），安提阿的基督信众们头一次被称为基督徒。"巴纳巴斯到了塔苏斯去接扫罗。找到索尔的时候，把他领到安提阿。巴纳巴斯和索尔在教堂整整一年，教了一大批人。信徒们被称为基督徒，最初是在安提阿"（使徒行传11:25-26）。

作为新的宗教，基督教还没有《圣经》这部书，他们的教义由云游的传教士到处传播。诺士替教强行灌输上帝的真谛和全部旨意。贾斯廷玛达尔（公元100-165 C.E.）就在宣讲者之列———他们多数人是研究哲学的，用谙熟的希腊知识对当时的神话、宇宙、哲学和异教提出了疑问。贾斯廷认为，基督教是真正的哲学，从此开始传播他的新宗教哲学。后来，他落了个颠覆罪名，被处死。

以下是贾斯廷玛达尔所界定的基督徒：

歪曲我们所传的教是没有道理的，恐怕有些人会想，我们说基督150年前诞生于球里纽斯，把我们所说的话教给我们。后来，他在邦球斯皮拉特的时候继续传教，要我们注意：所有的人在上帝之前出生，这么说是不负责任的———让我们怀着期望去解决这个难题吧。我们所知道的是：基督是上帝的长子，我们曾经声明，他是一切种族都包括在内的"道"；有理智的人都是基督徒，甚至是无神论者，也是基督徒。希腊有苏格拉底、赫拉克利特之流；野蛮人中有亚伯拉罕、亚拿尼亚、亚撒利雅、米沙利和伊莱贾士以及许多其他人，他们的名字和行为过于繁琐，在此不便一一列举。

由斯米乌士是研究教会历史的，他认为，基督教所传播的没什么新异的。新的是基督徒一族、基督教会。他们在一起生存，普遍地虔诚，逐渐扩大影响，这的确是没有过的，然而，他们所教的却不是新的。他们的教义几个世纪之前就已经有人从埃布尔接罕、摩西和晚期的先知们那里学了。他们祖先的宗教信仰和基督教是相同的。

All history was a contest between God, acting through Patriarchs, Prophets, and the Church on the one hand, and the Devil, instigating Jews, Persecutors, and Heretics, on the other. It is a contest in which the Devil always gets the worst of it in the long run, but the righteous suffer considerably in the process." (Lake, Eusebius, Ecclesiastical History (Locb Library), I, pp. Xv-xvi.)

Belief in the teaching of Jesus Christ is the duty of Christians, but it is a complete different matter in worshipping Jesus.

If Christians worship Jesus Christ as an intermediate god, Christianity is no different from any other religion. When Christians believe in the teaching of Jesus Christ, they worship the One creator God. The laws came from Moses, but mercy and truth came from Jesus. Jesus has been honoured as Christ because he carried out the mission of preaching the Word of God.

God is the Creator and is the God of all tribes and peoples. There is no other god like him. He is the almighty. It is the duty of Christians to follow the commandments of God, which is Christ.

All the scholars before Qin Dynasty were prophets. As the Book of Hebrew 1:1 states that God in many ways and at many times through the prophets instructed our forefathers. The Word is from the mouth of God and is the Word of God, the Logos or Dao. It is also the Word that created the world. Being the first word, it is also termed as the "first son" .(Hebrew 1:6)

Most Protestant Christians today follow the teaching of the "Church", without realizing that "Church" means the Roman Catholic Church. The Reformation of the "Church" by Martin Luther was able to remove some of the wrongs carried out by the "Church", then, without challenging the pagan religious believes, festivals and practices that had been dovetailed in. It was indeed an impossible task for Martin Luther to do it single-handedly, while the State and the Church had been enforcing their ultimate motives for centuries.

Some Christians still wonder how could there be Christians before Christ. It is simply that they do not know the overall purposes of God in human history and the meaning of Christ, the Word. Did not Jesus say that those who hear the word of God and put it in practice are his brothers, sisters and mother. The emphasis is on the "doing" of the Two Great Commandments.

In the similar vein, those philosophers and great teachers in China like Lao Zi, Kong Zi, Zhuang Zi, Meng Zi and Mo Zi and others were Christians before Christ. This applies to people all over the world disregarding race or nationality.

所有的历史都是一种纷争,这种纷争一方面是上帝与主教、先知和教会,另一方面是魔鬼、蛊惑的犹太人、迫害者和持异端者。从长远的角度看,这种魔鬼在这种纷争中总要处于下风的,然而,正义在这个过程中付出沉重的代价"(雷克、由斯米乌士《基督教史》,落克博图书馆馆藏,卷一,15-15.1)。

从信仰上来看,耶稣基督所传的是基督徒们的职责,但是,崇拜耶稣就完全不同了。

如果基督徒把耶稣当成媒介神来崇拜,那么,基督教与其他宗教就没有分别了。当基督徒相信耶稣所传的教的时候,他们崇拜唯一的创造神。律法出自摩西,惠真出自耶稣。耶稣被尊为基督,因为他的使命是传了上帝的道。

上帝是创造者,是万族万民的神,没有别神能与他相比,他是全能的。做个基督徒要遵从道的训谕,就是基督的训谕。

前秦诸子都是先知。希伯来书第一章第一节认为,上帝多次、多方地通过先知晓谕我们的祖先。这"晓谕"就是从上帝的口中说出的,是上帝的道,也是创世的道。作为第一个词汇,"道"也称作上帝的长子(希伯来书第一章第六节)。

如今,多数信教基督徒信奉教会所传的教,却没有意识到,这个教会是罗马天主教。马丁路德改革教会,只能除去教会的一些错误做法,却无法挑战异教根深蒂固的信仰、时庆习俗。马丁路德单枪匹马是不可能成事的,政府和教会强制推行极端政策已经数百年了。

有些基督徒还没弄明白,基督以前怎么会有基督徒呢?这是由于他们不懂上帝在人类历史和基督的意义也就是道方面的总体目的。耶稣不是说了吗:凡是听上帝的话,按上帝的话做的人,都是他的兄弟姐妹和母亲。"重点落在两大诫命的"做"上、即是行道者。

同样,中国的哲人和大师们老子、孔子、庄子、孟子和墨子等都是基督产生之前的基督徒。无论什么种族,什么国籍,道理都是一样的。

CHAPTER SEVENTEEN
Dao exists among the Heavens, the earth and People.

Chinese Philosophers argued that the heavens, earth and men exist in a unity, which implies that people should live harmonously within the enclosure of the heavens and the earth, as Dao exists in all of them. There are four elements in this statement.

Dao, "The Word" —was viewed as the means of creation.

Where did the universe and all creatures inhabiting it come from? This was one of the questions asked by the Daoists. Lao Zi argued that the Dao was in existence "before the creation of the heavens and the earth". It was "the source of all creation" and was present in all creation. Zhuang Zi explained that the Dao "created the heavens and the earth", but Dao had "its originality and its own root," and "was there in the beginning," "existing from the most ancient of times" It was through the Dao that everything was created. It was present in all creation. However, the Dao was not the creator God, but the means used by the creator God, a Way of God.

The heavens and the earth constituting the creation.

It is obvious that the heavens and the earth exist in an orderly system, a Way. They seem to be meticulously designed, and follow certain laws. Furthermore, as the heavens and the earth conform to the teaching of the Dao, "they do not exist for themselves, and that is why they can exist forever". The purpose of the heavens, besides regulating day and night, is to provide sunshine and rain, which give warmth, or energy, and water for the nourishment and growth of all creatures. And the earth, with the help of sunshine and rain, provides nutriment to vegetation of all kinds. This vegetation grows ceaselessly. In turn, it provides habitats and food for all creatures. The heavens and the earth never keep anything back for themselves. They perform their functions with generous diligence. They don't exist for themselves.

People and other creatures:

In the mythic celebration of creation, in the Judaic–Christian tradition, God is said to have created people in his image, after having first created other creatures that live in the air, earth, and water. The man was given a companion, and the pair was placed in the Garden of Eden, a paradise, to enjoy the beauties of creation. The only obligation placed on them was to obey the Way of God. Unfortunately they failed. As a result, they acquired the knowledge of good and evil. In a sense, this was inevitable, an inevitability the Yahist account of creation seeks to elucidate.

第十七章

道于天地人

中国哲学家认为，天地人之间应和睦相处，就是说，正如道存在于天地人之间一样，人在天地之间应该和谐生存。这里有四大要素：

1. 道是创造的工具。

宇宙万物从何而来？这是道家的发问之一。老子认为，道是"先天地生"。"道，似万物之宗也"，存在于万物之中。庄子认为，道乃"生天生地"，是"自本自根"、"未有天地"之前就有的，是"自古以固存"的。万物从道而成，存在于万物之中。但是，道不是上帝这个创造者，而是这个创造者所使用的方式，即"天道"。

2. 天地创造说。

天地显然存在于有序的系统，即道。道，其序严谨，循法而动。天地守道，则"天地之能长且久者，以其自生也"。天，掌管昼夜，施以雨露阳光，供应万物滋生的温暖、热量和水源。有了阳光和雨水，地便可以养育万种植被。植被便可不断生产，而且为所有生命提供栖居和饮食条件。天地从不留物自用，而是守道成勤。故，天地不自生。

3. 人与其它创造物

在犹太-基督教传统中，造物是神秘的祝福。据说，上帝在创造空中、地上和水里的生物以后，依照自己的形象造了人。上帝给人陪了个伴儿，住在伊甸乐园，享受造物之美。他们唯有遵从上帝的道是从。然而，他们没有做到，他们得到的是知道了善恶。某程度上说，这是免不了的，也就是说，耶和华所讲的造物存在着某种不可规避性。

Humans alone are created with the wisdom to know good and evil, and with the faculty of free will, which enable them to take charge of their lives. Lao Zi argued that humans should learn from the example of selflessness set by the heavens and the earth, and thus follow the Way of Heaven.

Dong Zhong Shu (.179 – 104 B.C.E.) argued that men are of the "same substance and structure" as the heavens and the earth. "Heaven helps vegetation grow in spring and ripen in autumn", and thus "men plant in spring and reap in autumn". Dong Zhong Shu, consistent with ancient Chinese tradition, had a fondness for analogy. He argued that, just as "there are 365 days plus in a year", "a man has 366 small joints of bones" in the body. Just as there are "four seasons" in a year, people have "four limbs". Just as there are "three months in a season" there are "three parts in a limb". Furthermore, "twelve months in a year represent the twelve big joints that keep the body erect". Rivers and valleys resemble vessels, veins and cavities in a body. If Dong's way of arguing and the analogies on which it is premised, are accepted, people should behave as the heavens and the earth do, and thus follow the Way of Heaven.

"Men live between heaven and earth", benefitting from both. We are the only animal that has sufficient intelligence to exercise dominion over other animals. This ability can be, and has been abused. The misuse of this capacity to dominate has contributed to many of the ills we face – wars, pollution, global warming, HIV, mad-cow disease, HIN1, etc. It is, therefore, of the utmost importance that we behave selflessly, like the heavens and the earth, and that we live economically – "little private possession and scarce selfish desire". We need to live with ecological responsibility. Unfortunately, there appears to be an unbridgeable gap between the "Way of Heaven and the Way of Men". Lao Zi argued that people are created by the "Word" of God (道生之 Dao sheng zhi), and need be "nurtured by integrity".

People's behaviour is the outcome of "their philosophy of life". This philosophy helps calibrate the maturity of their spirituality, that is, their in-touchness with the Dao and their capacity to live selflessly.

4. 人类一旦创造出来，便有了认知善恶的智慧；一旦掌握了自由意志，便有了操纵生活的能力。老子认为，人类应以天地无私为榜样，遵守天道。董仲舒则认为，天地"同质同构"，"天有春生秋衰而人有春种秋收"。董仲氏恪守中国古来传统，善于比类。他说，"天有三百六十五多些日，人有三百六十六小骨节。一年有四季，人有四肢。每季三月，每肢三节"。又，"十二月合于十二节相持而形体"，河流深谷如同静脉穴道。董仲舒的比类观一经认可，人类便应习天地，从天道。

人生天地间，天地人各利。人，只有人这种动物，才具有驾驭其它动物的聪明才智。这种驾驭才智如果妄用，出现的则是我们所见到的战争、全球暖化、艾滋病、疯牛病、猪流感等。所以，至关重要的是，我们活得应该像天地一般坦荡，活得应该寡欲无私。我们活着，应该具有生态意识。然而，天道和人道的鸿沟是无法逾越的。老子认为，人，"道生之"也，应以"德畜之"。

人的行为是取决于人生观，人生哲学可调节灵性的成熟度，换句话说，可调节近道的程度和无私生活的能力。

Dao exists among the Heavens, the earth and People.

Cao Cao (c. 190–260 C.E.) was one of the three leaders in the Period of Three Kingdoms Dynastries. He was ambitious and known for his craftiness and ingratitude. He fought hard and finally defeated the other two kingdoms. But, by this stage, he was very old and bitter about life. He was also remorseful, and wrote the following poem.

"Let us drink wine in place of singing songs (of joy), (Recollecting on the events) in the duration of a man's life, like the morning dew, , (Leaving nothing but) much bitterness over the past." .

Cao Cao died before the country was united. The effort expended by Cao Cao to secure the throne ended up benefiting his prime minister, Si Ma Yi. The experience of Cao Cao illustrates the fact that when people do not model themselves on the fruitful inter-relationship of the heavens and the earth all their efforts are futile. Demonstratively, they have not attained the Dao, the teaching of the Word of God. If Cao Cao had put "The Word" into practice he might have enjoyed a happier life in a united, peaceful kingdom. He would have been remembered as a more reputable and respectable character in Chinese history.

Some philosophers treated life as a passing phase, a dream, something that would pass away, like grass and flowers. The prophet Isaiah (40:6–7) said that all men were like grass, and their glory like flowers. Both wither and die. Life is temporary, a passing phase in the cycle of creation. Knowing that it is temporary, we should live selflessly and contribute to the wellbeing of others. Others have been stimulated by this insight into the transitoriness of life to suck the last ounce of pleasure from life, solely for their own benefit. Others, again, conduct themselves in a way that suggests that they expect to be served, even pampered. Some prefer to be served, even though they are young and strong. Lao Zi argued that if people are in their "prime of life" and yet demand others wait on them "as if they are old, they are acting against the teaching of the Dao, 'The Word, 'and shall soon perish" .

There are three stages of life according to Lao Zi, the early stage of infancy and youth, the adult stage, and old age. In the early stage of life other people nurse you, educate and serve you. The wheel turns full circle, and in old age people again serve and take care of you till death. During the middle, or adult stage, when you are strong, healthy and able, you should contribute your very best to society, taking your cue from the selflessness of the heavens and the earth. You should be prepared to "serve the world with love, like a hired servant", and should not ask what the world can do for you. This attitude promotes unity among the heavens, the earth, and people. This is in accord with the teaching of "The Word" and the Way of God.

曹操（公元190-260）是汉晋三国时期的三巨头之一。他奸诈，不义，野心勃勃。他艰苦卓绝，击败两国。到头来，苦乐人生，老迈不堪，悔故成诗：

对酒当歌，

人生几何，

譬如朝露，

去日苦多。

曹操国破身死，身前汲汲御位，身后拱手让于相爷司马懿。这说明，如果不效法天地间互动的成果，一生努力付之东流。这种现身说法讲的是，他们没有获得上帝的"道"。假如曹操能遵"道"而行，他可以平天下而后乐，也可以在中国历史上以受人崇敬的名人形象存留在人们的记忆里。

有些哲学家认为，生命不过是个过程，是一场梦，是花草易逝的什物。先知以赛亚说，人的生命如草，他的荣美如花，花草终凋残。人的生命是短暂的，是造物轮回中的一段经历。明白一切都是短暂的，我们才应该活得无私，造福于人。只有深深认识到这一点，短暂的生活方可完全独自亨有每刻的快乐。然而，有的人所作所为也在养尊处优，有的人年富力强，却让人养着。老子说，"物壮既老，谓之不道，不道早已"。

老子认为，人生有三个阶段：早期为青少年、壮年和老年。人生之始，你是保育、教育和服侍的对象。生命走到尽头的时候，你被侍候到死。中年或壮年的时候，身体硬朗，应该竭力奉献社会，用无私的爱来奉献社会。"爱以身为天下牧"，而不应该牧天下于己身。这样，天地人才能和睦，这也就是"道"的训谕、就是天之道。

Dao exists among the Heavens, the earth and People.

John F. Kennedy, (192? –1963) former President of United States of America, made a famous speech, in which he suggested to his people that they should not ask what the country can do for them, but what they can do for the country. This is the philosophy of a meaningful life, a life that benefits society. It is the Way of Heaven.

Zhuang Zi, though poor, did not yearn for wealth, fame, or power. He regarded death as inevitable, "returning" men to their origin in "extreme emptiness". He considered that funeral rituals are superfluous and wasteful. Even burial was wasteful! His attitude was not based on a pessimistic view of life. On the contrary, it arose from his awareness of the value and meaning of life.

Before his death, he questioned his students about why they were preparing an elaborate burial for him. They replied that they worried about the vultures, which might eat up his body if he was not properly buried. Zhuang criticized his students for being biased against the vultures. He argued that there was no difference between his body being eaten by vultures from the air or being munched by worms in the ground. However, because of Zhuang Zi's attitude of life – care-free and without any inclination towards luxury – people regarded Dao Philosophy as pessimistic.

The sense of the transitoriness of life, reflected in Zhuang Zi's outlook, was captured by Shakesphere in Macbeth, where he commented:

"Life is like a walking shadow, a poor player upon the stage, who frets and struts, full of sound and fury, signifying nothing."

How do Christians view life?

It was obvious from his behaviour that Jesus of Nazareth felt himself to be on a mission. Jesus preached for only three years, his messages spreaded over all the land from Galilee to Jerusalem. His mission was to reconcile people to God and to each other.

The Apostle Paul argued that his purpose was to live the Christ–life, and, through this, to glorify God. Paul wrote to the Romans (12), urging them to offer their bodies as living sacrifices, holy and pleasing to God. It was thus that their worship would be expressed. They were not to conform any longer to the pattern of this world, but to be transformed by the renewing of their minds. Through living this way we can help to bring reconciliation between men and God, as well as between individuals and communities and between humanity and the rest of creation. When this happens, it is expressed that "The Word" is in heavens, on earth, and among human beings.

美国前总统肯尼迪发表了一篇著名的演说，他向民众指出：不要问国家能为他们做什么，而应该问，他们能为国家做什么。这就是有意义的人生哲理，是造福社会的人生。这，就是天道。

庄子贫困，但不追逐财富和名利。他认为，死是不可避免的，是"复归于无极"。在他看来，葬礼是多余的浪费，埋了也是浪费。他看待人生的丧葬是悲观的。反过来看，这也是意识到了人生价值和人生意义以后才发出的。

庄子将死，弟子欲厚葬之。庄子曰：何以加此！对曰：恐乌鸢之食夫子也。庄子责之曰："在上为乌鸢食，在下为蝼蚁食，夺彼与此，何其偏也"。然而，人们从庄子放达、贱富的人生观中看到的却是不亦悲夫的道家哲学。

庄子的世界观所反映的人生的短暂性恰恰被沙士比亚在《麦克白》中捕捉了，台词是这样说的：

人生好比走动的影子，

好比台上差劲的演员，

一会儿愁眉不展，一会昂首挺胸，

有的全是怨言和暴怒，

实际上，一切毫无意义。

下面我们看看基督人生吧。

大家知道，拿撒勒的耶稣所作所为，就是出于一种使命感。耶稣传教只有三载，而他的传教之音遍布了加利利到耶路撒冷的每块土地。他的使命就是做个人与神及其彼此之间的协调使者。

使徒保罗在《罗马书》十二章中极力主张，门徒们应该富于献身精神，应该洁身自好，应该博得上帝的好感。保罗就是想过上基督徒式的生活，以此来为上帝争光。正是这样，从他们身上所表现出来的便是膜拜。世界是个什么样子他们不再效法，他们要改造的是他们的思想。只有这样活着，才可以在人神之间、个人和集体之间、人类和其它造物之间达到和谐。果真能够实现和谐，也便出现了天道、地道和人道。

Mother Teresa helped the hopeless. She spent her life in Culcutta in India, nursing the dying poor with dignity. Her purpose was to bring the love of God to people. She was a superlative example of the dictum that the heavens and the earth do not exist for themselves. It was because "The Word" was in Mother Teresa that she lived in harmony with the heavens and the earth.

When people are immersed in the Dao, or Christ, "The Word of God, " they are at one, or in harmony with the whole universe.

修女特丽萨接困济危,她的一生是在印度加尔各答过来的,她给予贫困在死亡线的人们是尊严,她的目的是向人们说,上帝是爱他们的。她以最为完美的实际行动实践了"天地不自生"这一宣言。因为修女特丽萨的心中只有"道",她以和谐的方式活在天地之间。

如果深深地领悟了"道",领悟了基督,领悟了上帝之言,那么,也就出现了天人合一,出现了道于天地人也。

CHAPTER EIGHTEEN
Search for "Truth, Goodness and Perfection.

Dao Philosophy attempts to suggest ways of realizing the ultimate purpose of human nature, the incarnation of the intuitions of the Dao. Were this to happen, the tireless search for truth, integrity and the perfect harmonious society would be at an end. By putting the Dao De into practice by "respecting the Dao (The Lord) and valuing Integrity", we come one step closer to achieving truth, goodness and wholeness.

The word "Dao" has a range of meanings, the most common being "road" or "way". It may be just a simple "way," but this way is not always easy to discern or choose. We may find the Way of Heaven a difficult Way, one to which we have a natural aversion.

The "Dao" can also mean "reason". Reason, as we speak about it in our everyday lives, can lead to true or false conclusions, depending on the accuracy of our reasoning or the validity of our premises. When the Dao is interpreted as "Reason," it represents the embodiment of "Truth" or "Reality."

It is little surprising, therefore, that the third meaning of "Dao" is the "Eternal Word". This Eternal Word is "true reason", that is, the palpable eternal "Truth" that reaches us through a process of revelation. The "zhen" in "zhen shan mei" is equivalent to "zhen li", the "Truth".

The second word "shan" in "zhen shan mei" means "good" or "goodness." It is an adjective used to describe a "kind deed", or a "good person", or "good behaviour".

The combination of "truth" and "good behaviour" produce "superior integrity", or "eternal integrity". If you possess the Truth, a right attitude will grow in you, which in turn will influence the quality of your dealings with others. The "truth" is like a power-house that generates good attitudes. So, if everyone in society, through being open to the Dao, is gifted with the truth, they will love others as themselves, and society will be harmonious and peaceful, a "perfect society". The key to "good integrity" and a "harmonious society" is openness to the truth, which is the fountainhead of the ideal, happy life. This "good" and "true" integrity is derivative. It is a consequence of flowing with the Dao, not of merely seeking to realize certain ideals.

第十八章

寻求真善美

道学试图探索实现人最高目标的方式，也就是道的直觉经验的内化。如果它能成为现实，那么，人们为寻求真理、寻求德行、寻求完美和谐社会的不懈努力也就可以告终了。只有通过"尊道而贵德"来实践道德，我们方可逐步接近真善美。

道有多义，最普通的是道是"道路"，再简单不过的"道"，然而，这个道抉择的时候并非易事。我们也许会觉得，"天道"乃不易之道，人的本性是与其相抵触的。

道也作"道理"讲。我们平常所说的道理真真假假，得出道理的准确度或摆出道理这个前提的有效度，也就决定了道理的真假程度。当把"道"译成"理由"，体现的是"真理"还是"真实"？

也难怪，道的第三个含义是"恒道"。恒道即真理，而这种真理是可感知的，它历经启迪人们的心灵，才被人们掌握。真善美的"真"说的是真理的"真"。

"真善美"的"善"就是"良好"或"良善"，是个形容词，用来描写"善事"或是"善人"，或是"善行"。

真理和善行产生"上德"或是"恒德"。如果你掌握了真理，那么，你就会滋长正向的观念，从而影响你与他人交往的质量。真理犹如发电厂，所产生的观念是良好的。社会的每个成员如果开怀向道，持有真理，则会爱人如爱己，社会也将成为和谐、平安的美好社会。关键在于，只有真理，才向个人的善性与和谐社会开放，成为理想快乐生活的本源。这个"好的"和"真实的"德行是生成的，是随道而行的结果，而绝非是仅仅为了寻求某些理想的实现。

This is why Lao Zi argues that in the absence of Dao – The Word – people try to realize De, integrity, as a consequence of their own efforts, which vitiates its essential qualities by introducing the element of self-orientation. "True, " or "good integrity, " De is the natural outcome of discerning and flowing with the Dao. Therefore, when a society respects "The Word" good integrity is its natural result, and is reflected in a peaceful and harmonious society.

Confucius differs from Dao Philosophy, contending that the Dao is so illusive that it cannot be discerned. On the basis of this understanding, he emphasizes the need to promote "good deeds". Thus, for Confucius, "integrity" is the result of cultivating a "kind heart", the heart being considered the source of our attitudes and actions. Confucius argues that there are "five elements of integrity", namely: "benevolence", "righteousness", "propriety", "wisdom", and "trust-worthiness". [95] These are considered ethical behaviours that can be cultivated on their own right. For this reason, the West regards Confucian teaching as ethical rather than religious.

In spite of the excellence of this system, it is difficult for Confucius to bring about an embodiment of "truth, integrity and a harmonious society" without linking people with the Essence, Spirit, or Energy that sources these qualities, without facilitating their engagement with "The Dao, " "The Truth". Confucius rightly says that integrity comes from the heart, and the heart cannot be directly manipulated, but can be influenced by thoughts, ideas and reason. Thoughts, ideas and reason, however, are not the only, or the most effective determinants of behaviour. Feelings and intuitions also play a part. Intuition, or openness to Reality, or Truth, can be a form of spiritual discernment. This spiritual discernment, or openness to the Dao, to the Spirit, the Word, whatever you like to call it, is a form of faith. Faith is not belief in a set of propositions, or doctrines, by the openness to Reality. Reality discerned within and beyond the phenomenological world. Truth, therefore, is ultimately spiritual. The "spirituality" of truth does not render it intangible, or sheerly mythical, though it is through forms of contemplative experience that it is discerned. There is a facility to truth, a materiality, forms of embodiment. Such spirituality is the foundation of moral life, of good integrity.

Long before both Lao Zi and Confucius, Guan Zi, the greatest regulator and reformer in Chinese history, and the founder of Fa Jia, "System Family", promoted "propriety, " "righteousness, " "honesty, or purity, or transparency" and "shame or disgrace" as the four important pillars supporting a perfect and harmonious society. He argued that, unless it possesses each of these four qualities, a society will be unbalanced.

正因为如此，老子认为，只有废道，人们才会努力实践德行，通过把握自己，使外在的基本质量失去了制约作用。真理也好，善行也罢，认识了道，随道而行了，自然也就有了德。一个社会如果尊"道"，其结果自然是产生好的德行，这从和谐、平安社会中反映出来。

儒学与道法不同，孔子认为，道为虚，识也难。在这种认识观支配下，他强调要修德。对于孔子而言，善行始于修得仁心，仁心乃观念和行为之源。孔子认为"仁"、"义"、"礼"、"智"、"信"这"德行五常"，是可以自己修养的道德行为。为此，西方把儒学看成是伦理的而不是宗教的。

儒学的优点且不说，讲到真理、德行与和谐社会，儒家不能不联系到与此相关的精气神，不能不渗透"道"和"真理"。孔子说得好，德行发于心，心是控制不了的，但是可以受思想、理念和推理影响的。然而，思想、理念和推理并非是行为唯一的或最有影响力的因素。情感和直觉也不可忽视。直觉力也好，道也好，神也好，什么也好，无非是某种形式的信仰。信仰并非是真实的，它无非是一套教条而已。在这个看得见摸得着的世界之内或世界之外，真实是存在。而真理最终表现为精神。真理的精神实质并非含混不清，也不是绝对的神化，它是经过种种思辨才被人们所认识的。真理是可以认识的，它是一种物化状态，体现着各种物化的形态。而道德生命、德行则恰恰产生了这种精神实质。

在老子、孔子以前，中国历史上最伟大的革新家和法家创始人管子曾经提倡"礼义廉耻"这完美和谐社会的四条准则。他认为，社会没有这四条准则，就会失去方向。

Search for "Truth, Goodness and Perfection."

If it is short of any two supports, a society will be in danger. In the absence of three components, a society will be topsy-turvy. If it has none of them, it will perish. According to Guan Zi, the requirements of "propriety" should not exceed normal formality. "Righteousness" is concerned with our avoiding promoting or edifying ourselves. "Honesty" is a form of transparency in which we don't seek to hide our shortcomings. "Shame" discourages us from reveling in the company of evil-doers. Guan Zi considered that these were the "four elements," namely, "propriety, righteousness, honesty and shame," essential to nation building. [96] It is obvious that different formulae have been applied by Chinese since earliest times in an endeavour to build a perfect and harmonious society. The result, however, has fallen short of the ideal.

When Jesus said, "I am the Way, the Truth and the Life," what did he mean?

First of all, Jesus was regarded by his followers as the "Word of God", in the sense of incarnating the Living Truth. When he preached in the synagogues, those listening were amazed. The Truth he delivered sounded very radical to them. They all thought it was new teaching, as Jesus spoke with authority, with an immediacy to which they were unaccustomed. [97] Jesus cut through to the essence of the Mosaic Law, as often by his deeds as by his words. The latter shocked and infuriated the authorities, as when he healed on the Sabbath, declaring that: "The Sabbath was made for man and not man for Sabbath." Responding to criticism, Jesus commented that he had not come to destroy the "Laws and the Prophets," but to fulfill them. Jesus placed emphasis on the intention of the law in commenting about murder, adultery, divorce, the law of recrimination, and loving one's enemy.

Jesus incarnated divine compassion, sometimes at great cost to himself. The invitation to those in need was without restriction. As he put it, "Everyone who asks receives; he who seeks finds; and to him who knocks, the door will be opened." [98] His action, which followed up this invitation, was an illustration of putting "goodness into practice".

In John's Gospel, Jesus described himself as "The Way". This gospel indicates that when Jesus spoke of being "The Way," he was stating that he was the way to God, as well as an example of the way God wants us to live. Christ is the way to God in that our association with him helps us draw close to God, like children to the bosom of their father.

如果其中任意两条准则没了，社会就危险了。如果其中任意三条准则都缺失了，社会就颠覆了。如果一个也没有了，社会就消亡了。管子说，"礼"不可超越平常的礼式，"义"就是不要推崇自己，"廉"是一种透明状态，不隐瞒自己的缺陷，"耻"是不要与恶人为伍。管子认为，礼义廉耻，为国之四维。从这里可以看出，中国在努力建设完善和谐的社会进程中很早就有了不同的定式。然而，结局往往不尽人意。

耶稣说："我是道，我是真理。我是生命"，他指的是什么呢？首先，信众们认为，基督是上帝的道，是活生生的真理的化身。当他在犹太人会堂讲道的时候，听众们吃惊了。他所传的真理在他们看来讲到了点子上。他们都认为，它所讲的道是没有过的，因为耶稣说的有权威性，直接得使他们感到不习惯。耶稣常常是身体力行，切透了摩西律法的实质。后者震惊了，掌权者恼怒了，特别是他在安息日治病的时候公开说："安息日是人设的，人不是为安息日造的"。耶稣对批评的反应是，他来的目的不是想搞垮律法和先知，而是要使之完善。耶稣在谈论杀人、奸淫、离异、斗殴法和爱你的敌人的时候，强调了法律的意图。

耶稣是悲悯的神圣化身，有时候自己付出极大的代价。凡是有难的，他都一应到底，绝不保留。正如他所说的那样："人所要求的得到了；寻找的找到了；他所敲的门打开了"。有所求就有所应，这就是行善"。

耶稣在《约翰福音》里把自己说成是"道"。福音认为，耶稣说他成道的时候，他是在讲，他是通向上帝的道，是上帝要我们行道的榜样。基督是通向上帝的道，意思是如果我们和他联手，会帮助我们接近上帝，犹如孩子接近父亲的怀抱。

Through his teachings and actions, Jesus demonstrated the humility, forgiveness, faithfulness, grace, and love of God. The eternal Word, of which Jesus was supposed to be an incarnation, was with God in the beginning, being responsible for the creation.

Jesus sacrificed himself, remaining faithful to his mission to the point of death, and thus brought us a powerful sense of God. He was compassionate towards the sick, widows, the poor and the needy. He mingled with tax-collectors and sinners. In Christ, we see God reaching out to people who were despairing. When we live as Christ lived, and in his strength, we will contribute to the peace and harmony of the societies in which we live. However, the hope of a "Utopia," which immediately realizes the sort of society Jesus envisaged, is a little too idealistic and it would be naive if we imagined it would be easily achieved, especially when we take into account the harsh realities of political life and the persistence of human sinfulness.

When Jesus said, "I am the Way, the Truth and the Life," he meant that whoever believed in him, and put his words into practice, would be a new creation, that is, would have their life transformed, and be indwelt by God. Through him we would understand the Truth, and the Truth would cultivate in us good integrity. The more people possess good integrity, the more love there would be in the world, and the more peace and harmony (美好社会 mei hao she hui). Thus, through the teaching of Jesus, and through our being in contact with his energies, we shall live, the Truth, good integrity, peace and harmony.

耶稣通过言传身教，展示了上帝的谦逊、宽恕、信实、恩惠和慈爱。永恒的道就是耶稣的化身，在太初与上帝同在，万物因此得到了创造。

耶稣牺牲了自己，至死忠诚使命，使我们强烈感受到了上帝的存在。他对病寡贫弱者施以怜悯。他把税吏和罪人列在一处。在基督里面，我们看到上帝向绝望的人伸出手来。如果当我们像基督那样地生活，我们会在他的感召下为我们所生活的和谐、平安的社会贡献力量。但是，迅速实现耶稣所设想的那种社会是"乌多邦"的期望，有点太理想化了。政治生活的残酷，人类的罪恶现象久久不去，如果我们这种期望很容易实现的话，那我们则是太天真了。

耶稣说："我是道，我是真理，我是生命"，他的意思是说，凡是他的人，把他的话付诸行动的人，就可以成为新人。也就是说，他们的生活会得到改变，他们会站在上帝一边。通过他，我们明白了真理，真理会在我们心中产生善德。善德的人越多，世界的爱就越多，就越安宁，越和睦。通过耶稣的教导，通过我们和他言行相接触，我们就会生活在真善美的平安和谐之中。

CHAPTER NINETEEN
The Difference between God and Man

When a Christian proclaims, "Jesus is Lord, " a Confucian asks "Why is it that your Christian God was born some 500 years after Confucius? And he died as Confucius did. Why then do you call him 'Lord'" ?

There are many reasons that Confucians believe that Jesus of Nazareth was one of the prophets, and that he consequently died as Confucius did.

1. Confucians believe that God is omnipotent and that he rules with righteousness.

In the Chinese belief system, there are three levels, with God at the top and men at the bottom, and in between are the ghosts and spirits. There is a distinctive division of spiritual and physical realms. When alive, men live in the physical world, and, when dead, they are in the spiritual world. In this system God is omnipotent. Though he is in the spiritual realm, he also supervises the government of the physical world.

Mo Zi wrote in Tian Zhi that "God loves righteousness and dislikes those who are unrighteous" (99)Mo Zi argues that everyone, even the emperor, is under the rule on the principle of righteousness. "There is Heaven that governs." "Those who obey the wishes of Heaven, righteousness rules". "In the world, the righteous shall live, and the unrighteous shall die". For wrongdoers, "there is nowhere to hide!" . (100)

Therefore, God is in charge of everything under Heaven, and everything is under his control. There is no reason for him to send down his "Son" to live under his own law and to die for the sins of men.

2. Confucians believe that God is supernatural and will not die as humans do. Only humans die. No god will have to undergo the process of death. As God is in the spiritual realm, he is beyond the clutches of death. In fact, all creatures go through the life cycle from birth and death, as Lao Zi argued – "everything returns to its origin" .(101) Only mystic martial art stories tell of some saints who walked up to heaven.

第十九章

神与人之分别

有个基督徒宣布:"耶稣是主",有个儒生则问:"为什么你们的基督教的上帝在孔子500年后才出生呢?他也和孔子一样,都死了,这怎样解释呢?

儒生有许多原因相信,耶稣是一个先知,所以,他也和孔子一样死了。

1. 儒家认为,上帝是无所不能的,正义是掌控的手段。

中国人的信仰系统有三层,顶层是天,下边是人,中间是鬼神。灵界和物界有明显的界限。当人活着的时候,生活在物质世界;人死了,灵魂属于灵界。在这个系统中,上帝是无所不能的。上帝是在灵界,其实,祂在俯瞰物质世界的运营。

墨子在《天志》中说:"天欲义而恶不义"。他认为,每个人,甚至包括皇帝,都得守持正义。"有天政之"(注:天代表上帝名称);"顺天意者,义政之";"天下有义则生,无义则死";作恶者"无所避逃之"。

天下万事尽在上帝掌控之中。上帝要"儿子"下界受自己的律令制约并为人的罪恶而死,是没有道理的。

2. 儒家认为,上帝是超自然的,不会像人类那样死去。只有人才会死,上帝是不会有死亡经历的。上帝处于灵界,超出了死亡的魔爪。而事实上,一切生物都经过由生到死的生命轮回过程。老子说:"复归于其朴,复归于其根"。

In Genesis 5:24 it is reported that "Enoch walked with God and then was no more, because God took him away." The Prophet Elijah was separated from Elisha and was taken away in a chariot of fire into heaven in a whirlwind. (102)

Jesus of Nazareth was spoken of as being the "Son" of God. The Gospel of John described Jesus philosophically as the Word become flesh, that is, he was of the "essence" of God. As God is Spirit, that essence is also spirit. So, Jesus was a "spirit", but spirit never dies. Confucians would therefore have a problem with the death of Jesus.

3. God does not have to die for the sins of men.

Confucians believe the Lord-on-high has human characters, but there is no necessity for him to atone the sins of men by giving himself as a sacrificial offering. Emperor Shang Tang thought God had caused the five years draught and offered himself as a sacrifice to appease the divine anger. Before he stepped into the burning pile of wood, there was a downpour. God forgave. And the Emperor did not have to die.

Confucians considered that God had the power to forgive and did not have to self-sacrifice for the sins of men. The most God could do was to forgive sins, pardoning people without punishing them. Besides, God does not want sacrifices as what he wants is the heart of man.

4. Why don't Christian theologians separate Jesus of Nazareth from Christ, the Word?

Christians believe that there is only one God, who created the universe. In this they draw on doctrines enshrined in the Hebrew Scriptures. The prologue to John's Gospel refocused the Hebrew creation story and edited the Logos, or Word that indwelt Jesus of Nazareth, into the drama. John made the claim that Jesus was a unique incarnation of the Word, the Thought, the Reason, and the Consciousness of God. It was argued that this Word, enfleshed in Jesus, was the agent in creation - "Through him all things were made; without him nothing was made that has been made." (103)

The consequent history of the world, and particularly of humankind, reflected in early Hebrew myths and sagas, indicates that, from the beginning, and continuing through to the present, contrary energies - good and evil - have struggled for ascendency within each of us, and within our communities. Jesus, in his death, was a casualty of this struggle. In dying he remained faithful to his guidance and transparent to the divinity that glowed within. So powerful was the effect of this transparency, that it was said of him that "God loved the world so much that he gave his only Son (that is, the Word of God) that whosoever believes in him shall not die but have everlasting life" (104)

《创世纪》第五章第24节有这样的记载:"以诺和上帝同行,上帝把他带去,他就不在世了"。先知伊莱贾和伊莱沙分开了,乘着一阵旋风坐着烈焰之车被带走了(列王纪下二章11节)。

耶稣被说成是上帝的"儿子"。《约翰福音》冷静地描绘了耶稣,说他是道的肉身,有上帝的"质"。由于上帝是灵,这种质也是灵。因此,耶稣是灵,而灵永远不会死的。儒家因此对耶稣之死提出了质疑。

3. 上帝不必为人的罪而死。

儒家认为,上帝有人的性格,但是,没需要自己当牺牲品去为人赎罪。商汤以为,上帝降下5年旱灾,便自我献身来平息圣怒。他还没有踏进火堆,就下了一场大雨。上帝宽恕了。皇帝没有必要去死。

儒家认为,上帝有宽恕的能力,就没有必要为人去赎罪。顶多是上帝赦罪,原谅人们,而不是惩罚人们。上帝要的不是牺牲,要的是人心。

4. 基督教神学家为什么不和基督耶稣分开来论?

基督徒认为,上帝只有一个,祂创造了宇宙。他们引用了希伯来《圣经》里的信条。《约翰福音》的序言改写了希伯来创世的故事,把耶稣体现的道编成了剧本。约翰宣称,耶稣是独特的道的化身,思想的化身,理智的化身,上帝意识的化身。论点是,耶稣肉身化的道是造物的介质----"万物通过他而被创造出来,凡是被造的,没有一样不是借着他造的。"

后来反映在早期希伯来神话故事中的世界史,尤其是人类史的观点是,太初开始,一直到现在,善和恶这对矛盾在我们心中,在我们集体内部一争高下。耶稣之死就是这种斗争的牺牲品。临危之际,他仍然坚守着自己的导向,燃烧在他胸中的神圣一览无余。这种通透的效果是这样的强大,人们提起他的时候,便认为"上帝是这么爱世人,舍出了仅有的儿子,凡是相信他的,都不会死,都会得到永生。"

Christians see in Jesus, called the Christ, or "the annointed one, " a powerful embodiment of the essence of God. It is for this reason that they call him "Lord." It is a respect that people encounter God in encountering him.

In 335 CE the Roman Catholic Church declared Jesus as "god" and after debating for 50 years, they decided that he was a man, walking on this Earth like his disciples. After tossing the two ideas for sometime, they decided that Jesus was both "god" and man, but he was part of the "Trinity God".

Why could Christianity embrace both Hellenistic and Roman cultures and be indifferent to the Chinese?

If Christianity had accommodated Chinese culture as Buddhism did, it would act as a bridge for both culture and religion. Culture and religion are interpenetratable.

基督徒在称作耶稣的身上看到上帝强大的化身。正因为如此，他们称他为"主"。人们在接触耶稣的时候接触了上帝，这是一种敬佩之情。

公元335年，罗马天主教会宣布，耶稣是"帝"，此后50年间产生了争论，他们认为，耶稣是人，如同他的门徒一样行走在这块"地"上。两种观点对抗一个时期以后，大家的结论是，耶稣是神也是人，某种程度上说，是三位一体的上帝。

基督教为什么接受希腊、罗马文化，而冷漠中国文化呢？

如果基督教像佛教一样适应了中国文化，那么，他就会搭起文化和宗教的桥梁。文化和宗教是互相渗透的。

CHAPTER TWENTY
"The Ambiguity of Sin in the Chinese Language."

A distinction has been drawn between crime and sin, between action that is against the laws of the land, and action that is a transgression against divine law. Chinese use the word "zui", for both crime and sin. Of course, sin is sometimes translated as "zui guo" or zui wu," but both expressions could also refer to crime. If one commits a crime, one is guilty.

Some theologians seem to think that Chinese have no "guilt-oriented morality." If this is so, then it would seem that 2500 years of Confucian teaching on ethics and integrity has been wasted and that Lao Zi's preaching on "morality" have been thrown to the wind!? Fortunately, neither is the case.

Confucian and Daoist philosophy conflates, or rather, does not distinguish between the realms of the personal and the communal, between personal, moral guidelines and civil responsibility, and therefore between sin and crime. This is little different from the approach of the ancient Israelites, who saw themselves living in a theocrasy, that is, being ruled by God. There was no difference, at least in theory, between one's responsibility to God and one's responsibility under the law. Fundamentalists, in many Islamic countries, are arguing that the Koran should be the basis of civil law. The distinction between the two is a consequence, in part, of economic and social developments, associated with industrialization and therefore with the rise of secular society.

The Chinese have a long history. The legendary kings lived more than 5000 years ago, at the time of Yellow Emperor. The written history of the Shang Dynasty began some 3700 years ago in their Bronze Age. The emperors, called the "Sons of Heaven", represented the Lord of Heaven on earth. In the past, any natural disaster was considered a punishment by the Lord-on-high for wrong-doing. Sometimes the people prayed and gave sacrificial offerings to appease their god, or gods.

Shang Tang, in c.1783 B.C.E., overthrew the tyrant, Xia Jie, and became king. Unfortunately, there was a drought, which lasted three years. He thought that the ancestor of Xia Jie was getting back at him, and that the drought could be punishment for bringing down the Xia Dynasty. He thought he might have offended the Lord-on-high. He was aware of the dictum that the "Emperor should bear the guilt, as the people were blameless" and they should not be punished. Therefore, he set up an altar of fire and offered himself as a burnt offering. He did "not spare himself as a sacrifice in his desire to appease the Lord-on-high and other gods".

第二十章

汉语"罪"的模糊性

违反当地法律和侵犯神的律法之间是犯罪和罪孽之间的关系。犯罪和罪孽中国都用"罪"字。当然，罪孽有时候翻译成"罪过"或"罪恶"。两者都可以指犯罪。人犯了错误，就是犯罪。

有些神学家认为，中国没有"罪德"。如果确实如此，那么，2500多年以来儒家的德行都作废了，老子所传的道德都随风而去了。然而，绝无此事。

儒道二合一也好，单拿出来也罢，在个人和集体之间、个人道德界限和公民责任感之间、罪孽和犯罪之间，没有加以区分。这与古代以色列人生长在神权之下受制于神没什么区别。对于上帝的责任感和法律下的责任感之间，至少理论上没有区别。在许多伊斯兰国家，保守派认为，《古兰经》是民间立法。两者之间的区分某种程度上是经济、社会发展的结果，与此关联的是工业化过程和由此兴起的世俗社会。

中国历史悠久，5000年前秭史里炎黄二帝。3700年前的青铜器时代开启了商史。皇帝称为"天子"，是天上的主在人间的代表。过去，一发生自然灾害，都被认为是上帝罚罪。有时候，人们祷告，贡献燔祭，讨好鬼神。

公元前1783年，商汤推翻暴君夏杰后自立为王。可是，出现了三年旱灾。商汤以为，夏杰的祖先向他报复，用旱灾来惩罚他灭了夏。他想，一定是得罪了上帝。他意识到了这句格言："朕身有罪，无及万方"。于是，他建了一座火坛，打算献身燔祭。他是"不惮以身为牺牲，以祠说于上帝鬼神"。

"The Ambiguity of Sin in the Chinese Language."

No sooner had he stepped into the fire then the sky opened and the rain came in torrents. (105) This incident epitomized the "guilt-oriented morality" characteristic of Chinese since that time.

The period of the Spring and Autumn Warring States saw the Golden Age of Chinese Philosophy. Lao Zi's thesis on "morality" was a compilation of philosophical thoughts on morality that had accumulated since the time of Yellow Emperor. It is for this reason that Lao Zi's philosophy is sometimes called Huang Lao Philosophy.

The morality advocated by Lao Zi was a "guilt-oriented morality," even though he camouflaged his subtle allusions, so as not to offend the emperor and court officials. He talked about the presence of "The Word" in the world, and contended that people should "know The Heavenly Word". He argued that people should respect "The Word", and that those who act against it will die young. The insinuation of the latter was that those who transgress against the teaching of "The Word" are guilty, and that their guilt will result in an early death. (106)

There is no ambiguity about sin in the Chinese language, because crime also represents moral wrongdoing. The Chinese expression, "the committing of a crime", can refer to either crime or sin, because they do not have a deity against whom they could be seen to have sinned. Therefore, any wrongdoing, any "commiting of crime", can also be interpreted as the committing of sin (犯罪 fan zui), though that sin is seen to be against "Heaven" rather than against a personal deity. All crimes evoke guilt and are punished by law. Even today, Chinese will say to those who waste food that "Heaven will punish them". This surely represents a "guilt-oriented morality." Chinese consider any wrongdoing as "against Heaven", and expect that judgment will eventually ensure." For all there will be judgement at the end, and, if the judgement has not been metered out, it is because the time for judgement has not come.

The Chinese word "sin", is made up of two parts with si above and fei below. Si means four and fei means wrong or wrongdoing.

他一踏进火堆，天窗大开，大雨倾盆。这个故事证明，自那时起，中国已有了"罪德"观念。

春秋战国时期是中国哲学的黄金时期。老子的道德论集中了黄帝以来道德哲学思想的大成。因为这个缘故，老子哲学也常称作黄老哲学。

老子所倡导的道德思想"罪德"思想。为了避祸帝王将相，他打扮起来，绕着弯子说话。他说，天下有道，人应该知天道。他说，人要尊道，不道蚤己（不尊重道的人早死）。他暗指，违背道的人是有罪的，有罪的不得长寿。

中文的"罪"字并不模糊，因为犯罪也代表不道德的行为。中文的犯罪可以是"律法上的罪"或是"道德上的罪"，缘出是人们看不到对某个神所犯下的罪行。因此，凡做错了事或犯了罪，都可以解释成犯罪，尽管所犯的是滔"天"罪行，而不是犯了某个神的罪行。一切犯罪行为都是犯罪，都是按律惩罚的。今天中国人还说，浪费粮食遭天罚。这肯定是一种"罪德"。中国人认为，伤天害理是要有报应的。"善恶始终将有报，善恶未报，时辰未到。"

中文的"罪"字为上下结构，上面是个"四"，下面是个"非"。四是一二三四的"四"，"非"意思是做错了事。

"The Ambiguity of Sin in the Chinese Language."

The word zui includes four self-inflicted bad habits or wrongdoings, such as: "prostitution", "gambling", "drunkenness", and "smoking (opium, tobacco or heroin)". Even self-inflicted wrongs are considered crimes by society. The notion of 'crime" in Chinese tradition bears a close correspondence to the notion of "sin" in Judo-Christian tradition.

Confucius taught people to have "a heart of benevolence" and to "behave with integrity", whilst Lao Zi advocated "respect for The Word (of God) and the valuing of integrity", the penalty for disobedience being death. It is not true that Chinese lack a "guilt-oriented morality;" their guilt-oriented morality, associated with the Way of Heaven, is merely differently configured.

In Christian thought, there is a great difference between the "Way of Heaven" and the "Way of Man". There is no debate about the wrongness of acting against the "Way of Heaven", for sin will be judged by God. As for wrongdoings against the "Way of Man," the punishment, or otherwise, that is metred out, will depend on the nature of the society, and the character of its ruler, or rulers. Under autocracies, laws represent the whim of the ruler. Democratic rule contains safeguards against the arbitrary exercise of power, though it is not perfect. Access to the law, and its remedies, is enhanced for those with wealth and influence.

The West has not always lived the truth it has proclaimed, in spite of its Christian orientation. It has been given to self-aggrandisement, annexing countries less powerful or developed than itself. European gunboat diplomacy opened China to exploitation. Though those nations participating in the colonial grap-for-land were not all fully fledged democracies, many called themselves "Christian." Slave trade, dealing mainly in African slaves, and later industrial slavery in the early period of the Industrial Revolution, were facts of life in Britain and North America. It was those who could least defend themselves who were most at risk. While the yoke of the older style of colonialism has mostly been lifted, an economic colonialism has taken its place, with multinationals, and other commercial interest often exploiting the physical and human resources of poor countries. The negative aspects of globalization work against the wellbeing of the latter.

While contemporary democracy was largely a product of the Industrial Revolution, and the pluralism and wealth it spawned, its philosophic roots lay in ancient Greece. While democracy, and industrialisation, the economic foundation on which it rested, have exerted a powerful and ameliorating influence on the world, it has not been without its fault-lines, or failures. Because most workable democracies are strong and resilient, they are in a position to conduct themselves with dignity, humility, and compassion, particularly towards the needy, without vaunting either their power or charity. Unfortunately, this is rarely the case. Convinced that democracy, particularly their form of democracy, is the way forward for all nations, they insist on other nations democratizing.

"罪"字包含四种自己犯下的恶习,做过的错事,如:吃喝嫖赌抽。自己做错了,从社会意义上说也是犯罪。中国传统上"罪"的概念和犹太-基督教传统"罪"的概念是相近的。

孔子教人们有"仁心",重"德行"。老子提倡"尊道而贵德",违德者死。认为中国没有"罪德",这是不真实的;中国的"罪德"就是天之道,不过是说法不同罢了。

基督教的思想中,"天之道"和"人之道"是有很大差别的。做错了事,违背了"天之道",不用考虑,罪是由上帝判定的。干了坏事,违背了"人之道",是要根据社会性质,根据统治者或统治者们的意志进行惩罚的。封建时期,法律体现统治者的意志。民主制度虽不完善,但是可以防止弄权。对于有钱有势的人来说,是要有法可依,违法必究的。

西方尽管信仰基督,然而生活的实际状况并不总像宣扬的那样。西方有的是自我膨胀,以大欺小,以强凌弱。欧洲的炮舰政策打开了剥削中国的大门。虽然那些参与瓜分殖民地的国家并没有充分的民主,许多国家却以"基督"国度自诩。以非洲奴隶为主的贩奴活动和后来工业革命初期的劳工,都是英美所干的事。凡是自卫能力最差的,就是最不安全的。当老式殖民主义的枷锁基本被打开的时候,跨国组织和其他大企业的经济殖民又来了,掠夺穷国的自然资源和人力资源。全球化的负面影响给穷国谋的不是福利。

当今的民主政治基本是工业革命和所产生的多元文化和财富的产物,它的哲学基础根植于古希腊。它所依赖的民主、工业化、经济基础对世界产生了强大的、具有推动作用的影响,然而,它并非没有瑕疵和缺点。多数民主政体操作性强,灵活机动,行为高尚,具有悲悯之情,对需要接济的国家不耍威风,不摆架子。然而,这种情况毕竟是少数。坚信民主,尤其是民主的形式,是一切国家的必由之路,其他国家一定要进行民主化。

"The Ambiguity of Sin in the Chinese Language."

This may not, at least in the near future, be the most appropriate way forward for these nations. Furthermore, those propounding this thesis are often oblivious to the fact that the weaker nations, which they are seeking to coerce, are off-put and sometimes angered and offended by the caviller way the more powerful democracies behave towards them, and by the contradiction between rhetoric and practice. Most nations find it difficult facing their shadow side. The more powerful the nation, the less likely it is that they will be given to self-reflection.

Wealthy democracies would do well to heed the words of Isaiah 58:6–7"to loosen the chains of injustice, to set the oppressed free, to break every yoke, to share food with the hungry, to provide the poor wanderer with shelter, and to clothe the naked." Genuine democracy is committed to the wellbeing of all, particularly those least able to fend for themselves.

Sometimes, in seeking to create a more sustainable world, rich and less populated countries have sought to foist their perspectives on others, perspectives that demonstrate an abismal lack of understanding of the dilemmas faced by other countries. At the Fourth World Women's Congress in Beijing in 1999, an American leader asked Chinese women to stand up for their human rights and insist on having as many children as they wanted. This would be lunacy, particular in a country that is grossly overpopulated, and where the Chinese leadership has sought to curtail population growth by their responsible "one child policy."

Democracies call loudly for the establishment of "human rights" in countries where they feel they are being denied. One cannot fault such a call. However, those taking up this mantra often fail to discern where they themselves are denying "human rights" to sections of their community. Even less do they appear to appreciate the complexity of the political landscape in those countries being criticised. In many of the latter there is no free press or independent judiciary, let alone a sizable middle class or economic infrastructure necessary to provide the conditions necessary for a national commitment to the sorts of "human rights" envisaged by wealthy democracies. Such calls, for the awarding of "human rights" to the citizenry, in the absence of a nuanced understanding of conditions in the country concerned, became little more than slogans, or what Lao Zi called "trading with beautiful words" ! (Note: The speaker has given birth to one and only daughter.)

Our ethno-centrism can also blind us to the fact that situations can be viewed differently by different people and nations. Tibet is a case in point. While most Christian democracies lament China's treatment of Tibet, and, at least offer moral support to the Dalai Lama, many Chinese view the situation quite differently. They argue those who support human rights should condemn Tibetan Lamaism, which impoverished the peasants and made them perpetual serfs for generations. [107]The fact that Christian countries champion the Dalai Lama's cause is considered ironic. From what we have been arguing, it is obvious that laws can be immoral. However, when we are in a powerful position, we are less likely to recognize our sin or guilt.

至少是在不远的将来，民主制度对于这些国家来说，可能不是最合适的选择。另外，有些说法认为，本文忽略了下面这个事实：民主国家想法欺凌的弱国对于强权的民主国家对他们的指手画脚感到窘困、恼怒和反感，口头上说的和实际行动之间两厢矛盾。多数国家难以面对这个阴暗面。国家越强大，就越不自省。

富裕的民主国家应该倾听以塞亚（58：6-7）的箴言："打开不公正的锁链，解开套在脖子上的枷锁，使被欺压者得到自由，挣脱条条锁链，把食物分给饥饿的人，给无家可归的人找个窝住，让衣不蔽体的人穿上衣服"。真正的民主要考虑大家，特别是那些无助者。

有时候，在寻求创建一个可持续的世界过程中，人口较少的富裕国家将自己的想法强加给别国，而这些想法完全不顾别国所面临的困境。1999年，第4届世界妇女大会在北京召开，美国一个领导人号召中国妇女争取人权，想生多少就生多少。在一个人口极度超量的国度里，此言纯属狂言，中国领导人想办法削减人口增长，负责任地提出"一对夫妇一个孩"的政策。

搞民主的人在他们以为没有民主的国家里喧嚣"人权"。这种喧嚣你不可能说他错了。然而，唱喜歌的人往往认不清自己，认为自己的社会中有些方面是没有人权的。他们甚至也不怎么考虑挨批的国家所存在的复杂的政治环境。挨批的国家很多没有出版自由，没有独立的法制，更没有相当规模的中产阶级或经济基础来保障富裕民主国家所设想的那种人权的国家义务。

对于一个不觉人权条件差异的国家，怎样强迫给他们总不超过一种口号吧了，或者正如老子说的，"美言可以市"。

我们的民族优越感也可能一叶障目，认为不同国家不同民族看问题的角度不同。西藏就是个例子。多数基督教民主国家哀悯中国处理西藏问题，对达赖喇嘛打打气，而许多中国人认为，完全不是那么回事。他们认为，那些支持人权的人应该谴责西藏喇嘛教，是它害苦了农民，使他们沦为一茬又一茬的农奴。基督教国家支持达赖喇嘛活动的事实被认为是一种嘲讽。我们认为，法律明显是不法的。如果我们处于权势位置，我们不可能认识到自己的罪过。

"The Ambiguity of Sin in the Chinese Language."

    This is how the Japanese Government is able to avoid admitting their responsibility in the "Massacre of Nanjing." It is a mistake for Western theologians to imagine that the Chinese lack a "guilt-oriented-morality," that is, that sin is somehow an offence against God, or Heaven, or that Confucian teaching is just ethical. If we were to focus merely on the West's more reprehensible actions, it could equally be argued that the West lacks "guilt-oriented" morality, and that it often conducts itself on the basis of self-formulated laws designed to preserve the advantages it enjoys.

就是因为这样,日本政府才能够拒不承认"南京大屠杀"。在西方神学家的想象中,中国人缺少"罪德",他们搞错了。所说的罪就是触犯了上帝或天,实际上,儒教恰恰是讲究伦理的。假如我们反过来非难西方的行为,同样也可以认为,西方也缺少"罪德"———西方往往按自己的利益模式制定了法律,并以此为基础大行其事。

CHAPTER TWENTY-ONE
Love others as yourself

Confucius argued that love comes from the "kind heart" of a person. That is why it is important that the heart be benevolent, so that you can love others as yourself. But there is often "differentiation or distinctions in our loving" based on one's status or the nature of the relationship.

Confucian teaching considers that there are different ways of showing love to persons of different status, ties and relationships, and also in terms of distance from oneself. For example, one ought to love the emperor more than his court officials. One ought to love himself more than his parents. One ought to love his parents more than other members of the family. One ought to love members of his family more than others in the community. One ought to love close neighbours more than distant neighbours. Love is dispensed according to these different measures.

This sounds logical and sensible. It is little wonder that it was favoured by the emperors, who put it into practice in China for thousands of years. Those in government in China today favour this approach, but often for ulterior motives. In certain circumstances, it can be seen to appeal to selfishness, hypocrisy, favouritism and discrimination. This love, which depends on emotional and relational ties, can be insincere. It may not arise from a "benevolent heart." However, Confucius's maxim that "What you do not like, do not give to others" is more likely to promote "acts of integrity", acts that come from a "benevolent heart".

Confucian "love" is discriminative and not universal. Love, based on status, is likely to be artificial and forced. It contains an element of fear ("favour and disgrace are alarming, or fear inducing"), and sometimes such love is merely an expression of propriety, one of the five elements of (Confucian) integrity. Confucian love, if it is graded, does not issue from a benevolent heart, and is not freely given or spontaneous. It does not necessarily have to be, but it is often a forced "love." What Confucius did not explore was how to make the hearts of people benevolent! If our hearts are benevolent, the love that flows from them will not be discrimatory and insincere. It is almost impossible to love your neighbour as yourself when there is inequality in your love.

Mo Zi, on the other hand, advised: "Love others doubly as yourself". He argues that when there is more love for one another in the world, or more universal love, nations will not attack one another, and people will not fight. Eventually, there will be no disunity in the family, no thieves and robbers, and no lack of filial piety.

第二十一章

爱人如己

孔子说，爱来自一个人的"仁心"。关键是人要有慈心，这样才会爱人如己。而现实往往是"爱有差等"，理由是地位不同，关系有别。

儒家认为，爱分远近、亲疏、高下。比譬，爱皇上胜过爱百官，爱自己胜过爱父母，爱父母胜过爱家人，爱家人胜过爱别人，爱近邻胜过爱远邻。爱，因为对象不同，而有所差别。

这听起来合情合理，难怪几千年来被皇帝们所推崇。但动机往往是秘而不宣的。在某些情况下，人们认为这含有自私、虚伪、偏袒和歧视的成分。这种爱靠的是情绪和关系，可能有失诚信，而不是出自仁心。孔子有句名言："己所不欲，勿施于人"，可以用来促进源自仁心的德行。

儒家的爱是歧视性的，不是普世之爱。爱分等级，可能造成娇柔之和强迫之爱。爱包含着宠辱若惊的成分，有时候，爱只是个礼仪，是个德行五常。儒家的爱有等级之分，就不会发自仁心，就不是自然而然的。人们不一定非爱不可，爱往往是逼出来的。孔子没有探索过怎样才能使仁心变得仁慈。假如我们的心仁慈了，所流露的爱就不会是歧视性的，就不会是不虔诚的。如你的爱失衡了，那就不可能爱人如己。

墨子也认为，"兼相爱。"他说，世上多了一份爱，多了一份博爱，那么，国不攻国，民不斗民。最终，家庭不会不团结，世上不会有贼盗，也不会没有孝顺的。

If one respects the body of the other person one will not harm him. He says that if one loves others first, others will reciprocate this love. Therefore, people should love one another with this super-abundant love, and they will live in peace and harmony. Likewise, larger and stronger nations should learn how to handle smaller and weaker nations without desiring to dominate them, without imposing unilateral and unfair conditions on them. When this sort of love is demonstrated there is equality among the nations.

Lao Zi agreed that love comes from a benevolent heart, but only when the heart possesses "The Word" of God. Then it will become benevolent. He goes one step further, arguing that "one must sacrifice oneself for his love of the world". He describes the qualities of a sage, or leader, as one who does not act against "The Word" of God, is not selfish, and does not have coveteous desires, but puts his people first and does not foresake them. Such a leader "serves the world like a hired servant". He considers the wishes of his people as his own. It is only in the absence of the teaching of "The Word" of God that one is constrained to bring out the importance of "benevolence and integrity". He argues that this deep love arises out of the respect for "The Word" (of God), which will not "trade flattery in the market place".

According to Jesus of Nazareth, the second of the two great commandments is concerned with our loving our neighbours as ourselves. There is a sense in which we love God in loving our neighbour. Our loving of our neighbour is not merely a means of our loving God, but is a spontaneous expression of that love. Loving our neighbour as ourselves is a universal love, a love that, in its object, reaches beyond those who are likely to love us in return. The agape love advocated by Jesus Christ is proactive, and is in line with his advice to "treat others as we would have them treat you."

In the parable of the Good Samaritan, recorded in Luke 10:25-37, Jesus extended love's reach to the stranger, in this case, a stranger belonging to a despised racial group. The Samaritans were considered bastardized Jews, half-casts. It was this stranger, rather than the Jewish priest or Levite, who stopped to help a man who had been robbed and left by the side of the road. He attended to his wounds and provided for him out of his own purse. The nub of the story, however, lay at an even deeper level. What Jesus was saying to his fellow Jews was: "Those you despise are acting in a more neighbourly way than you are." The love shown by the Samaritan issued from a benevolent heart, extended beyond a neighbour to a stranger, and asked for nothing in return. He did not expect to be repaid. This love transcends racial boundaries and social status. It is a compassionate love with a universal reach.

假如人爱惜他人的身体，就不会去伤害他。墨子说，假如人先爱他人，他人必以爱来报答他。人彼此之间的关爱是无穷的，只有这样，才会生活平安，相处和睦。同样，大国强国应该研究对待弱弱小国家的方式，而不要去统治他们，单方面地把不平等的条件强加给他们。有了这种爱，国家间就平等了。

老子认为，爱发自仁心，人心有了道，才会仁慈。他进一步说："爱以身为天下"他说，圣人或领袖的品质是不违上帝之道的，是不自私的，是没有贪欲的，要以民为先，不可疏忽百姓的力量。作为领导人，要"爱以身为天下牧"。他认为，要以百性之心为心。如果不讲究上帝的道，才会不得已去强调仁慈和德行。他认为，大爱出自对上帝之道的敬畏，并非"美言可以市"。

耶稣认为，第二大诫命是爱邻如爱己，意思是爱邻居也就是爱上帝。我们爱邻居不仅仅是为了爱上帝，爱邻居是一种自然的表露。爱邻如爱己是博爱，这种爱客观上说，是不必回报的。耶稣所倡导的爱不是没有前提的，他倡导过："你们愿意人怎样待你们，你们也要怎样待人"（《路加福音》6：31）。

《路加福音好撒马利业人》（第十章第25-37节）中，耶稣把爱延伸到了陌生人，甚至是被蔑视的种族"。撒马利亚人不是纯粹的犹太人，是混种。撒马利亚人路遇被盗后遗弃路边的人以后，伸出了援助之手，这不是犹太祭司也不是利未人所为，所为的是个陌路之人。撒马利亚人为他的伤口敷药，解囊相助。这件事还有更深的含义。耶稣对同族的犹太人说："你们所蔑视的人在行为上比你们更有爱邻之情"。撒马利亚人所表现的爱是出于仁心，超越了邻居，惠及给了陌路人，不求任何回报。他也是不求回报的。这种爱超越了种族界线和社会地位。这是怜爱，是普世。

Consistent with this story, Jesus, in Matthew 5:43–44, argued that we should love even our enemies. Jesus demonstrated just such a love as he hung dying on the cross. He prayed, referring to all who had had a part in his death, "Father forgive them for they know not what they do." This was a love free from hatred or resentment, a gentle but tough love that brimmed over with compassion.

Unlike Lao Zi, who argued that people should sacrifice themselves out of love for the world, yet gave up on a corrupt emperor and his court. Jesus sacrificed himself for the cause to which he had committed himself. Jesus "sacrificed himself for his love for the world". Surely, there is no greater love than this.

The Apostle Paul's advice in Romans 12:9–21 bodies out the essence of a Jesus-style love. "Love must be sincere. Hate what is evil. Cling to what is good. Be devoted to one another in brotherly love. Honour one another above yourselves. Never be lacking in zeal, but keep your spirit fervor, serving the Lord. Be joyful in hope, patient in affliction, faithful in prayer. Share with God's people who are in need. Practice hospitality.

Blessed those who prosecute you; bless and do not curse. Rejoice with those who rejoice; mourn with those who mourn. Live in harmony with one another. Do not be proud, but be willing to associate with people of low position. Do not be conceited.

Do not repay anyone evil with evil. Be careful to do what is right in the eye of everybody.

If it is possible, as far as it depends you, live at peace with everyone. Do not take revenge, my friends, but leave room for God's wrath, for it is written: 'It is mine to revenge; I will repay, 'says the Lord. On the contrary: 'If your enemy is hungry, feed him; if he is thirsty, give him something to drink. In doing this, you will heap burning coal on his Head, ' Do not be overcome by evil, but overcome evil with good."

Paul's great hymn of love in Corinthians 13 is unsurpassed in its depiction of the love to which Christ calls Christians.

"Love is patient, love is kind. It does not envy, it does not boast, it is not proud. It is not rude, it is not self-seeking, it is not easily angered, it keeps no record of wrongs. Love does not delight in evil but rejoices with the truth. It always protects, always trusts, always hopes, always perseveres. Love never fails... And now the three remain: faith, hope and love. But the greatest of these is love."

The Second Great Commandment is to "love your neighbour as yourself." Christian nations are urged to live up to their faith. It is indeed a tragedy and irony that rich and developed nations often develop policies that "beggar their neighbours." [108]

耶稣就这则故事在《马太福音》5：43-44中认为："我们甚至得爱我们的敌人"。耶稣被钉死在十字架上，证明了这种爱。他为那些害死他的人祷告："天父啊，赦免他们吧，因为他们不知道他们做了什么"。这种爱脱离了仇恨和愤怒，是一种温存而又坚韧的爱，这种爱漾过了同情。

老子认为："爱以身为天下"，便离昏庸的皇帝和朝廷而去。相比之下，耶稣为了自己所从事的事业牺牲了自己。耶稣是"爱以身为天下"，没有别的爱比这个更伟大了。

使徒保罗在《罗马书》12：9-21的谏言指出了耶稣之爱的实质所在："爱人不可虚假，恨恶扬善，以兄弟之爱彼此衷心。以对方的荣誉为上。要热情，心里要有激情，要为主服务。希望之中要有欢乐，痛苦之时要有耐性，祈祷之刻要有忠诚。与上帝的子民分享所需吧，待人殷勤是行动指南。

迫害你的，要祝福他们；只要祝福，不要咒诅；喜与人同喜，哀与人同哀。彼此和睦的生活吧，不要翘尾巴，去和卑微的人沟通吧，自负是要不得的。

不要以恶报恶，要和大家平安地生活。不要有报复心，我的朋友，给上帝留个发泄的空间吧，上帝是这样说的：'报复是我的事，我会偿还的'。从另一面来说，'如果你的敌人饿了，给他吃的；如果他渴了，给他些喝的。这么做，你是在往他的头上堆燃烧的煤炭。'不要被邪恶所征服，而要用善良去征服邪恶。"

《哥林多前书》是保罗伟大的爱的赞美诗，它是描写基督召唤基督徒的爱的绝唱。《哥林多前书》第十三章如是有言："爱是耐心的，爱是善良的。它不嫉妒，它不夸张，它不自傲，它不粗鲁，它不张狂，它不易激怒，它不记着错误。爱不因恶而喜，却因真而欢。爱总是保护，总是信任，总是希望，总是忍耐。爱从不失败。现在，剩下的有三点：信任，希望和爱。三者最伟大的是爱"。

第二大诫命是："爱邻如爱己。"基督国家主张守信。而富裕、发达国家往往制定"掏空邻国"的政策，的确是个悲剧和讽刺。

CHAPTER TWENTY-TWO
In the beginning the nature of man was originally good.

"In the beginning the nature of man was good." This saying is attributed to Confucian teaching. These are the first two phrases in the Classic of Three Words. No one is sure of its author. Some say it was the work of Wang Yinglin of the Song Dynasty, but critics disagree. Others argue that it was written by Ou Shizi, during the last years of the Song Dynasty.(109) In spite of the fact that the author of this piece is unknown, the Classic of Three Words is the first book students in Confucian schools have to learn by heart. The sequence of thought, and the rythmic wording make it easy to recite, in a singing characteristic of oral tradition.

The Chinese define "man" as a child born of natural descent to a married couple, or as the product of the consummation of marriage. This person is flesh and blood. The word "man" is the common noun for human beings. The "nature" or "character" of men consists of the "inherited part before birth or genetic inheritance" and the "developed part after birth", an interplay of nature and nurture. (110)

That people should be good, and tend towards perfection, seems to be a common expectation in all cultures, indeed, a moral demand. In Jewish and Christian societies, it is argued that people were created in the image of God, who, of course, was perfect. The reality does not live up to the expectation. This tension is reflected in the history of Western Philosophy, and in Christianity, between those who emphasize human perfectability, and those who stress the flawed nature of human beings. (111)

Confucians argue that the "nature" of men of integrity should reflect the qualities of their hearts. These qualities encompass "benevolence", "righteousness", "manners or propriety", "knowledge" of good and evil, and "trust-worthiness". The behaviour of a person expresses the desire of their heart, whether or not they are conscious of this. Genetic inheritance makes a big difference in behaviour, a factor that is increasingly becoming evident. While we can't do a great deal about our genes, except through the embryonic science of gene therapy or through medication, we can attempt to provide a more helpful environment for our children.

第二十二章

人之初，性本善

"人之初，性本善"。这是儒家，是三字经里的前两句。作者是谁不得而知，有人说是宋朝王应麟，但被否定了；也有的人认为是末宋区适子。虽然不确定作者是谁，但三字经却是儒学必背的第一本书。三字经脉络畅通，朗朗上口，复述犹如歌咏。

汉语界定的"人"是夫妇人是传承血脉的孩子，是完婚的结晶。此人有血有肉。"人"字是代表人类的通用名词。"性"字是先天遗传和后天培养的性格，是先天和养成相互作用的产物。

人要善良，要十全十美，似乎成了各种文化中的普遍埋想，实际上是一种道德的要求。在犹太和基督教社会里，人们认为，人是依照神的形象造的，当然是完美的。但是，现实并不等于理想，西方哲学史和基督教史反映了人性善和人性恶之间的张力。

孔子认为，品性应该反映德行五常，包括仁义礼智信。人的行为表达了他自觉或不自觉的欲念。遗传对行为影响较大，行为因素体现的越来越明显。我们对自己的基因是不会有太大作为的，除非通过基因胚胎疗法或药物治疗，这样，我们才可能为孩子们创造一个有益的环境。

In the beginning the nature of man was originally good.

This was realized thousands of years ago by the Chinese, as is evident from the comment: "Close to cinnabar one turns scarlet, and nearer to black dye, or ink, one turns black". This was illustrated by the mother of Meng Zi, who shifted house three times in order to find an ideal environment to bring up Meng Zi, who became a great Confucian scholar.

Confucians believe that human nature was originally good, but men's actions worked against this inborn inclination. It is therefore important that we provide our children with a good upbringing. In other words, good in-born character must be reinforced with an up-bringing that will facilitate the development of this innate goodness. That is why sages sought to re-model people's characters by establishing guidelines, such as "patriotism", "filial piety", "benevolence", "trust-worthiness", "propriety", "righteousness, "honesty", and "shame".

Among the philosophers of the period of the Spring and Autumn Warring States, one philosopher, Xun Zi (.316–213 B.C.E.), argued a contrary point of view. He contended that people's basic nature is evil. But he did not disagree on the interplay between heredity and environment. He argued that people are born with inherited evil desires, for example: eyes desirous of looking at beautiful things, ears straining to listen to what pleases, mouths that crave delicious foods, and hearts that yearn for selfish gratification. Therefore, if the nature of a man is allowed to develop without restraints and control, he will become fiercely competitive, pugnaciously aggressive, jealous, utterly self-centred, debauched and vicious. This is why the sages wish to remodel the evil in-born character of individuals and encourage them to acquire good character through education, where they learn to live co-operatively and productively in society with others. Xun Zi therefore placed importance on the "efforts of men".

Xun Zi argued that propriety, righteousness and good behaviour re-enforced by the society are remedial measures, capable of reforming in-born evil.Xun Zi uses a number of analogies to illustrate his argument that remedial actions are required to improve people's characters: ie. a knife is not sharp before it is sharpened; a piece of crooked wood needs to be staightened before you work on it and make furniture out of it; a lump of clay is of little value until a potter kneads and moulds it into a vessel of value. This is why Xun Zi emphasizes the importance of improvement in the "works of men". (112)

这一点几千年以前中国人就实现了，明显地体现在"近朱者赤，近墨者黑"上。孟母三次搬家给孟子找个理想的育人环境也是个例子。孟子成了儒学大师。

孔子相信，人的本性本来是善良的，然而，人的行为往往有违天性。因此，我们要好好培育自己的孩子。换句话说，好的天性必须通过培养加以强化，以此养成内在的善良品质。因为，圣贤们通过制定规则，来寻找重新塑造人的性格的办法，比如，忠孝仁爱，礼义廉耻。

春秋、战国时代诸子中，荀子持相反的观点。他认为，人的本性是恶的。他并不认为遗传和环境之间有什么关系。他的观点是，人生来就有恶念，比如，眼睛爱看美的东西，耳朵爱听悦耳的音调，口爱吃美味佳肴，心怀着自私的欲念。因此，假如一个人的品性任其发展，他就会拼命地争，狠命地斗，嫉妒心强，彻底地自私、堕落和邪恶。所以，圣人希望通过教育重新塑造这种邪恶的天性，鼓励他们养成好的品性。通过教育，学习合作共赢的社会生活之道。由此可见，荀子注重的是"人为"。

荀子认为，社会施加的礼义善行是能够改变天性恶的补救手段。荀子使用许多类比，以此证明改善人性需要补救行为的论点，比方说，刀子不快了得磨一磨；木头弯了得直一直，才能下料做家具；一块泥没什么价值，陶工捏成有价值的用器。这就是荀子所强调的改善"人为"环境的重要意义。

In Christianity:

Judaism and Christianity have similarly emphasesed the polarity between good and evil in humankind. While made in the image of God, we nevertheless discover ourselves to be flawed. The flawedness, in the Yahwistic account of creation in Genesis 3, has been the despair of interpreters from earliest times. Some, following Augustine, have argued that we fell from a state of perfection. Others, following Irenaeus, have contended that the mythic account of creation in Genesis 2 and 3 was meant to convey, not a fall from perfection, but an inevitable process of human growth, involving the making of mistakes and the damaging of ourselves and others. These chapters are seen to have captured the essence of the developmental process.

Judaic–Christian tradition, and with it, Western Philosophy, concurs with Chinese philosophy, represented by the polarities of Confucius and Xun Zi, that human nature is both perfectable and flawed, and needs to be carefully nurtured and educated to encourage the good to emerge to supplant the evil.

基督教的观点：

犹太教和基督教同样重申人类善恶两个极端。我们是以上帝的形象造的，然而，我们却发现自己的缺陷。耶和华《创世纪》(3)中讲述了这种缺陷，有史以来一直成为译者最挠头的。有些人根据奥古斯丁的思想认为，人类是从完美状态下走向堕落的。也有的人追随依兰苦的学说，认为《创世纪》第二章和第三章所讲的神秘造世不是完美的堕落，而是为了让大家知道人类成长的必由过程，其中当然包括我们自身以及其他人的失误和损害。这些章节被看作是捕捉到了发展过程的实质。

犹太-基督传统及其西方哲学与中国哲学是一致的，孔子和荀子的思想虽然走两个极端，认为人性有善恶，需要细心调教，以此来扬善抑恶。

CHAPTER TWENTY-THREE
Ancestral worship or veneration?

The earliest, extant, written records of Chinese history, from the Shang Dynasty (c. 1766–1122 B.C.E.), indicate that Chinese worshipped their ancestors, paying them respect and asking for their protection. In ancient China, ancestor worship, especially the worship of the "high ancestors" or aristocrats, was held in ancestral temples. Most Chinese consider themselves descendents of Huang Di. Even today, both in China and in Taiwan, the birthday of Yellow Emperor is celebrated with a big festival, when thousands of Chinese, mainly Han, travel thousands of miles to pay their respects.

Ancestor worship is normally performed in the house of the worshipper. Delicious foods are offered, and "gold and silver" papers are burnt, both of which are seen as provision for ancestors in the other world. On All Souls Day Chinese pay an annual visit to the graves of their ancestors for memoral services and at the same time, tend their graves.

Filial piety, and the benevolence from which it springs, is traditionally considered by Chinese to be one of the major virtues. In the absence of benevolence, the world would be in turmoil. Filial piety is the basis of the family system, binding members together and reducing their isolation. The community and the nation also benefit from the practice of this virtue. Filial piety, which involves treating parents with reverence and affection, extends to all elders. Interestingly, the word xiao has no equivalent in English.

Confucius once said that a man, who fails to support his parents with reverence and affection, is not human. Even dogs and horses can offer support. Moreover, parents care for their children and carry them lovingly in their arms for at least two years before they can walk. They provide them with all neccessities and educate them until they become independent. It is only right that children should in return support their parents with tender and loving care, relieving them of heavy chores when parents grow old, weak and feeble.

In supporting and caring for parents, we are doing no more than what other creatures do. To emphasize this point, Confucians told a story about caring for the aged in the Book of Civics, where the comment is made:

"Crows build their nests in trees and breed their young chicks. They search for worms and bring them back to their nests to feed their young chicks. When they grow old and become immobile, by which time their young chicks have grown into big and strong birds, they feed their old ones in their nests with worms." One good turn deserves the other.

第二十三章

崇敬父母

　　中国历史现存最早的书面记录起于商代（公元前1766-1122），证明中国人拜祖，敬祖，祈求庇佑。中国古代，拜祖，尤其拜"远祖"或贵族祖先，在宗祠里举行。多数中国人认为，他们是黄帝子孙。甚至今天，海峡两岸同胞在黄帝生日的时候，数以千计的中国人，多数是汉族人，从千里以外赶来举行盛大的祭拜活动。

　　拜祖一般在家里举行。供上丰盛的食物，烧金银纸钱，供祖先们在另一个世界享用。每逢清明，中国人到祖坟去进行每年一度的祭奠活动。

　　中国人认为，孝敬及其仁爱是个传统美德。人无爱心，世界会不成样子。。孝敬是持家的基础，把家庭成员捆在一起，不至于掉队。这种美德也有利国家和社会。孝敬不但是对父母表现尊敬和爱心，而且惠及所有长辈。有趣的是，英文里却没有"孝"这个对等的单词。

　　孔子说过，人不孝，非人也，狗彘不如。父母养孩子，怀里至少抱两年才会走路，要什么给什么，供他们念书，直至成人。子女理当关爱父母，报答养育之恩，父母年老体弱的时候，要减轻他们繁重的家务。

　　关爱父母，我们所做的不过和其他动物一样罢了。儒家为了强调这一点，儒家在公民必读里面编了一篇老有所养的故事，说的是乌鸦在树上筑巢养小乌鸦，到外面找虫子回来喂它们。乌鸦老了飞不动的时候，小乌鸦长成健壮的大鸟了，它们就给窝里的老乌鸦喂虫子。这就是反哺的故事。

Ancestral veneration among the Chinese is more a cultural than a religious performance. Veneration, by way of bowing, or otherwise showing respect, is equally acceptable. Veneration, as an act of filial piety, does not amount to idolatry. The function of ancestral veneration serves to unite every member of a Chinese family. It is part and parcel of Chinese culture, except for those Chinese in foreign countries who are strangers to their heritage.

In the early days of Christian missions in China, some missionaries considered ancestral veneration as ancestor worship, and forbade converts to practice it. They regarded it as contrary to the Christian faith. This brought serious conflict with well-established Confucian society. They were opposed by the weight of Chinese high culture. It was not until the arrival in 1582 of Matthew Ricci (1552-1610), who began to study the thorny problems faced by the missionaries, that missionaries began gaining an insight into the distinctives of Chinese culture. Not only did he try to find Chinese equivalents for Christian terms, he also sought to reconcile Chinese customs and Christian principles. After a thorough study and careful consideration, Ricci decided that the rites in veneration of dead ancestors had civil rather than religious significance and concluded that it was OK for Christians to engage in them. It was for this reason that the more ethno-centric Franciscans regarded Jesuit converts as semi-pagan. However, those missionaries who were tactless and behaved with imperialistic disdain, that is, those who strictly adhered to the Vatican line, were driven out of China by the Emperor Kang Xi. Only those who accepted the rules laid down by Matthew Ricci were allowed to remain in China.

In Christianity:

The ancient Greeks and Romans developed ansectral cults. The nomadic ancestors of the patriarchal Hebrews not only cerebrated their ancestors but also worshipped animals, trees and stones.

Joshua told his people that the God of Israel remembered their forefathers, who had worshipped other gods. He advised them to throw away those gods, which they had worshipped when they lived beyond the River Euphrates and in Egypt. (113)

When Jacob planned to leave his father-in-law, Laban, his wife Rachel waited for her father to go to shear the sheep, and, when he was absent, stole his household gods. (Genesis 31:19). These household gods were figurines in human shape. Such human figurines could have been symbols of their forefathers, or of the gods worshipped by their forefathers.

These stories show that Israelites did have some form of ancestor worship in their early history. There is little doubt that ancestor worship was common in most ancient cultures, both East and West.

中国人拜祖属于文化，而不是宗教。常见的拜祖自然是磕头作揖什么的。拜祖是一种孝敬行为，没有上升到崇拜偶像。拜祖的目的是团结成员，这是中华文化的一部分，这个传统海外华人是陌生的。

基督教传到中国初期，有些传教士认为，拜祖就是祖先崇拜，不让皈依的人拜祖。他们以为，这种行为有违基督信仰。这在根深蒂固的儒教社会引起了激烈冲突，被中华高深的文化压倒了。雷芝马太（1552-1610）于1582年来到中国以后，开始研究传教士们面临的难题，洞悉了特殊的中华文化。他不但发现了中国和基督教对等的术语，而且试图把中国习俗和基督教原理整合起来。经过仔细研究和认真思考，雷芝认为，祭拜先祖只是民间活动，不含宗教色彩，由此得出结论，基督徒可以参与进来。这是这个缘故，比较民族化的法兰斯士教徒认为，耶稣教会的皈依者是半异教徒。但是，那些缺乏圆通、摆起帝国主义架子的人（也就是唯梵蒂冈阵线是从的人）都被康熙帝从中国撵了出去。只有遵守雷芝马太定的规矩，才可以留在中国。

基督教的观点：

古希腊、罗马都有拜祖的祭礼。希伯来人的先祖不但拜祖也拜动物、树和石头。

《乔舒亚记》第二十四章第2节里，乔舒亚告诉人民说，以色列人的上帝记得他们的先祖，尽管他们的先祖也崇拜其他神。他劝他们抛弃那些他们所拜的神……它们不属于幼发拉底河流域和埃及。

雅各布打算离开岳父拉比的时候，妻子拉结等她父亲去剪羊毛的当儿，偷了父亲家中的神（创31：19）。这些家神雕成人形，可能是他们的先祖的形象，或者是先辈们祭拜的神的形象。

这些故事说明，以色列人早期也有某种形式的先祖崇拜。东西方远古文化中，拜祖是普遍现象，这是毫无疑问的。

As for filial piety, Jesus is reported as saying, in Mark 7:13, that the Pharisees and teachers of law often aborted the intention of the commands of God by overlaying them with their own traditions. One such instance allowed a man to escape the responsibility of providing for his parents. Even though this was merely an illustration used in the course of a broader argument, it did indicate that Jesus endorsed the obligation to care for aging parents, while he asked followers to demonstrate an allegiance to himself, which overrid obligations towards family. It is obvious from the general tenor of his remarks, and from his behaviour, that he was not suggesting that his followers were immune from family, including parental obligations.

Jesus argued that the 10 Commandments, enshrined in the Hebrew Scriptures, could be reduced to two, – "Love the Lord your God with all your heart and with all your soul and with all your mind, " and "Love your neighbour as yourself." (114)Loving one's neighbour begins with loving one's parents the fifth Commandment of Moses. On another occasion Jesus argued that if a man did not care for his family he was worse than a heathen, Christians should honour their parents when they are alive – making sure that they are well provided for, giving them emotional support, minimising their hard chores, and giving them the love they deserve.

Ancestral veneration, and respect for parents, are synonymous, and inform the ethic of both Judeo–Christian and Chinese traditions.

A story on the origin of Ancestral Worship.

Once upon a time there lived a poor old widow and her only son, who worked as a hired shepherd. With his meagre wage, they lived from hand to mouth. The old widow grew frail and weak as the days passed. But her love for her son was unchanged. She did all the household chores; gave the better portion of food to her son; and mended his clothes. No matter whether it was raining or sunny, she always took his lunch to him in the field, which, at times, was quite far away from their home, as the flock moved from pasture to pasture.

The young man was spoiled and ungrateful. He did not appreciate what his mother had done for him. For reasons only known to him, presumeably owing to frustration, poverty, boredom with his job, he would find fault with his mother. He would beat her up for being too early or too late in delivering his food, or for the fact that it was too hot or too cold. The old widow endured this treatment, blaming only her fate.

One fine day the young man saw, to his great surprise, that the little lambs sucked their feed on bended knees. The scene of piety shocked him, and jolted his conscience. Suddenly, he realized that even the little creatures, which he tended, were grateful to their mother for their food. He was moved and ashamed of his behaviour towards his own mother. Tears rolled down his cheeks. He broke down and sobbed.

关于孝敬，《马可书》第七章第13节记载，耶稣说法利赛人和文士们经常用自己的传统罩住上帝的训令，以此来遏制懿旨。比如，允许人逃避奉养父母的责任。这个论题比较宽泛，在这里不过是打个比方，但的确证明了耶稣是赞许扶养老人的义务的。他吩咐门徒，忠实于自己，要胜过对家庭的责任感。他所说所做的主旨很清楚，他并不是让弟子们摆脱家庭，也摆脱对父母的义务。

耶稣认为，铭记在希伯来经文的十诫可以压缩成两点："你要尽心，尽性，尽意爱主，你的上帝"和"爱邻如爱己"（马太22-37-40）。爱你的邻居，从爱你的父母开始，这是摩西第五条诫命。耶稣还说，如果人不家，连异教徒都不如。只要父母在世，基督徒们就要孝敬父母，保证他们的供给，给他们精神安慰，减轻他们繁重的家务，给他们应得的爱。

尊敬祖先，孝顺父母在犹太-基督教伦理和中国传统中是同义的。

神子牌拜祖的故事：

从前，有个穷寡妇就一个儿子，给人家放羊。工钱很低，刚够糊口。日子一天天过去了，寡妇老了，日渐衰弱。可是，她爱儿子的心没有改变，所有的家务她都做了，把最好吃的给儿子吃，给儿子缝缝补补。无论是晴天还是阴天，她都到地里给儿子送饭，有时候，要走很远的路。因为羊群从一个草场啃到另一个草场。

年青人宠坏了，不懂得感恩。母亲为他做的，他没反应。也只有他自己才知道的缘故，大概是穷的吧，不如意吧，活儿干够了吧，他总找母亲的别扭。饭送早了或送晚了，凉了热了，他总要打母亲一顿。老寡妇忍着，认命了。

有个晴天，年轻人很惊奇地看到小羊们跪着吃奶。这种孝敬的情景震动了他，使他良心发现。他突然意识到，连他看的小动物也懂得感谢母羊给的吃的呢。他感动了，渐愧对母亲的行为。泪水滚下了他的脸颊，他呜咽地哭了。

Ancestral worship or veneration?

At this very moment, he saw his mother climbing the hill with a heavy basket of food. He could see her exhausted, walking. She staggered, struggling and dragging herself along. He was filled with compassion. Without hesitation, he ran towards his mother, wanting to relieve her of her heavy load. He wanted to tell her that he was sorry for ill-treating her and wished to ask for her forgiveness.

Having been beaten each day, the old woman was used to approaching her son with anxiety and fear, wondering what he would accuse her of next. Now she saw her son running towards her. Her heart jumped to her mouth. Her legs trembled. She almost fell under the weight of her frail body. She was at her wit's end. Then she saw a lake nearby. She put down her basket and ran as quickly as her legs would carry her. "Splash!" She jumped into the lake, making ripples that moved out towards the other side of the lake.

The young man, when he saw his mother stumbling towards the lake, shouted to her, "Ma ... Ma " Alas! It was too late. He quickly dived into the lake at the spot where his mother had fallen in. He reached the bottom, but could not find her body. He surfaced to take a deep breath and dived to the bottom again. He searched for his mother, but in vain. He thoroughly combed the bottom of the lake, but could not find her. There was no trace of his mother.

The commotion did not destroy the serenity of the lake and its surroundings. The lambs grazed quietly by the side of their mothers, and tiny birds chirped merrily upon the bough above them. It was unbelieveable that the young man's mother could have disappeared into thin air. He made a final dive into the bottom of the lake, and, to his great disappointment, all he could find was a piece of wood. One final time he called out, "Ma ⋯!" But there was no response. Thinking that his mother had turned into a piece of wood, he took it home and treasured it. Whenever he looked at it he thought of his mother.

People heard about how piously he respected his mother. They imitated him by keeping wooden tablets with the names of their ancestors written on them, for the purpose of remembering them.

In China today, despite the impact of the Cultural Revolution, the Chinese still build "ancestral halls", where wooden tablets are arranged in tiers on a long high table and photos are hung on the two side walls of the hall of rememberance. The ancestral hall also serves as a community meeting place for social gatherings, such as, planning for festivals and national public holidays, etc. Village elders, or clan elders, ─── many villages are occupied by one single clan – hold regular meetings in such buildings to make decisions on developments or improvements in the village. In this way the hall acts as a seat of local government.

就在这时,他看见母亲背着重重的饭筐,爬上了小山。他见到的是她疲惫的步履。她一走一摆,脱着身子往前挣扎着。他充满了同情。他毫不犹豫地朝母亲冲了过去,想卸下她的重担。他想告诉母亲,过去虐待她,他是多么的后悔,希望能得到她的原谅。

老妇人每天都挨揍,每每到儿子跟前的时候,都是胆胆突突的,不知道这回怎么指责她呢。看到儿子朝她跑来,她的心都要跳出来了,她两腿发抖,羸弱的身子险些倒了。她没法没法的,瞧见旁边有个湖,放下篮子,奔了过去。"扑通",她跳进湖里,溅出的水纹儿传到了湖的那一边。

年轻人眼见母亲笨笨咔咔地朝湖里去了,大声喊道:"妈……妈!"可是,太晚了。他马上潜入母亲跳进去的地方。他潜到湖底,也没找到妈妈的尸首。他浮上水面,深深吸了一口气,又潜到湖底。他找哇找,结果没找到。他搜遍了湖底,怎么都找不到她。湖里没有妈妈的踪影。

一气儿的折腾没有打扰湖水和周围的宁静。小羊静静地在母羊旁边吃草,小鸟在羊群上方的树枝儿上啁啾着。信不信也好,年轻人的母亲可能消失在薄薄的空气里了。他最后一次潜入湖底,让他大失所望的是,他所找到的只是一块木头。他最后一次喊道:"妈…..!"没有回音。他想,妈妈变成了一块木头,就把它带回家,珍藏起来。每逢见到它的时候,他就想起了母亲。

人们听到他是多么虔诚地爱着他的母亲,都纷纷效仿,把自己祖辈的名字刻在木板上,来祭奠他们。

今日的中国虽然经过"文革",一部分中国人依旧建造宗祠,长长的供板上安放一排排的牌位,纪念厅的两壁悬挂照片。宗祠也是逢年过节社交聚会的去处。老亲少友(不少村子是一家子)早在这里定期碰个面,研究研究村子怎么发展。这样以来,宗祠就有了会所让地方政府召集村民一样的功能。

CHAPTER TWENTY-FOUR
Self-discipline, Family Management, National Government, and World Peace.

The aspiration of a Confucian is to be either a sage or a leader. In order to achieve such an ideal, one must first of all develop the qualities of a sage inwardly, and the noble characters of a leader in outward behaviour. This is always more easily said than done. It takes tremendous effort and perseverance to arrive at this ideal state.

Confucians argue that even the seemingly impossible task of world peace begins with individuals. That is why they consider first of all self-discipline, then management of a family, and finally governing a nation. When these different levels are attended to world peace is brought closer. These are the four stages in life's journey. The Book of Da Xue comments: "you must discipline yourself first before you manage your family; you must manage your family first before you govern your nation; and you must govern your nation first before you are in a position to bring peace to the world". (115)

Unless you take charge of yourselves and set a good example to others, you will not be able to command respect from others and acquire persuasive power in your words. As you live with high moral standards, your thoughts and deeds will influence the society in which you live. And this society will be orderly, systematic and harmonious. The importance of self-discipline cannot be over-emphasized. Self-discipline is not only a basic moral standard for individuals, but is also the foundation of good government.

As Confucians are scholars, they encourage learning and the honing of dialectical and logical skills as the first step in self-development. One then develops a capacity for understanding and for identifying causes. You must control your emotions and avoid losing your temper, to the extent that you do not see objects around that distract you, nor hear words that disrupt you. You must be sincere and refrain from deceiving others, or even yourself. Your words and deeds will be closely watched, even when you are alone. As Lao Zi argues discipline involves "self-adjustment", "self-criticism", and "self-appropriation". (116)

第二十四章

修身，齐家，治国，平天下

儒士的志向是成圣成贤，当个官。为了实现这个理想，必须做到内圣外王。这个说来容易做到难，需要百折不挠，方能达到这个理想的境界。

儒家认为，即使是天下太平这样的难事也要从个人做起。所以，要修身，齐家，治国，平天下。这是人生四步走。《大学》说："先修身而后齐家，先齐家而后治国，先治国而后平天下。"

如果你不担起责任，给别人做个榜样，你就得不到别人的尊重，也就说服不了别人。如果你道德高尚，你的思想和行为就会影响你所处的社会，社会就会有条有理，平安和睦了。自我修养怎么提都不为过，它不但是个人基本道德的准则，也是良性管理的基础。

儒士们鼓励向学，把研磨辩证逻辑方法当作自我修养的第一步。然后再提高理解和鉴别能力。必须控制情绪，不要使性，要达到视而不见、听而不闻的程度。要真诚待人，不要欺骗别人，也不要欺骗自己。即使独处的时候，你的言行也会被密切关注。老子说，人要自正、自视、自均。

Self-discipline, Family Management, National Government, and World Peace.

Family management is concerned with putting one's family in order consistent with the second stage of Confucian teaching. The emphasis is on paying filial piety to one's parents, and respecting elders, and loving sibling and children. Self-discipline also involves the development of a "benevolent heart". Family management represents the initial stage in the development of "good deeds" in community living. Self-discipline and family management are considered internal affairs. The following stages relate to external matters. Family members are your immediate kin. One must have a good grounding within one's family before one takes on larger responsibilities. There is a transition between the first two stages and the remaining two.

In serving your nation, whether you are a general or a governor, you must be patriotic in your support of leaders above you, and you must implement and fulfil the wishes of the people under you. Lao Zi argues, leaders in government must be just in all dealings, encouraging just behaviour in leaders, subordinate officials and the common people. He also argues that one must be concerned for the poor and needy. Leaders must act humblely and moderately, and not tax the people excessively so that they go hungry. They are advised to stay close to the wishes of the people. If we disregard the masses, we will be like a fish out of water. We must value the lives of others and not send them off to war at the other end of the world. (117)

Finally, world peace is to be sought, by "way of moderation". Confucians favour moderation as a way of life, which in Lao Zi's terms is to "keep to moderation". Lao Zi argued that in international affairs one should not use military might to overpower others. When one is forced to use weapons, the situation often gets out of control, and one takes delight in killing. A large state should maintain a humble attitude towards smaller states, and win their support and co-operation. Smaller states should seek to gain protection from and an alliance with a larger state. Diplomacy should be sincere, with mutual accommodation and obligation. This is one reason why China, which had been a strong nation from time to time, has not been aggressive, or become a colonial power acquiring territories around the world over the last two thousand, five hundred years! John Merson, an Australian historian, in his book The Road to Xanadu, says that China had the largest naval power with ocean-going ships and military might in the 14th Century which could have been used to conquer the world.

"Self-discipline, Family management, the government of a nation, and "world peace" are closely attached to the maxim "patriotism, filial piety, benevolence, love, courteous manners, righteousness, honesty and 'awareness of' shame", which were promoted by Guan Zi (685 B.C.E.). (118)When one is equipped with these characteristics, one is disciplined, and well able to bring peace to the world. This maxim has been the basic principle in Confucian teaching, and is still inculcated in modern education.

| 修身，齐家，治国，平天下

　　儒家学说的第二个阶段是齐家，就是要处理好家庭关系。重点落在孝敬父母，尊敬长辈，爱护兄弟姐妹和孩子。修身也就是仁心的养成，齐家是步入社会生活培养德行的第一步。修身和齐家被认为是内部事务，接下来就是涉外了。家人是自己的亲人，肩负起更大的责任之前，务必在家里打好底子。头两个阶段是向后两个阶段的过度。

　　治国的时候，无论是武将还是文官。都要忠君爱国，圆满完成人民的嘱托。老子认为，有司凡事要讲公道，在同僚、属下和百姓中树立正气。他还认为，要关心疾苦，虚以下人，不横征暴敛，让人民吃不上饭。要倾听群众的意愿；如果不考虑群众，就像离水之鱼。要珍惜别人的生命，不要让他们到异乡他国去送死。

　　最后是守中庸之道的平天下。儒家把中庸之道当作人生观，用老子的话说，就是"守于中"。老子认为，国家之间不应该使用武力来压服别人。被迫使用武力的时候，常常控制不住局势，把屠杀视为儿戏。大国要谦让小国，要争取他们的支持与合作。小国要寻求大国的保护，和大国结盟。要进行诚信外交，互相包容，互进义务。正是这个原因，中国过去2500年间时兴时衰，并未曾侵犯过别人，也未曾成为殖民势力，霸占世界领土。澳大利亚历史学家约翰·默尔森在他的著作《路向赞安都》中说，中国在十四世纪时拥有最强大的海上力量和军事力量，是完全可以征服全世界的。

　　"修身、齐家、治国、平天下"的基本原则和管子的"忠孝仁爱，礼义廉耻"非常贴近。一个人如果有了这些品质，也就有了素质，也就能给世界带来和平。这个格言成为儒学的基本原则，至今还在教育中反复灌输。

Self-discipline, Family Management, National Government, and World Peace.

The upbringing of children within the Judeo-Christian tradition is more God-oriented than the equivalent Confucian system, and involves seeking divine wisdom. The Book of Proverbs provided a stock of wisdom sayings, which were designed to mould character.

The Book of Proverbs says that parents should not spare the rod, otherwise their children will be a disgrace of their mothers (29:15). If you spurn your father's discipline you are a fool (15:5 and 29:15). You should respect God, for he will bless you with knowledge and wisdom. Only fools despise wisdom and discipline (1:7). One should not be lazy, which brings poverty, but be diligent, which will lead to the acquisition of wealth (10:4). One should be honest in business dealings. If you are righteous, your integrity will guide you (13:6) You should be generous to the poor and kind to the needy (14:31) When you are a man of knowledge and understanding you will restrain your words and will not lose your temper easily (17:27) You should not be proud in your heart, but humble (18:12).

The Covenant demands of Yahweh, in the Book of Leviticus, are comprehensive. First of all, you must respect your mother and father and love your brother. You must uphold justice, and refuse to show favouritism to people with wealth or status, and despise the poor and lowly.

As rulers and officials, you must administer justice, save people from the hands of oppressors, give alms to orphans and widows, and not ill-treat aliens. [119]Yahweh forbade rulers to enjoy luxurious palaces at the expense of the poor.

In his Letter to the Romans, the Apostle Paul said that we receive grace from God through our faith in Jesus Christ. Not only do we rejoice in the hope of the glory of God, but we will also rejoice in the sufferings, for it is sufferings that give us perseverance, and perseverance produces character, and this character brings hope, which leads on to an experience of the love of God (5:1-5).

Paul also argued that Christians must submit to authorities, who were God's servants, and pay taxes when they were due. (13:1) Furthermore, he advised in his final letter to Timothy that
"God did not give us a spirit of timidity, but a spirit of power, of love and of self-displine." [120]

Jews and Chinese are of two different traditions, relating to the Middle East and the Far East. Character was grounded similarly in the two traditions, except for the fact that Jesus and later Christians were directly responsible to God in whatever they did, while for Confucians the Lord-on-high was remote and "Heaven" is too big and indifferent. The good deeds of Confucians depended on the state of their benevolent hearts, though acts consistent with the Way of God.

和儒家教育体系相比，犹太-基督教传统更注重子女的神学教育，内容涵盖求索神的智慧。《箴言书》中有一堆智慧格言，是用来塑造人格的。书中说，家长舍不得棍棒，孩子就会给家长丢脸（29：15），不听父亲言，傻瓜在眼前（15：5），敬畏上帝，上帝用知识和智慧保佑你；只有傻瓜才蔑视智慧，不受约束（1：7），懒汉受穷，勤劳致富（10：4），诚信经商，正当做人（13:6），慷慨待贫，仁慈救急（14：31），有知识的人要慎言戒怒（17：27），谦虚戒傲。

《利未记书》记载，耶和华的约书内容广泛。首先，要孝敬父母爱护兄弟。要主持公义，不要偏袒高官厚禄的人，不要看不起穷人和卑微的人。

当了官掌了权，要公正；拯救人民摆脱压迫者的魔掌，接济孤寡，善待外人（杰里迈亚 21:12，22:3）。耶和华不许统治者鱼肉百姓。

使徒保罗在《罗马书》中说，我们通过耶稣基督的信仰接受上帝的恩惠。我们幸福，不仅是从上帝的荣耀中获得了希望，而且是在痛苦中得到幸福，因为痛苦磨炼了我们的意志，意志练就了性格，性格带来了希望，希望引导我们去体味上帝之爱（罗马13）。

保罗还认为，基督徒要听官方的，因为他们是上帝的仆人，到期的时候是要交税的(13:1)。他在给第摩西的最后一封信中还认为，"上帝没有给我们胆怯的灵魂，而是给我们力量的灵魂、爱的灵魂和自律的灵魂。"

犹太人与中国人是中东和远东两个不同的传统，性格的基础是类似的，只是基督徒直接对上帝负责，儒家则认为皇帝太远，天太高，因此，不太在乎。儒家行善靠的是仁心，尽管他们的行为是在尊上帝之道。

CHAPTER TWENTY-FIVE
In a company of three, definitely there is my teacher(121)

Confucius argued that we live and learn. The longer we live, the more we learn, and we continue to learn even when we are in our senior years. He also encouraged people not to be ashamed to "stoop, " that is, to lower oneself in order to make an inquiry. As a matter of fact, Chinese use two words xue wen, to describe "knowledge." xue, denotes "learn" or "learning, " and 问 wen, means "ask" or "inquire." The inquisitive mind probes the unknown.

Most of our learning, especially conscious learning, takes place after birth. But there is a hereditary aspect, "in-born intellectual potential" or a capacity for certain skills, which must also be taken into account. Chinese describe the latter rather picturesquely as "before heaven" .This genetic inheritance is a gift, and is not easily explained.

We also learn from the experience of others. Suppose you are with two others in a company of three, and the other two are older and wiser than you are. Their wisdom is at your disposal. If only one is wiser, then you can learn from this person. The worst scenario is when both of your companions are not as wise as you are. Is there anything to be learned in these circumstances? If the other two are stupid, and make a lot of mistakes, you can learn from and avoid their mistakes. Therefore, when you are in the company of two others, no matter how developed, or otherwise the other two are, you can learn from what they have to teach you and avoid their short-comings.

Learning involves more than mere academic knowledge, we also learn from the successes and mistakes of others. It also includes learning from personal experience, which involves both practical and theretical knowledge. It is because not everyone has the same experiences that we need to learn from each other. We can pick and adapt the good experiences and discard bad ones, or avoid the shortcomings of others.Learning from others requires a certain degree of humility.

Proverbs 22 contends that it is the Lord who gives wisdom, and that knowledge and understanding come from his mouth. If you accept the words of the Lord, then, you must adjust your ears to wisdom and give your heart to understanding; you must plead earnestly, asking for insight and understanding; and you must look for wisdom with the same commitment and intensity that you search for gold or silver.

第二十五章

三人行必有我师

　　孔子认为，人"生而知之"。人活得越长，学得越多，"活到老，学到老"。他还鼓励人们"不耻下问"。中国人用"学问"这两个字来形容知识，"学"就是"学习"，"问"就是"询问"。好奇心（注：心和头脑通用）探索的是未知。

　　多数学问，尤其是意识到的学问，是在出生后学到的。然而，也有先天的因素……"天生的智力潜能"或掌握某些技巧的能力---不能不考虑进来。遗传是天赋，在此不便解释。

　　我们也可以学习他人的经验。如果三人为伍，其他两人比你大，比你聪明，你可利用他们的才智。如果有一个比你聪明，你可向这个人学习。最糟糕的情形是：两个赶不上你聪明。这种情况下，你还学什么呢？如果另两位都是个笨蛋，尽是搞事，你能学的就是不犯他们的错误。因此，你和他们在一起，不管怎么发展，也不管他们怎么发展，他们所能教你的你学到了，他们的短处也就避开了。

　　学习不单单是学术知识，也可以从别人的成败中学习。学习也包含"格物致知"，其中有理论的，也有实践的。因为每个人的经验并不相同，需要互相借鉴学习。"三人行，必有我师；择其善者而从之，其不善者而改之"。向别人学习得谦虚点儿。

　　《箴言书》第二章第6节认为，"主给人以智慧，知识和理解力都从他那里脱口而出。"如果你接受了主的话，你就得侧耳聆听智慧，专心去理解；你得虚心求教，以求顿悟；求索智慧，一定要像寻找金银一样下功夫，专心致志。

Practical experience is an important part of learning, such as "Not climbing up a high mountain you do not realize how high the sky is, and not coming near a deep valley where you do not know how thick the crust of the earth is". Confucians do not stop at acquiring knowledge. They argue that knowledge is only good when you put it into practice – "Not having heard it, it is better that you hear it; hearing it, it is better that you see it; seeing it, it is better that you know it; knowing it, it is better that you put it into practice. The route is from learning to practice. Practice brings a more complete understanding, and it is only this complete understanding that qualifies a person as a sage.". (122) This is similar to Lao Zi's philosophy about knowdege and putting it into practice. (123)

Through reading and thinking we receive theretical learning or head-knowledge. This head-knowledge is bodied out with practical experience, which involves our senses, among other things. However, there is a third kind of "knowledge," often referred to as Wisdom, which comes by way of revelation. This style of Wisdom is the gift of spiritual inspiration. While the initiative, in the gifting of this wisdom, lies with God, we can prepare ourselves for it through respect shown for God, or through openness to God, to the Spirit. This sort of knowledge is sometimes called inspiration, creative inspiration.

This phenomenon is illustrated by a story about Si-ma Guang (司马光 c. 1085 C.E.). When the subject of the story was a little boy, he was playing hide and seek with a few other children. One of the little boys thought it was a good idea to hide inside a huge earthen jar. With the help of a stool, he climbed inside the huge jar, not knowing that the jar was full of water. The little boy fell inside the water. "Help! Help! ...", he cried, for he was drowning. Everyone gathered around the huge jar, but the jar was too huge and heavy for the boys to move. It was too high for them to reach the drowning boy. They were at their wit's end, and did not know what to do. They were very frightened, staring blankly at one another. Suddenly, Si-ma Guang had an inspiration. He ran out of the house and brought in a big stone. He threw the big stone at the side of the huge jar with all his might. Clonk! The jar cracked and broke. Water rushed out through a big hole, bringing the little boy out with it. By this action, Si-ma Guang saved the boy's life. (124)

Si-ma Guang did not have the practical experience, or the theoretical knowledge to save the drowning boy. However, we can say that he had presence of mind, or that he was a clever lateral thinker. The inspiration, the idea of cracking the jar, appeared out of the blue, and was therefore a type of revelation.

实践经验是学习的重要组成部分，比方说："不登高山，不知天之高也，不临深渊，不知地之厚也"。儒生们不断地求学，他们认为，知识得活学活用---"不闻，不若闻之；闻之，不若见之；见之，不若知之；知之，不若行之。学至于行而止矣。行之，明也，明之为圣人"。这话类似老子实践出真知的哲学观。

通过读书和思考，我们获得理论知识。理论知识要通过各种感知等实践经验才得以体现。不过，还有第三种知识，常称为来自启发的智慧。这种智慧是灵性的启迪。智慧的天赋具有能动性，是上帝给的。通过敬拜上帝，通过向上帝坦开心胸，我们才能走向这个灵性。这种知识有时候叫做灵感，创作的灵感。

司马光（公元1085年生）有个故事，说的是他小时候和小伙伴捉迷藏玩儿。有个小孩儿以为藏在大缸里不错，就借着个凳子爬进一个大缸。殊不知缸里一下水。小孩掉进水里。"救命啊！救命！……"他喊道，快要淹死了。孩子们围着大缸，缸又大又重，搬不动。缸太高，无法够到快淹死的小朋友。大家袖手无策了，非常害怕，互相大眼瞪小眼。忽然间，司马光心血来潮。他跑到门外，抱着一块大石头，用力朝着缸的一侧酷了过去。"呼"的一声，大缸破了，水花的一下从洞里冲了出来，也把小伙伴冲了出来。司马光这个举动救了孩子的命。

司马光没有实践经验，也没有救落水儿童的理论知识。然而，我们可以看到，他有头脑，善于联想。砸缸这个灵感仿佛从天上掉下来一样，是一种灵感的体现。

Some would argue that what the boy did was no more than the application of "common sense." However, one has to ask what "common sense" represents.

I know of the son of a wealthy family in Malaysia who attended Geelong Grammar School, in Australia, where Prince Charles received part of his education. After schooling, the young man went to Cambridge University, in England, to study Economics.

While there, he tried to fry an egg. This was his first experience working in a kitchen. The egg stuck to the frying pan, and when he tried to flip the egg over, he made a mess of it. He telephoned his mother in Malaysia, and asked her why this had happened. After listening patiently to his description of his proceedure for frying eggs, the mother asked her son whether he had heard of something called "oil." It was not a non-stick pan that her son had used. He was trying to fry the egg without using oil! Yes, it was commonsense to fry an egg with oil. However, if someone has had no experience in the kitchen, how does one acquire the "common sense" understanding that one uses oil to fry eggs? Commonsense, therefore, is practical understanding, employed in everyday life, which derives from teaching or experience, which becomes common knowledge, at least to the individual concerned.

Confucius was the most knowledgeable teacher of his time. One day he was travelling from one state to another. There was a group of little boys playing along his path, and thus blocking his carriage. Confucius thought he could use friendly persuasion to obtain a passage. He requested the boys to let him pass, but they refused, saying that they would let him pass if he answered a question from their leader. Confucius gladly agreed, and promised them that if he failed to do so, he would return home. The leader of the boys asked Confucius to tell him the number of stars in the sky, to which Confucius could not give the correct answer. He pointed out that the stars were too far away to allow him to give a correct answer. He requested the boy to ask him something that his eyes could take in. Consequently, the boy asked him to name the number of his eyelashes! Confucius was dumbfounded! The eyelashes were really close to his eyes, but they were too close for him to see properly, and therefore to count. There was silence, as both groups stared at each other. Then, slowly, the carriage turned to face the direction from which it had come, and Confucius bid the boys farewell. Are such awkward questions artful? Are they witty questions? Or are they deliberately nasty and impossible?

Proverbs 30 says that we can learn even from tiny creatures like ants, coneys, locusts and lizards. The importance is on our attitude. Advices fron the Book of Proverbs encourages us to be humble and persistent as we approach the learning task, that is, to learn from the ants.

The prophet Jeremiah argued that we have to wait patiently on the Lord for his revelation. To gain wisdom we need to be humble and respectful. As wisdom is a gift of God, it transcends the scope of ordinary education.

When Jesus was teaching in a crowded house, his disciples informed him that his mother and brothers were outside. He told them that anyone who had heard the Words of God, and put God's will into practice, was his mother and brother and sister.[125]This highlighted the importance of grounding theory in practice.

有人会认为，这个小孩儿所做的不过是用了一下常识而已。但，我们要问，这个常识代表什么？

我认识马来西亚有个富裕家庭的孩子，他在澳洲芝隆文法学院念书，也就是查尔斯王子就读过的地方。毕业后，年轻人去了剑桥大学读经济学。

有一回他想煎个蛋，这还是他头一次下厨哩。蛋粘在煎锅上，他想把蛋翻个身儿，结果弄得一团糟。他给马来西亚的妈妈打电话，问是怎么回事。他妈妈耐心听完他煎蛋的过程，就问儿子，听没听说有一种叫"油"的东西呢？儿子用的不是不粘锅。他想煎蛋，但没用油！对了，煎蛋放油是个常识，可是，如果没做过饭，怎么会知道煎蛋还得用油这个常识呢？所以，常识就是日常生活中的实践性了解，它来源于教学或经验，成为至少是个别人的普通知识。

孔子是当时最有知识的人。有一天，他周游列国，有一群小孩正在路上玩，挡了他的车。孔子想，还是劝他们让个道吧，就要求孩子们让路，但是，他们就不让，他们说，让路可以，但得回答他老大的一个问题。孔子高兴答应了，说答不上来就折回去。孩子头儿要孔子说出天上有多少颗星星，孔子无法捏准答案。孔子指着星星说，太远了，没法答对。他请这个孩子出个能看见的。孩子头儿问他，他有多少根睫毛！孔子哑口无言！睫毛的确近在眼前，但是太近了，没法看啊，也没法数哇。一片沉寂，双方你瞧瞧我，我瞧瞧你。后来，车慢慢地掉头朝原路走了，孔子告别了孩子们。这些蹩脚的问题是耍滑呢，还是斗智呢，还是刻意刁难呢？

《箴言》第三十章说，我们可以向蚂蚁啦，兔子啦，蝗虫啦，蜥蜴啦这些小东西学习。重要的是我们的学习态度。《箴言书》要我们谦虚，有恒劲儿地面向学习任务，那就学学蚂蚁吧。

先知杰里迈亚认为，我们要静候神的启示。要想得到智慧，就必须谦虚，必须尊重人。智慧是上帝的恩赐，是超越普通教育的。

当耶稣在一家传道的时候，满屋子都是人。他徒弟告诉他，他母亲和兄弟们没在家。他告诉他们，不管是谁，听了上帝的话，遵行了上帝的旨意，就是他的母亲、他的兄弟姐妹（马可书3：35）。这强调了基础理论付诸实践的重要性。

Proverbs 13:20 contends that "He who walks with the wise grows wise, but a companion of fools suffers harm." This highlights the fact that we are influenced, both consciously and unconsciously, by the behaviour of our companions.

There is no end to learning, as the Confucian saying argued. We continue learning into our senior years. There are three important elements in learning, – humility, eagerness and moral choice. We must be humble enough to learn from anyone, even fools. We must be hungry for more knowledge. Finally, we must be wise enough to differentiate between right and wrong, and between conventional wisdom and the Way of God, or Heaven.

《箴言》第十三章第20节说："与智者同行必增智，和愚者为伍必受害"。这里所说的是，我们有意识或无意识地受着身边人的行为的影响。

孔子说学无止境。人要学到老。学习的重要因素有三：不耻下问，如饥似渴，学风正派。只有不耻下问，才能从任何人甚至是傻瓜那里学到东西；只有像饿了一样，才能学到更多的知识；只有明辨善恶，把凡夫俗子的智慧和天之道区分开来，才是明智的。

CHAPTER TWENTY-SIX

Bringing up children without discipline is the fault of the father Uncut jade not finely honed does not represent something precious

"Feeding without teaching" or "bringing up children without educating them, " is the fault of the father. A father is responsible for disciplining children, and therefore he is called, literally, "strict or stern father" , while a mother, responsible for feeding the children, is called "loving mother" "Jade which is not cut or carved, and also finely honed, " "will not be transformed into useful vessels" .

The Confucians emphasized the importance of two types of education --- family education involving discipline and academic education in schools. Academic knowledge is the foundation on which one builds a career, while family discipline helps to mould character, attitudes and behaviour. Someone who has not been well disciplined at home, or adequately educated at school, is like a piece of uncut, precious stone, be it jade or diamond. Jade is of no use unless it is fashioned into a vessel or instrument of intrinsic or utilitarian value. There are many stories in Chinese history to compliment this saying.

(1) The mother of Mencius moved house three times in search of a suitable neighbourhood which would furnish a healthy and nurturing environment for her son. They first lived near a cemetery. Mencius learned how to cry and wail, becoming familiar with funeral rituals. His mother thought that this was not what she wanted her son to learn. They moved to a place near the butchers, where Mencius played with the butcher's children. He began to pick up the language and behaviour of butchers. Realizing the future consequence of this could be disastrous for her son, she quickly made another move. This time they chose a house next to a school, because she wanted her son to be a scholar.

Once Mencius played truant from school. On his reurn home, his mother was so angry that she cut the unfinished cloth in the weaving machine. Mencius, observing her action, expressed surprise. He quickly kneeled before his mother and inquired why she had acted this way. His mother explained that, in making a piece of cloth, she used threads one by one and undertook each stitch patiently to weave them into a pattern, just like he needed to do with his study, consistently, day by day, if he wished to succeed. However, if he stopped his study half way, which would deny him future success, it would be like her cutting the unfinished cloth. Her lecture was like a thunderbolt, and jolted him into reality. He learned the lesson, and thereafter worked hard at his studies. (126)

第二十六章

养不教，父之过，玉不琢，不成器

"养不教，父之过"。当父亲的责任是要管教儿女，所以被称为严父。母亲的责任是养儿育女，所以叫作慈母。儒家说，"玉不琢，不成器。"

儒家注重两种教育，也就是家庭教育包含育和教。教是立业的基础，育有助于塑造人格、态度和行为。家庭教养不良，学校受教不足，好比没有雕琢的玉或钻石一样。玉的价值在于按照内在的或实用的价值雕塑成某种器具。中国历史上有许多故事说明了这个格言。

(1) 孟子的母亲三次搬家，找个适合的邻居，给儿子创设个健康、补益的环境。第一次住在墓地附近。孟子学会了哭号，熟悉了葬事。孟母想，儿子不应该学这个。他们搬到了屠宰场附近，孟子和屠夫的孩子成了伙伴，言行举止开始学屠夫了。意识到这样卜去会害了儿子的，她马上搬走了。这一次，选了个靠近学校的住了下来，她想让儿子成个学者。

有一次，孟子逃了学，回家时，母亲非常忿怒，把织机上没织完的布剪了。孟子见到母亲的举动非常惊讶。他随机跪下，问为什么这样。孟母说，织一匹布得有耐性，要一针一线，才能织成花色，学习也是这样，要日复一日地坚持下去，这样才能学成。如果半道扔了，将来不会有作为的，就像布织了一半剪断似的。她的话好像晴天霹雳，一下子把他霹进了现实。他有了记性，以后就用功读书了。

Bringing up children without discipline is the fault of the father
Uncut jade not finely honed does not represent something precious

He is today recognized as the greatest disciple of Confucius and is honoured, along with Confucius, in Kong Meng Philosophy. Not only education, but also environment contributes to the making of a great and successful man.

(2) Once upon a time, there was a robber. He was a terror in his district. He not only robbed people of cattle and goods, but also burnt down their houses. Finally he was arrested. The district governor sentenced him to death. Before the execution, the governor asked him whether he had a request. He said that he wanted to speak to his mother. The governor sent for his mother, who came and saw her son, whose hands were tied behind his back, kneeling in the town square. She burst into tears, running towards him, hugging him and crying aloud. The robber asked his mother to put her ear nearer to him so that he could whisper to her. She thought that there might be an important secret he wanted to tell her. She put her ear closer to him. "Crunch!" He bit her ear off. He argued that had his mother disciplined him when he was a small child he would not have gone astray and become a robber and would not be losing his head now. This story further highlights the importance of parental discipline in character building.

(3) Zuo Zongtang was a great general in the Qing Dynasty. He had, in his army, a supurb warrior, Zhang Yao, who fought and won many battles. Zuo Zongtang recommended this warrior to the post of governor of a prefecture. The emperor later withdrew his approval, because someone reported that Zhang Yao was illiterate. Realizing the lost opportunity of a good education during his childhood, Zhang Yao engaged a teacher to teach him day and night. After a few years of hard work he became well educated and the emperor restored him to the post of governor.(127)

Zhang Yao, without higher education, was like a piece of uncut jade. He was not refined enough to be a governor, though he was a skilful and wise warrior. What he needed was a higher education to complement his other qualities. The finishing touch to a piece of jade is to be finely honed, which enhances its value, making it both more beautiful and useful.

Mo Zi stressed the importance of "actions taken by men" in shaping their characters, as well as qualities acquired through conscientious learning. Bringing up children without educating them sounds very irresponsible. The responsibility for educating their children is the task of fathers, according to Confucian teaching. The fathers provide them with the means as well as the aspiration for higher learning. The children pick up on their father's aspirations for their lives and careers. They "work" on the children, making sure that they are encouraged to realize these aspirations.

Without higher education it was impossible to obtain a good and honoured job in ancient China. Technical tasks were considered "rough jobs." Scholars were considered above other professions in the occupational classification, which ran from "scholars to farmers, workers and businessmen" This was the reason why many struggled to succeed in their studies.

他被称为孔子的大弟子，和孔子并称为孔孟之道。教育和环境塑造伟大的成功人士。

(2)从前，有个强盗，为害一方，抢人家牛羊，烧人家房屋。最后，他被逮住了，地方官处他死刑。行刑前，地方官问他还有什么说的，他说要和妈妈说句话。地方官派人把他妈妈找来，妈妈见到儿子双手反绑跪在场子上，流着泪奔向儿子，抱着儿子大哭。强盗叫妈妈把耳朵凑过来，说句悄悄话。她想，有什么秘密告诉她吧。她把耳朵凑过去。"喀嚓"一下，妈妈的耳朵咬掉了。他说，小时候妈妈管他的话，就不会走错路，也不会被砍头的。这个故事说的是培养人格过程中家长管教的重要性。

(3)清朝大将左宗棠手下有个能征惯战的张曜，左宗棠保举他当了一个省的提督。因为有人参奏，张曜是个文盲，皇帝后来撤奏。张曜知道童年没机会念书，就请了个教师爷日夜攻读。几年苦读，学问长进，皇帝赐他官复原职。

张曜没念过大书，就像一块粗玉。虽然打起仗来条条是道，当个提督还欠练。他缺的就是长进学问，品质互补。玉得细细地磨，才能增加它的价值，好看又好用。

墨子强调"人为"，通过有意识地学习，来塑造性格和品质。养而不教是不负责任的。儒家认为，教子，父之道。当父亲的要让孩子想念书，同时给他们创造念书的条件。孩子不能有负于父亲对他们成家立业的渴望。他们在孩子身上"下功夫"，为的是了了这份心愿。

中国古代，不好好念书，就找不到什么像样的营生。技工被认为是"粗活"，各业之中，学者排在前面，依次是"士农工商"。所以，许多人为仕途拼命学习。

Bringing up children without discipline is the fault of the father
Uncut jade not finely honed does not represent something precious

Proverbs 13:24 advised parents not to spare the rod, if they loved their children. It is obvious that the disciplining of children was equally stressed in Hebrew society. Only a fool would despise discipline and wisdom. Parents were to train their children in a manner that would develop in them positive character. (22:6)

| 养不教,父之过,玉不琢,不成器

　　《箴言》第十三章第24节劝告家长,如果爱自己孩子的话,就不要吝惜棍棒。希伯来社会也很注重管教。忽视管教,忽视智力培养,只能是愚蠢的。家长要培养子女走正道。

CHAPTER TWENTY-SEVEN
"The Righteous shall live by Faith" , Peter's Vision

All religions centered on the Dualism, that is, "good and evil". The moral teaching is always on doing good deeds and avoiding evils. This is the reason why many people say that all religions are the same, teaching people to do good deeds. However, there is a slight variation in their philosophy. Christianity, according to the gospel preached by Jesus Christ, emphasized on universal love and God is that love. This Creator God is the God of all nations and, therefore, God has no favouritism. The Jews may be given the laws to keep and the Gentiles are given the conscience. Both have to do the right thing. Whosoever does the right thing is righteous in the sight of God and he shall live by faith.

In Acts Chapter 10 records an incidence where a Gentile has been accredited righteousness.

"One fine afterneen in Joppa, Peter went on the roof to pray. He became hungry and wanted something to eat. Suddenly he fell into a trance. (Note: The afternoon sun might be too hot and made him drowsy.) While he was in the semi-conscious state, Peter saw a large sheet fell from heaven, holding by its four corners. On the sheet, it contained all kinds of animals, such as kookabarras, kangaroos and crocodiles etc. Then, Peter heard a voice from heaven, saying, 'Peter, get up. Kill and eat'.

Peter was shocked. He replied, 'Oh no! Lord, surely not with anything impure or unclean.' The voice spoke again, 'What God has made clean, you do not call them unclean.'

This happening repeated three times before the sheet was taken up to heaven.

Peter got out of the trance and was wondering what that vision about. At this moment, three men sent by Cornelius, the centurian of Caesarea were at the gate, asking for Peter. The spirit asked Peter to get up to meet the three men, whom Cornelius had sent.

The messengers told Peter about their boss, Cornelius, who was a righteous and God fearing man, who was loved by all the Jews people. They told Peter that a holy angel had told Cornelius to invite Peter to the house and to hear him preach.

The next day, Peter left Joppa and went to Caesarea. Cornelius was expecting Peter. He gathered all his relatives and close friends, waiting in his house.

第二十七章

公益者因信得活：彼得的异像

一切宗教都有两面性，即：善与恶。德育往往是行善祛恶。因此，不少人说，所有的宗教都是一样的，都叫人做善事。不过，这种观念不是完全没有差异的。耶稣基督传播的福音基督教强调博爱，这爱就是上帝。造物的上帝是所有国度的上帝，上帝是没有偏向的。犹太被赐予了可规守的法律，非犹太被赐予了良心。犹太和非犹太都不能做错事。在上帝眼里，谁做对了，谁就是正义的，就有活着的信誉。

《使徒行传》第十章里记载，有个非犹太人被人认为是正义的，故事是这样的：

约帕城的一个晴朗的下午，彼得上房祷告，饿了，想吃点什么。忽然，他迷昏过去了（注：太阳把他晒晕了）。他神智半醒地看到天上掉下来一大块布，展着四角，布上有各种动物，有鹰鸟啦，袋鼠啦，鳄鱼啦什么的。彼得听到天上传下来个声音："彼得，起来，杀了吃吧"。

彼受惊了，答道："不，不！主啊，不纯的或不干净的，是不能吃的"。

这个声音又说，"上帝弄干净的，你不要说不干净"。

这话重复了三遍，布被天收了回去。

彼得清醒过来，猜疑这种异像是什么意思呢。就在这时，撒利亚的百夫长科尼列斯派来三个人到了门口，召唤彼得。圣灵叫彼得起来，去迎接科尼列斯派来的三个人。

使者们告诉彼得，他们的主人科尼列斯是个正人，敬畏上帝，全犹太的人都爱他。他们告诉彼得，有一位天使告诉科尼列斯来请彼得到他家去听讲道。

第二天，彼得离开约帕，去了撒利亚。科尼列斯正等着他来呢。他聚集了所有的亲戚朋友，在家里等着他呢。

At the house of Cornelius and after a brief introduction, Peter began to preach, saying that he now realized how true it was that God did not have favouritism, but accepted men from every nation who feared him and did what was right'..."

This story indicates that:

1. God is the God of all nations.

2. God has no favouritism.

3. God's revelation is more than what the Bible holds, and indeed, he speaks from time to time to his prophets of every tribe on the earth.

Before Peter's vision, the Roman centurion had a vision. An angel of God spoke to him, saying that both his prayers and gifts to the poor were remembered by God. This means that God is not only a god of the Jews, but also the God of all nations. This God watches over his peoples, Greeks, Jews and Romans alike. God like and accept those who are devout and obedient, and also who give generously to the poors.

God accepted Cornelius not because 'he was a circumsized Jew'. It was not the question of 'a baptized Christian'. In fact, God accepted all righteous people disregarding race or creed.

Besides Bible, are other religious scriptures "unclean" ? Let us establish the funfamentals. First of all, the Creator God is the God of all nations and he has no favouritism. His only demand is our obedience to the Commandments, namely, love God and love our neighbours. Helping the poors and needy is a way of loving our fellow man. It is considered as a righteous act. For that God was pleased with Cornelius.

Cornelius was a Roman centurion, an oppressor in the enemy's government. But he feared God, obeying the words of God and doing what was right in helping the less fortunate ones by giving alms to the poor and needy. He was well-respected by both Romans and Jews. His righteousness had transcended the racial boundary.

The Jews always regarded Gentiles unclean. It was unclean because of different race without consideration of the quality of the characters of a person. It was a racial discrimination and also was under the wrong assumption that the Gentiles had different gods and that they were under different moral codes.

The same wrong assumption applies to Christians today, regarding other people of different religions, or even of different denominations, or same denomination but not of the same sect. To some Christians today, God speak only through the Bible. There is no other way. It is sad that the Creator God is now restricted to only one means of communication with man through the Bible. And, also, God communicate with only one sect of Christians.

进了撒利亚这幢房子，寒暄寒暄以后，彼得开始传道，说上帝不偏心，这话千真万确呀……不管哪个国家的，只要敬畏上帝做善事，上帝一概接纳了。

这个故事说的是：

1．上帝是万邦之神。

2．上帝不偏心。

3．上帝的训谕不是《圣经》所能容纳的，其实，上帝常常晓谕世上每个种族的先知们。

彼得出现异像之前，罗马百夫长也出现过异象。上帝的天使对他说，他的祷告和他施舍给穷人的上帝都记着呢。这说明，上帝不单是犹太人的神，也是万国的神。上帝俯瞰着他的子民，不分希腊人、犹太人还是罗马人。上帝喜欢接纳虔诚、顺从的人们和慷慨接济穷人的人们。

上帝接纳了科尼列斯，不是因为他是受割礼的犹太人，也不是因为他是受洗的基督徒。上帝接纳所有正义的人，不分种族，不分信仰。

除了《圣经》之外，其他的宗教经文是"不干净"的吗？首先，造物主上帝是万邦的上帝，不偏不倚。他只要求服从诫命，也就是，爱上帝的话，就爱你的邻居。扶困济贫，是爱同胞之道，是正义之举。所以，上帝对科尼列斯是满意的。

科尼列斯是罗马的百夫长，在敌手的政府，他是压迫者。但是，他敬畏上帝，听上帝的话，扶困济贫，接济不幸的人们，他做的是对的。他收到了罗马人和犹太人的敬爱，他的仗义之举超越了种族的界限。

犹太人常常认为异教徒不干净。为什么不干净？因为种族不同，性情不同吧。这是搞种族歧视，认为非犹太人还有个上帝，还有道德法则，那就错了。

如今，基督教徒也犯了同样的错误，认为其他人宗教不同，教派不同，教派相同但旁门左道。如今，在有些基督徒看来，上帝靠《圣经》说话，除此以外别无他法。上帝仅仅被当成了通过《圣经》来和人交流的一个工具上了，这是可悲的。而且，上帝交流的只有基督徒的某一个教派！

If Cornelius could be considered righteous and God was pleased with him, he must have complied with the moral laws or have done the demands required by the conscience that God had planted in his heart. Though he was a Gentile, God had sent angels to give him the vision about Peter's presence in Joppa. There remains a big question that anything which is not in the tradition of the church, or is beyond the individual scope of knowledge, either through learning or experience, would be pushed aside or dismissed as "unclean".

It is mentioned many times in the Bible that God have no favouritism. (Refer Romans 2 and Acts 10) God reveal his wisdom to various people around the world and from time to time. We uphold Greek philosophy on democracy and human rights. God gave Chinese Dao Philosophy and Confucian ethical codes. Do we consider them "unclean" because they are not in the Bible?

Is it too radical to consider philosophy of all races come from God? Clement of Alexandra commented about the wisdom said that all rivers come from one source.

Jesus Christ was the most radical of all, accusing the Pharisees and Scribes as hypocrites, who held on to the traditions and neglected the essence of the laws of God. Like Cornelius, men in every nation observe the laws of God and do all the right things are all righteous in the sight of God. "The Righteous shall live by faith" transcends all faiths, if we believe there is one Creator God.

Therefore, the bottom line is: "Man must do the right thing". This brings back to the beginning of the chapter that "the teaching in every religion is the same, requiring every man to do the right thing". The consequence depends on one's faith in God. If there is non-existence of God, there is no fear of God. Then one may do whatever one likes, even killing people. Unless an atheist has good moral and does the right thing according to the good conscience in his heart, there is no difference to him about the existence of God. If there is God, then, there is fear of God, and this is where religion comes in, building one up in faith in God. The rituals and even the creeds in a religion are extravagance. It is the "doings", which reflect the attitude of the heart, that are important. Jesus Christ said that if anyone heard the word of God and put it in practice he/she would be his brother or sister. Religion can, therefore, help to harness one to do the right thing like the laws instituted by the governing authority.

如果科尼列斯被认为是正义的，上帝对他是满意的，那么，他一定是遵守了道德法则，或者是受了上帝给他根植的良心所驱使。他是个非犹太人，上帝派了天使给他显现了彼得现身约帕的异像。这问题就大了，教会传统中所不存在的东西，超越了个体认知范围的东西，习得的也好，实践的也好，被踢开了，被否定了，因为它们是"不干净的"。

《圣经》中多次提到，上帝不偏不倚，屡次把智慧启示给世界上各个民族。我们推崇希腊哲学的民主和人权。上帝赐给中国人道家哲学和儒家伦理，我们能因为它们不在《圣经》里就认为它们"不干净"吗？

认为所有种族的哲学都来自上帝，是不是太极端了呢？亚历山大的克莱门特说："所有的河流来自同一个源头"。

耶稣基督是最极端的，责备法利赛人和哥利流文士们，说他们是伪君子，只维护传统，忽视了上帝法律的内核。这样的人在各国都遵守上帝的法律，做了上帝眼里正确的事。假使我们相信只有一个造物的上帝的话，那么，"正义有了信义才得以存在"大于一切信仰。

综上所述，最后要说的一句话是："人得行善"。这又回到了本章的开篇：每个宗教的教义都是相同的，要求每个人都做好事。这个结论取决于对上帝的信仰。如果上帝不存在，也就不用怕上帝了。那么，人就可以胡作非为了，甚至是可以杀人了。如果无神者德性好，凭良心做好事，上帝存在与否没什么意义。如果上帝存在，就敬畏上帝，宗教就是这么来的，上帝就是这么被信仰的。宗教仪式，甚至是宗教信条是一种浪费。行动上反射出心的态度，才是重要的。耶稣基督说，倘若任何人听了上帝的话，并把这话落实到行动之中，他/她就是他的兄弟姊妹。因此，宗教有助于规范人们行善，正如政府机构制定法律一样。

Postcript

After writing the last chapter, we pause to wonder whether this book is for the consumption of oversea Chinese, informing them of Chinese traditions and culture, or for Chinese in Mainland China, convincing them that Shangdi, whom they used to worship, is none other than the Creator God. Or is it for the general public, for people interested in sampling the trade between Chinese Philosophy Before Qin and Christianity. Or, should it be received as an encouragement to enthusiastic missionaries to recognize the need to sinify Christian theology for the Confucian Chinese.

There are many questions to answer, we will touch on the following:

1. Is there religious fereedom in China?
2. Does the Chinese Government prosecute Christians?
3. Is there morality in China today?
4. Christianity for the Confucian Chinese.

These are not the problematic questions. As tourism in China is responsible for foreign exchange dollars, and the country is virtually open for study and investigation. China today is very different from China in the 90s, let alone the China of the 50s or 60s. The real problem lies with Western media and certain parties interested in establishing spheres of influence.

1. In China today, there is a Religious Council, consisting of leaders from Buddhism, Islam, Daoism, Catholicism and Protestantism etc. The first three are well established and are Chinese in most respects. Because Christianity has for so long been associated with colonialism, the Chinese government insisted on the importance of "Three Self-Movements," hoping to encourage an indigenous Christian theology and ethos. Politically, Christian churches should not take orders from either the Vatican or the USA.

During the second half of the 90s there were numerous rebuildings or renovations of temples, either Daoist or Buddhist, as well as churches, all over China. There are many temples with a long history behind them. There are hundreds of temples, so much so that a tourist complained that none in his many tours of China has he ever lacked a temple. Most of these temples are thronged with worshippers, burning josticks and "gold and silver" papers.

后 记

写完最后一章，我想了一下，这本书是不是给华侨写的，给他们讲讲中华传统文化，是不是给大陆华人写的，使他们相信，他们所拜的上帝正是造物的上帝。本书的对象是普通读者还是把兴趣放在先秦哲学和基督教进行比较的读者。本书是否是在鼓励热心的传教士们，让他们认识到，有必要使基督神学在儒化的中国人面前中国化。

答案是不少的，下面来谈谈吧：

1. 在中国有宗教自由吗？
2. 中国政府迫害基督教吗？
3. 今天的中国有道德观念吗？
4. 儒化的中国人眼里的基督教。

这些都不是问题的问题。中国旅游业创外汇，国家敞开大门让人调研。今天的中国和九十年代不同，和五、六十年代更不同。症结所在是西方媒体及其某些党派的兴趣在于建立势力范围。

1. 今天中国，宗教协会包罗了佛教、回教、道教、天主教和基督教的教主们，前三者建设得很好，几乎被中国化了。因为基督教历来和殖民主义走得太近，所以，中国政府坚持"三自运动"，希望鼓励产生本土化的基督教神学和民族精神。从政治上来说，基督教会不应该受控于梵蒂冈或美国。

九十年代后期，中国各地重建或改建大批佛道庙宇教堂。许多寺院历史悠久。寺院好几百个，游客抱怨说，在中国观光，不进寺院的时候没有。多数寺院到处都是烧香、烧纸的。

Churches in Shanghai are packed with believers. Away from the commercial and developed cities of the Eastern region, people are surprised to see a huge catholic cathedral in the middle of Guilin City in Guangxi among the minorities. Similarly, one can find a mosque in Quanzhou on the east coast of Fujian, where Arab traders used to visit, or in Guilin, or in Kunming in Yunnan in the southwest region of China. To the surprise of many Australian tourists, the Dongba Culture is very much alive among the Mosuo and Naxi minorities in Yunnan. Their religion is a mixture of Lamaism, shamanism with its nature gods represented by water, tree and mountain etc., and Buddhism. These groups have their own dialects as well as their ancient pictorial wrting.

On the whole, Chinese are very pragmatic as far as religion goes. Maybe they considered it a personal choice and are liberal in their attitude. We know a family living in the capital of a northern state in Malaya in the 40s and 50s. The father was the last consul of National Chinese Government in that state. He was a Muslim, and his wife a Buddhist. Their children were converted Christians, both Catholic and Protestant. They lived under one roof. There are similar stories all over China.

From these accounts, one can safely say that there is religious tolerance and freedom among the Chinese in China, because God is regarded as a personal deity.

2. With regard to the question of the prosecution of "Christians," one must be circumspect. When the government of China prefers Christians to be associated with the "Three Self Movements" as distinct from the underground church, the West acuses it of prosecuting Christians. Every government wants to protect the wellbeing of its people and to know what is going on under its nose.

What is prosecution?

In an Islamic country like Malaysia no one is allowed to preach Christianity to the Malays. It is an offence under the law. We are told that in Bhutan Christians are registered and are asked to declare that they will not preach Christainity to the people of Bhutan. Australia and other countries prohibit certain cult-like religious bodies. The Singapore government de-registered Jehovah's Witnesses and has recently asked many European Catholic priests and nuns to leave the country. The US government sent in the FBI to quash The Branch Davidians at WACO on 19th. April, 1993, an action that resulted in 86 charred bodies. "Missionaries," have been active in politics notably in South American governments, where they further the political and economic interest of their national governments. Can one blame the Chinese Government for being cautious about the underground church!

Three Self Movements (self administration, self supporting and self propagation) encourage Christians to be transparent in their faith, without falling under the control of foreign powers. (128)Three Self Movements give Chinese Christians a chance to develop their own theology and ethos. It is a good opportunity for them to inculturate Christianity free of external interference and influence. If this happens, Christianity in China will become an authentic Chinese Christianity, similar to authentic Chinese Buddhism, which incorporates Dao and Confucian philosophies. Christianity for its own survival and growth in China must embrace and merge with Chinese high culture. The product has to be locally grown, processed and packaged for both local consumption and export overseas. Though Christianity originally developed in the Middle East, it has been westernized. As China became industrialized, it could not avoid Westernization. However, rural socio-economic structures cannot cope with the pace of industrialization and modernization. It is like installing a Rolls-Royce engine in a bullock cart. The two are not compatible. It is little wonder that the Government intends to check the speed of Westernization so that the country will not be fractured into pocket-size kingdoms.

Governments of the world have a moral obligation to concern themselves with the welfare of their people, and policies should be designed to benefit all.

3. Is there morality in China?

The Philosophies Before Qin laid the foundation for a high standard of morality in China. Even before that period, the legendary emperors had also ruled by "benevolence, righteousness, integrity and morality".

Once the legendary emperor Tang Yao asked his nominated successor, Yu Shun, whether it would be good for him to raise an army to rein in the remaining three small countries. Yu Shun replied that if the three small kingdoms experienced his benevolence and integrity, they would naturally come and merge with him.

Throughout history, those leaders who ruled by their swords fell upon their swords. Only leaders who knew how to dispense love, benevolence, righteousness and good integrity survived and enjoyed long reigns. Lao Zi argued that those who "acted against the teaching of Dao would die early", and Mo Zi argued that those who exercised "righteousness would live".

三自运动（自治、自养、自传）鼓励基督徒要信仰公开，不受国外势力管制。三自运动使中国的基督徒有机会发展自己的神学和文化品格。这是个让他们不受外来干涉和影响的情况下来培养基督教的好机会。假如是这样的话，中国的基督教将成为正宗的中国基督教，正如中国佛教一样，融汇了道教和儒家哲学，变成了自己的东西。基督教想在中国生存、发展，必须和中国高尚文化相结合。其结果必须是在本土成长，本土改造和本土完善，然后在本土吸收，同时推向海外。既然基督教起源于中东，然而，它已经西化了。由于中国已经工业化，免不了要西化，但是，农村社会、经济结构跟不上工业化和现代化的步伐，就像牛车安装个劳斯莱斯发动机一样，两不相称。难怪政府想抑制西化进程，以保证国家不会分化成无数个小国。

世界各国政府有责任为人民谋福利，制定的政策是面向大家的。

3. 中国有道德吗？

前秦哲学为中国打下了深厚的道德基础。甚至是先秦以前，传说的君主们也以"仁义道德"来进行统治。

传说尧帝问继承人舜，可否兴兵接管其他三个小国。舜回答说，如果这三个小国没有仁德，他们会自然归顺的。

历史上，所有靠武力征服的统治者都死于武力。只有讲仁义道德的人，才长治久安。老子说："不道者早已也"，墨子也说："义则生。"

Postcript

What is "Moral Development and Socialism"?

China in the year 2003 experienced a smooth transfer of power from the "Third to the Fourth generation of leadership," against all the negative forecasts of some Weatern political analysists. With the opening of China to world trade, China has discarded communism for democratic socialism. In his "Swan Song" at the 16th. Party Congress in October, 2002, Jiang Zemin argued that China would work towards "slightly well-to-do or comforable society", that is, a reasonable level of comfort.

If we care to comb through the sayings in Mao Zedong, Deng Xiaoping and Jiang Zemin on Moral Development and Socialism, we soon discover that they do not depart from the ancient philosophy of love and integrity, and a high standard of morality. No wonder when Henry Kissinger met Zhou Enlai for the second time in late 60s, he remarked to his entourage that Zhou was a man of high moral character. Chinese leaders today argue that "the country must be governed with integrity", [129] "centering on service of the people" in "a spirit of humility". [130]

It is argued that the government must "promote fine, ancient moral traditions" and "adapt the best achievements of human morality" in order to create a "Special Sinified Socialism". This socialism will incorporate the principles of "The Three Represents" that our Party must always represent the requirements of the development of China's advanced productive forces, the orientation of the development of China's advanced culture, and the fundamental interests of the overwhelming majority of the people in China, they are the foundation for building the Party, the corner stone for its exercise of state power and a source of its strengthen, only by doing so can we really ensure that our Party always stand in the forefront of the time and maintain its advanced nature. [131]Ibid. page 37. In the opinion of foreign observers China has forsaken communism and is moving towards social democraic government, similar to Labour Parties of Britain, Australia, New Zealand, and the People's Action Party of Singapore. As a consequence, China, with her high morality, will be acceptable as an advanced, developed, democratic country like Britain or Australia.

后记

什么是"讲道德,讲社会主义"?

2003年,中国经历了第三代领导人到第四代领导人的平稳过渡,这是西方政治分析家们消极预测所没料到的。中国已经向世贸开放,似乎已经放弃了共产主义,进入民主社会主义。2002年10月,在党的十六大上,江泽民声明,中国即将奔向小康社会(也就是生活比较舒服的水平)。

如果我们细读"毛泽东、邓小平、江泽民谈论道德和社会主义",我们就会发现,里面都包含着古代的仁义和尚德哲学。难怪基辛格在第二次会见周恩来的时候,告诉自己的随从,说周恩来是个道德高尚的人。今天,中国领导人要"以德治国",本着"公仆精神"去"为人民服务"。

政府必须"弘扬中国古代优良道德传统","吸取人类一切优良成就",以便建设具有中国特色的社会主义。这个社会主义体现在"三个代表"上:必须代表中国先进生产力的发展要求,代表中国先进文化的前进方向,代表中国最广大人民的根本利益,是我们党的立党之本、执政之基、力量之源,是我们党始终站在时代前列,保持先进性的根本体现和根本要求。在外国观察家看来,中国已经放弃共产主义,在朝着民主社会主义政府迈进,类似于英国、澳大利亚、新西兰的工党和新加坡的人民行动党。其结果是,中国以自身高尚的行操被世人接纳为英国和澳大利亚这样先进、发达的民主国家。

4. Christianity for the Confucian Chinese.

"What is Christianity?" This question was asked of a group of Christians in a Bible study.

The answers given were:

"It is belief in God who created the heavens and the earth and all creatures in it."

"It is the teaching of Christ."

"Christianity is the belief that Jesus Christ was born of the Virgin Mary; that he came down from heaven to save the sinners; that he died on the cross and was resurrected from death, and that he is coming again to judge the living and the dead."

One member added, "And he was baptized in the River Jordan."

Another one quickly corrected him, saying, " He was immersed in water."

One radical in the group said quite innocently that all these doctrines were less important than the Gospel message that Jesus of Nazareth preached. He was immediately shot down by those who responded with: "What is Christianity without these doctrines?"

The nonplussed radical meekly replied, " Christianity is based on the sayings and doings of Jesus Christ. The message in the Old Testament, as I understand, is based on obedience to the Ten Commandments and not on the 603 rules and regulations of the Tamud as formulated by the Pharisees and the Teachers of Law. Jesus Christ warned his followers that unless their righteousness surpasses that of the Pharisees and the teachers of Law, they would not enter the kingdom of heaven. Jesus summed up the Law and Prophets in Two Great Commandments: Love God and love your neighbours. He went on to argue that those who hear the Word of God and put it into practice are his brothers, sisters and mother.

The Gospel Jesus of Nazareth preached was not the doctrines of the various denominations, but love and peace. There are more than three thousand, three hundred sects in Christianity, each accusing the others of being wrong. God is love. This love transcends denominational differences and is the centre of the Gospel. God so loved the world so that he sent Christ to be born in the person of Jesus of Nazareth to bring his Word to the world that whoever embraces this Word has eternal life. Those Christians who live in love live in God. They love God and love their neighbours.

4. 中国儒家的基督教

"什么是基督教？"一帮基督教徒在研究《圣经》的时候问道。

答案有以下几个：

"基督教就是对创造天地和万物的上帝的信仰。"

"它是基督所传的教。"

"基督教是一种信仰，相信耶稣基督是圣母玛丽亚生的，是从天上下凡拯救罪人的，被钉死在十字架上又复活了，现在又回来审判活人和死人了。"

也有人说："他在约旦河里受洗的"。

还有一位马上纠正说："他在水里淹了"。

这伙人里，有个观点激进的人很天真地说，所有这些教条都赶不上耶稣所传的福音重要，于是立刻遭到了围攻："没这些教条哪来的基督教？"

激进者不知所措，和顺地说："基督教以耶稣基督的言行为依据的。依我看，《旧约》里的内容以遵守十戒为根本，而不是伪善、教条所圈定的塔木德经里的603条规章制度。耶稣告诫门徒，除非他们的正义不再伪善，不再教条，否则，他们进不了天堂。耶稣总结了两大诚命中的律法和先知的训谕：爱主吧，爱你的邻居。他接着说，听了神的话，办了神的事，便是他的兄弟姐妹和他的母亲。

耶稣所传的福音并不是所有宗派的教条，而是爱与和平。基督教有3300多个教派，各派互相指责对方是错误的。上帝是爱，这种爱超越各派的分歧，带来的主要是福音。上帝是这么爱世人，派出了基督，以耶稣化人的方式把道带给这个世界，凡是接受道的，都得到永生。那些活在爱中的基督徒们，活在上帝那里。他们爱上帝，爱他们的邻居。

Postscript

God continually works through the Church to return her to this simple, pistine basis. In the 1500's, Martin Luther (1483–1546), challenged the authority and mystic power of the Pope and gave the church freedoms she had not enjoyed for centuries. Thomas Campbell (1777–1844), wanting to unite the churches in North America in the 18th Century, found it necessary to discard the use of creeds as tests of fellowship. The Declaration and Address was part of a new religious revolution. (132)In the 20th Century, Christian theologians attempted to de-mythologize the gospels, underling the fact that this Jesus of history should be distinguished from the Christ of faith.

It is important for an ancient country like China that possesses such a high culture, to get their Christian theologians to work on a distinctive Chinese, Christian theology, freeing them from the theological yoke of their humiliation under Imperialisms. It is better and healthier for Chinese Christians to inculturalise Christianity for their own consumption rather than being forced-fed by Western Christian tradition and dogma.

Given to the fact that Marxist Communism has been Sinified into the "New Chinese-style Democratic Socialism, " it should not be difficult for the Christian theologians to develop their own theology and ethos.

The progress of China, from patriarchalism and authoritarianism to democratic socialism in just 50 years is both amazing and heartening. The maintenance of high morality without surrendering to materialism and individualism) is commendable. (133)

It is unfortunate that the most populous country in the world, with its high morality, is without a Creator God. Christian nations, which claim to be God fearing, have not shown enough integrity, love, benevolence and righteousness to influence the Chinese population. Without integrity, one has no righteousness. This righteousness is the gift of God, of the Logos, the Dao, the Spirit of God, and is available to those who are open to receive it, that is, those who exercise faith.

| 后记

上帝通过教会的不懈努力,又回到了这个简单而又古老的原则上来。15世纪,马丁·路德(1483-1546)对教皇的权力和神秘的权威进行了挑战,使教会几个世纪都没得到自由。18世纪,多马士埃贝尔(1777-1844)为了联合北美一些教会,因为他认为,该抛弃信条了,这样才能检验会众。《宣言和演说》是宗教的一个新的革命。20世纪,基督教神学家们试图剥开福音的神秘色彩,认为历史上的耶稣要和信仰上的基督区分开来。

像中国这样拥有如此博大文化的古国是必须使其基督神学工作者们开创具有中国特色的基督教神学的,把他们从帝国主义屈辱的神学枷锁下解放出来。中国基督徒将基督教中国化,为我所用,这是有利的,健康的,从而也摆脱了西方基督教传统和教义的束缚。

马克思的共产主义已经中国化,成为中国新式的民主社会主义,那么,基督教神学工作者就要发展自己的神学和神学思潮。

中国在过去60年中,从家长制独裁统治发展成了民主社会主义,这是令人惊奇的,是令人鼓舞的。维护高尚道德,去除拜金思想和个人主义,这是可钦可佩的。

然而,在这个世界上人口最多的国度,讲了道德,但没有造物的上帝。基督国家说是敬畏神,却没有用仁爱道德来影响中国人民。无德则无义,而这个义是神的恩赐,是理性的,是神灵的,只有坦然接受它,并且行使信义的人们,才能体现正义的。

Postscript

It has been suggested in the Silk Road that the foundation on which a distinctive Chinese theology can be developed are the Philosophies Before Qin, – such imperatives as Guan Zi's "Propriety, Rigtheousness, Honesty or Modesty, and Awareness of Shame", Lao Zi's "Respect The Word and Value Integrity" and "Do not act against the Way os Heaven", Kung Zi's "Five elements of Good Integrity", and Mo Zi's "Love others Doubly in Mutual love and Benefit others More in Social Dealings". With these moral understandings as a basis, we could reflect on the teachings of Jesus about the nature of God and the import of His Will. In this way, we could, as Matteo Ricci put it, be crowning Chinese philosophies and morality with a Deity – the Creator God.

Christianity started well in the first century, following the teaching of Jesus of Nazareth. Jesus himself did not write anything down. It was after his death that his followers felt it necessary for them to record his words and deeds. They tried to write anything available even materials from the "Q" (questionable) source.

In the third century the Roman Emperor felt that Christianity had grown by leaps and bounds and it was inevitable that Roman Empire had to accept it sooner or later. However, paganism was very popular and active. (The Romans worshipped Venus and Apollo; Greeks Ophism and Aphrodite/ Isis; Egyptians Isis and in Asia Minor people worshipped the sun god Sol and Mahna Mater, the Great Mother of God.) In order to achieve both unification of East and West Roman Empire and preservation of paganism, a creed was created to synchronise paganism into Christianity. It was enforced with swords and burning stakes.

Christianity was all about the Universal Love, Agape, preached by Jesus Christ. Yet the Crusaders fought for that "little acre" in Jerusalem. Did not Jesus teach that "neither on this mountain nor in Jerusalem" that we worship God, as true worshippers must worship the Father in Spirit and in truth" ? Up to date men have not learned this solemn teaching, as it is displayed in all cathedrals all over the world, figures of Jesus, Mary and other saints, putting men before God.

When I visited Berlin in May 2008, I learned that Hans Kung was promoting Global Ethic. It is based on Inter–faith dialogue, crossing the divide. Have not all World religions promote "ethic" in their teachings? Though the followers of all religions know the truth of Agape, Universal Love or Global Ethic, they do not "speak and act truthfully". Christians are, in fact, very arrogant in declaring that their faith is the only way to salvation. Pope Pius XVI has even gone a step farther, saying that he doublts the salvation of the Protestants! The teaching of Jesus Christ has all gone to waste

后记

  人们认为，在这条丝绸之路上，中国特色神学发展的基础是先秦哲学，其中值得一提的有管子的礼义廉耻、老子的尊道而贵德和无违天道、孔子的德行五常和墨子的兼相爱、交相利原则。以这些道德为基础，我们可以对耶稣关于上帝的本质和上帝意志的含义的训言中得到反映。正如雷芝马太所说的，只有这样，我们才会用神造物的上帝来指导中国哲学和道德。

  基督教起源于一世纪，信奉耶稣所传的教义。耶稣本人没有写下什么，他死后，他的门徒才觉得必须把他的言行记录下来。凡是相关的他们都尽力写下来，甚至包括人们所提出的问题。

  三世纪，罗马皇帝觉得基督教发展得过快，罗马帝国接受它是早晚的事。但是，异教非常盛行（当时，罗马人信奉维纳斯女神和阿波罗；希腊有奥菲士教和阿佛洛狄特-伊希斯女神；埃及有伊希斯，小亚细亚人崇拜太阳神索尔和大母神梦那马特等）。为了把联合东、西罗马帝国统一起来，保住异教，搞出了一套信条，来把异教并入基督教。这是用刀枪和烙刑强制执行的。

  基督教全是耶稣基督所传的博爱，无私的爱。十字军为耶路撒冷那块弹丸之地争战起来。耶稣的训谕不是说了吗？我们拜神，不是在这座山上，也不是在耶路撒冷，真正的崇拜者用心灵和诚实来拜上帝。直到今日，人们还没有掌握这个严肃的教诲，全世界所有大教堂里都有这则教诲，也有耶稣像、玛丽亚和其他圣徒像，然而，人类被排在了上帝的前面。

  2008年5月我去柏林的时候，发现汉氏孔正在推广"善世（全球）道德"活动。这是基于跨宗教的多种信仰。世界一切宗教不是推介自己的"规范"吗？尽管所有宗教信徒都知道神对世人的爱、博爱或全球伦理，但是，他们的言行是不诚实的。其实，基督徒非常骄傲地宣告，只有他们的信仰才能得救。教皇匹尤斯十六世甚至走得更远，对新教徒能不能得救产生怀疑。耶稣基督的教诲快要废了。

Postscript

Both Christians and Confucians know "What you do not wish for yourself, do not do to others". The question is not that they do not know this teaching. It is indeed short of carrying through or in the golf language, the full swing with following through. Confucius taught more than 500 years before Jesus Christ. The behaviour of Confucians had not changed an iota.

Without the weight of the First Commandment, the Second Commandment is like a toothless tiger. And no physical organization can achieve "Global Ethic" without the "fear of God' at the back of one's mind. Without the "fear of God" it is almost impossible to submit to the demands of God. That is the downfall of all ethical teachings.

The Two Great Commandments must be performed simultaneously. Jesus interpreted that the Second is equally important as the First. Confucian teaching compromised for the Second Commandment because God is spirit and invisible. As such, there is no motivation or obligation to honour and respect God and, therefore, to fulfil the demands of God in loving the neighbours.

Lao Zi, on the contrary, proposes "respect Dao and value integrity", which is equivalent to The Two Great Commandments. He explains that "respect Dao" must go through four progressive stages: listening about Dao; understanding about Dao; securing what Dao is and putting Dao into practice. Jesus Christ said that "those who hear the word of God and put it into practice are his brothers and mother". However, Christianity has been hijacked and Confucius Analects has overshadowed Lao Zi's Dao De Jing. That may be the reason why there is no Global Ethic.

后记

基督徒和儒家都知道:"己所不欲,勿施于人"。问题并不是他们不明白这个教诲,而是无法贯彻始终,用高尔夫球的语言讲,就是"举打没打全"。孔子行教早耶稣500年,然而,儒家之风一点儿也没改变。

没有第一诫命的压力,第二诫命好比没牙的老虎。如果不从心里敬畏上帝的话,任何机构组织都难以做到普世道德。如果没有"畏神"观念,就不可能遵从上帝的意愿,这便是一切讲道德行为的沦落。

两大诫命必须同步进行。耶稣认为,第二诫命和第一诫命同等重要。儒学在第二诫命上采取了折中办法,因为上帝是灵,是看不见的。由此,也就不存在敬重上帝的动机或义务了,也不用去落实上帝"爱邻"的意愿了。

比较而言,老子提倡"尊道而贵德",这一点等于两大诫命。他认为,尊道分四步进行:问道、进道、得道、行道。耶稣基督说:"听了上帝的话,按上帝的话去做的人,就是我的兄弟,我的母亲"。但是,基督教早已被挟持了,孔子的《论语》也被老子的《道德经》掩盖了。这也许是没有普世道德的原因吧。

Bibliography

1. Lu Yuling, Peng Yongjie, Li Zhengang, 中国道家 Zhong Guo Dao Jia, Religious Culture Publication, Beijing, China, 1996.
2. Chen Zhiliang, Jia Runguo, 中国儒家 Zhong Guo Ru Jia, Religious Culture Publication, Beijing, China, 1996.
3. Li Yabin, 中国墨家 Zhong Guo Mo Jia. Religious Culture Publication, Beijing, China, 1996.
4. Wei Donghai, 中国法家 Zhomg Guo Fa Jia, Religious Culture Publication, Beijing, China, 1996
5. Edited by Guo Xue Ji ben Cong Shu, 老子 L ao Zi, Zhi Yang Publication, Taipei, China, 1991.
6. Edited be Guo Xue Ji Ben Cong Shu, 庄子 Zhuang Zi, ZhiYang Publication, Taipei, China, 1991.
7. Edited by Guo Xue Ji Ben Cong Shu, 墨子新释 Mo Zi Xin Shi, Zi Yang Publication, Taipei, China, 1992.
8. Author unknown, 三字经 S an Zhi Jing, Zi Yang Publication, Taipei, China, 1992.
9. Wang Sen, 荀子白话今译 Xun Zi Bai Hua Jin Yi, China Book Store Publication, Beijing, China, 1985.
10. Li Dan, Yong Ting Jin, 管子白话今译 Guan Zi Bai Hua Jin Yi, China Book Store Publication, Beijing, China, 1997.
11. Luo Shangxian, 老子通解 Lao Zi Tong Jie, Guangdong High Education Publication, Guangzhou, China, 1989.
12. Edited by China Historical Society, 太平天国 Taiping Tian Guo, Shenzhou Guoguang Company Publication, undated.
13. Edited by Zhang Duan Cheng, 孙子兵法 Sun Zi Bing Fa, Xinjiang People Publication, Urumqi, China, 2000.
14. Edited by Zhang Yu Lou, 古文观止 Gu Wen Guan Zhi, Fu Yuan Publication, Tainan, China, 1989.
15. Stephen Neill, A History of Christian Missions, Penguin, Middlesex, U.K., 1982.
16. Patrick Tyler, A Great Wall, Public Affairs Publication, New York, USA, 1999
17. Steven Hassan, Combating Cult Mind Control, Park Street Press, Rochester, Vermont, U.S.A., 1988.
18. Witold Rodzinski, The Wall Kingdom, Fontana Paperbacks Publication, U.K., 1984.
19. Han Suying, Han Suying's China, Doubleday Publication, Sydney, Australia, 1988.

20. Jin Zhu, Is Tibet the Last Shangri-La?, New Star Publication, Beijing, China, 1991.

21. Chen Qingying and Feng Zhi, Administrative Division of Tibetan Areas, China International Press, Beijing, China, 1995.

22. Hans Kung and Julia Ching, Christianity and Chinese Religions, Doubleday and Collins Publication, New York, U.S.A., 1989.

23. Moa Zedong, Deng Xiaoping and Jiang Zemin, Socialism and Moral Development, Xue Si Publication, Beijing, China, 2001. 24. J. Stevenson, A New Eusebius, SPCK Press, London, U.K., 1957.

25. J. Stevenson, Creeds, Councils and Controversies, SPCK Press, London, U.K., 1966.

26. Edited by Wang Fei and Song Youwen, 诗经 Shi Jing- "The Analects," China Social Science Publishers, Beijing, 2000.

27. Philip Stevenson, A Poor Case for Globalisation, Financial Times, London, U.K., 2001.

28. James Rupert, Making Mischief in Tibet, The Australian Financial Review, Sydney, 2002.

29. Johanna McGeary and Karen Tumulty, The Fog of War, Time Magazine, New York, May 7, 2001.

30. Edited by Zhong Gong Zhong Yang Xuan Duan Pu, Mao Zedong, Deng Xiaoping, Jiang Zemin on Moral Development and Socialism, 毛泽东，邓小平，江泽民 论社会主义道德建设，Xue Si Publication, Beijing, 2001.

31. Edited by The Rev. Alexander Roberts and James Donaldson, The Writings of The ante-Nicene Fathers, Vol. 1, Apostolic Fathers, Justin Martyr, Irenaeus, W.M.B. Eerdmans Publishing Company, Michigan. Undated.

32. Thomas Campbell, Declaration and Address, Birmingham, The Berean Press, 1959

33. Susan George, A Fate Worse Than Debt, Penguin Books, London, U.K, 1990.

34. A Collection of Historical stories 历史小故事丛书, Henan People Publication, Zhengzhou, 1981. (Stories as told by various authors.)

35. Ante-Nicene Fathers: The Writings of the Fathers Down to AD 325 (www.ccat.sas.upenn.edu/jod.html)

Suggestions for further reading:

1. Paul Bracken, Fire in the East, Perenial, an imprint of Harper Collins Publisher, 2000.

2. Tariq Ali. The Clash of Fundamentarism, 2002.

3. Wen Yi, Approaching Tibet, China Intercontinental Press, Beijing, China, 1995.

www.ingramcontent.com/pod-product-compliance
Lightning Source LLC
Chambersburg PA
CBHW061136010526
44107CB00068B/2964